Lost Sheep

Lost Sheep

Aspen's Counterculture in the 1970s

A Memoir

KURT BROWN

CONUN
DRUM
PRESS

CONUNDRUM PRESS
A Division of Samizdat Publishing Group, LLC.

Lost Sheep: Aspen's Counterculture in the 1970s—A Memoir. Copyright © 2012 by Kurt Brown.

ISBN: 978-0-9713678-7-6

Library of Congress Cataloging-in-Publication Data is available upon request.

Conundrum Press books may be purchased with bulk discounts for educational, business, or sales promotional use. For information please email: info@conundrum-press.com

Conundrum Press online: conundrum-press.com

Cover photo by Tommy DiMaggio

Special thanks to:

Tommy DiMaggio, Bruce Gordon, Virginia Slachman, Anne and Cheryl Burrows, Lorna Daley, Sandy Munro, Joannie Starbuck, Adrienne and John O'Donnell, Dan Sadowsky, Victor Garrett, Cecily Anne Killingsworth, Nancy Dunton, Scott Myers, Russell Carter, Bruce Berger, Steve Cole, Bo Hale, Pat Flynn, Peter Michelson, Al Lyons, Joe Popper, Steve Cohen, Matt Martz, Michi Blake, David Rothman, and Barry Burchell.

Martha Durgy Pitkin County Library, Aspen

Steve Huff: who read the whole thing

Caleb Seeling and Sonya Unrein: matchless editors

Laure-Anne Bosselaar: who rescued me

And everyone else who was there to make the town what it was:

Thanks for the memories.

Contents

Oh the shepherd is asleep
Where the willows weep
And the mountains are full of lost sheep.

— Bob Dylan "Ring Them Bells"

Foreword

All come to look for America . . .
—Paul Simon

Is there really such a thing as the American dream? For some of us who came of age during the tumultuous decade of the 1960s, our dream meant escaping America itself, its smog-laden cities, violence and crime, its arrogant posture in the world, corruption and annihilating power and unseemly wealth. Our American Dream meant rejecting the values of empire, the industrial juggernaut the nation had become in the late nineteenth century, the mechanized murder and savagery of two world wars. For some of us in the generation born during and immediately after World War II, a war which had reduced Europe to a hell of ashes, the situation had become intolerable. When Vietnam was foisted upon us, we recoiled. We suspected if there were an American dream, it lay outside of America, or somewhere within it that had been untouched by the suffocating mores, hypocrisy, and militaristic soul of the existing state.

To speak of one's life in such a context might seem pompous. Individual lives mean little, in historical terms, and the

details of such lives are engulfed by currents larger than any
one person can imagine. No one I ever knew said: "I want to
escape the industrial juggernaut the nation has become," or "I
reject the arrogant posture America has taken with respect to
other nations in the world." But from the perspective of forty
years, it is also possible to see one's life as part of a larger pattern, something that invests individual existence with meaning,
while at the same time, absorbing it almost completely. We live
in history as if it were an element, like fish live in water, and it's
impossible to divorce ourselves from our choices, the actions we
take in the course of an ordinary life. We are the actors and en-
actors of history, whether we are aware of it or not.

   The exodus that took place once the 1960s ended has been
pored over, analyzed, and recorded by historians and social crit-
ics, as well as by artists who shaped it in fundamental ways.
Many of the so-called "baby-boomers" became refugees. It
would be an abomination to equate ourselves with the suffering masses of World War II Europe. We were trying, rather, to
avoid a system that would destroy us with privilege and poison
us with plenty. We were ethical insurgents, moral exiles experi-
menting with the idea that we could live full, decent lives if only
we rejected materialism. We were the children of the Beat generation, though we called ourselves—or were called—hippies,
a term which holds no real weight. We failed, and for the most
prosaic of reasons: initially we wanted only to satisfy our appetites, to live free of mundane responsibility and devote ourselves
to immediate experience. When we finally took up the yoke of
personal and social responsibility, we ended up as our parents,
give or take a technological advancement or two.

   Just a handful of us washed up in Aspen, but there were
other pockets of experimentation—mostly in the West—

where people sought to gain a foothold on the unencumbered life: Bend, Oregon; Telluride, Colorado; Sand Point, Idaho; and Taos and Santa Fe in New Mexico. And there were those who probably melted into the woods and fields of the countryside to live as simply as they could on what they could harvest and grow. They were subsistence level settlers struggling to remain off the grid as long as was possible, or wise. Some *did* become small farmers in communities like Fruita and Paonia, Crested Butte and Montrose. But it is dangerous to generalize. The collective pronouns *us* and *we* have questionable antecedents. No one can speak for a whole generation—or even a considerable part of one. At best, such pronouns mean "some other people probably felt and acted as I did, more or less." A community of like-minded people only comes clearly into focus when regarded from a distance. Up close, it is a fractious mass of individuals leading singular lives, and no one quite fits the ideal generational mold.

Aspen in the 1970s offered just the right balance of geographical and socio-political elements to pursue a respectable life without giving in to the self-alienating demands of the greater culture. For a brief decade, it seemed possible to build a community that was tolerant but fundamentally law-abiding, hedonistic but practical. This vision of harmony was an illusion. Hardly a single person of color existed anywhere in the Roaring Fork Valley, making Aspen a ghetto of white hegemony and privilege. Racial anxiety was reduced to zero. Poverty was nowhere to be found. This compositional unity helped to create the feeling that Aspen was a place of unusual peace and sanity.

To live our lives, we had to turn our backs on the rest of the country. We had to compromise our sense of compassion and pretend we were unconnected to what was happening in the outside world. A large portion of the population of Aspen was decidedly non-conventional and strenuously opposed conformity with the rest of the country. America's ideals were not ours, and its values found no favor in "the old mining town" that had resurrected itself in the image of Bob Dylan and Walter Paepcke. Any *normal* American visiting Aspen at the time would have noticed the difference. America, however, has a genius for accommodating its dissidents by adopting their rebellion as fashion, thereby defusing any movement that might effectively oppose it. Eventually, you could buy headbands and bell-bottom trousers at any style emporium in Los Angeles or New York. Like most places, whatever Aspen once was, it was not to be sustained. When the 1970s were done, so were we, and Aspen began its real evolution towards the exclusive luxury resort it has become.

Prelude to a Journey

I came up through west Texas in a '55 Ford panel truck bought off a used car lot in Dallas and customized to fit my needs. It was May, 1970, and those needs were simple: travel as far and as fast as I could and always have a place to sleep, a place to retreat to in all weathers. I'd graduated from a respectable state university back east, majoring in English with the vague notion of becoming a writer, though my head was filled with romantic ideas about what that meant. I'd read *On the Road, Been Down So Long It Looks Like Up To Me, Howl* and several other books extolling the virtues of bohemian life, and most of the music of that era proclaimed freedom and a lack of responsibility. My father had been a ship's captain in the merchant marines and traveled all over the world, and I liked to tell myself that wandering was in my blood. Now my father was retired, and lived with my mother in a small suburban house in Arlington, with its clipped lawn, two-car garage, and flagstone walk leading up to the front door. They also owned a one-bedroom bungalow with three acres of land on the shores of Lake Arlington, and it was there that I took refuge after my college years, to plan what I would do next.

* * *

Ford panel trucks were plentiful in the 1950s, and roomy enough in back to accommodate a full-sized mattress and enough baggage for an extended trip. The front had two bucket seats, a stick shift on the floor, and two wide doors that swung open in the rear. Before I bought it, the truck had been used for deliveries by a business in Fort Worth. I could still make out the name of the bread company on the outside panels, half erased by the weather and the lack of new paint. The panels were a faded white, while the truck as a whole was a powdery, pastel turquoise, not very attractive, but I didn't care. What mattered was its size and durability. I paid the dealer five hundred dollars and towed it back to the small garage on my little estate at Lake Arlington.

The engine had to be overhauled, and I took it apart, piece by piece, laying each part on a tarp in the same order in which I'd removed it. That way, I could clean and oil them, and remember where they all went when I was ready to reassemble and lower the engine back into place. Strangely enough, this method worked. I listened to an old radio. Songs like "Moondance" by Van Morrison, and Simon and Garfunkel's "Bridge Over Troubled Water" wafted out of the garage, along with the stink of kerosene and burnt grease. But the song that caught my fancy was Crosby, Stills and Nash's "Wooden Ships," with its poignant ironies about setting out to find a new world, and its defiant valediction: *We are leaving / you don't need us.* Something about the will to search for another world, another way of living, struck a deep chord. I'd witnessed the violence and mayhem of the 1960s, with its assassinations and wars, its corruption and disillusionments, and I wanted no more. If the world of my parents had led to the world of the 1960s, then I was going to find a way to leave it all behind. My ship wasn't made of wood, but I meant to set out in it across the mountains and deserts of the west, headed toward Haight-Ashbury and what might be left of that ebullient, experimental community.

I didn't consider myself a hippie. I came from a solid middle-class background and I had seen enough hippies to know that I wasn't quite as militant and violent as some, and certainly not as wildly iconoclastic in my behavior or dress as others. But the Beats had been there first, in North Beach, and then the hippies in Haight Ashbury, so I assumed something about California, and San Francisco in particular, might be to my liking. None of this impressed me as being quintessentially American, though I was headed west like so many others before me in search of a new life and new opportunities. I had grown up in New England, and California seemed to me to be about as far away as I could get and still be in the country. Maybe I'd find somewhere to live that would suit my temperament and soothe my soul.

* * *

All that March and April I worked on my truck. I bought two six-by-eight sheets of laminated kitchen siding, imitation walnut a quarter-inch thick, to line the walls. With my father's help, I made large cardboard templates of how they would fit inside, then cut the siding into that shape with a coping saw, sanded the rough edges, and screwed them in to a metal band that ran along the interior walls on both sides. I bought a piece of new carpet, cut it to fit the floor, and tucked it in all the way around. It was beginning to look like home. Later, before I em-

barked for the endless highway to the coast, I shoved a new
mattress and bedding into the back. Whatever else happened,
and given that the engine would continue to function, I'd be
comfortable wherever I went. I could eat at diners or buy my
own groceries and eat them in the truck. Gas stations would
provide toilets, maps, coffee, and other sundries for the road. I
planned to park in rural areas, woods, and state parks, bathing
in any lake, stream, or public facility I could find. I would want
for nothing, and I'd be free.

I had some money I'd saved from a bartending job I'd
worked at for a year at the country club on Lake Arlington.
It would be enough to get me to the coast, and to set me up
in an apartment and a new job. The *pièce de résistance*, however, came near the end, just before I dropped the engine back
into place and fired it up for the first time. The truck lacked
a front bumper, and instead of buying a real one from a junk-
yard, I bought a clean two-by-eight, cut it into a six foot length,
stained it, shellacked it until it glowed, and bolted it onto the
bumper mounts on the front end. The first time I nudged a
railing in a parking lot, it split smartly in two. So much for
homemade comfort. But for the whole trip up through west
Texas and on into New Mexico and Colorado, it looked handsome indeed, giving the impression of a kind of boat—a yacht,
perhaps—swiftly plying the asphalt.

* * *

Finally, the day came for me to lower the engine into its com-
partment in the front of the truck. Draping a winch over one
of the beams in the garage, I hoisted the engine up, then ma-
neuvered it down again onto the motor mounts and bolted it
home. I was admiring my handiwork when the music stopped

and an announcement came over the radio: four students had been shot dead by the National Guard at Kent State University in Ohio. I was stunned. I felt blood drain from my head, and when it came swirling back it brought with it a sense of outrage and injustice I couldn't control. I rushed out of the garage and around the side of the bungalow, where my father was standing on a ladder, daubing paint on the eaves.

"They shot four students!" I yelled. "They killed them!"

"Who?" he said, looking down at me tembling on the ground.

"The National Guard, they shot four students for demonstrating at Kent State. They're *dead*," I wailed, still trying to come to grips with it. My father came down off the ladder.

"Good," he said, wiping his brush on an old rag he pulled out of his back pocket. "That's what you get if you attack the government and threaten the country."

He said it so calmly, with such conviction, that his manner infuriated me even more.

"What?" I shouted. "They were throwing bottles and sticks—and they killed them!"

"They were breaking the law," my father said. "They were there to get an education, not threaten the soldiers. If they don't like this country, they can leave."

"You're crazy," I screamed. "They weren't doing anything wrong. They were only protesting!"

He gave me a pathetic, measured look. There was sadness in it as well, sympathy for me perhaps, for the pain and fury I was feeling, and the knowledge that this moment might sever us completely, might widen a gulf that had been there all along when we spoke about events or tried to discuss what had happened in the United States over the past ten years. The '60s

were an explosion of energy and emotion, the coming of age
for an entire generation that seemed determined to remake the
world into its own vision of universal brotherhood and peace.
How stupid and naïve it must have seemed to those who had
been through two world wars and a crippling global depression. My father and I stood there in the dust under a searing
Texas sun, regarding each other from the shores of different
worlds. He studied me carefully, unfazed. I was volatile, half-
mad with righteous anger.

"You gotta be crazy," I said again, choking back tears. "You . . ."

But I never finished my sentence. I ran back to the garage,
nearly blind with rage. My stomach was churning and my
hands were shaking. When I picked up a bolt and tried to fasten a cable to the engine block, I dropped it into the tire-well
and had to fish it out, skinning my knuckles in the process.

"God damn it!" I muttered to myself through clenched
teeth. "God *damn* it!"

* * *

That night I walked down to the club and drank until I could
drink no more. Out on the lake I watched the lights of a few
boats heading for the marina on the far shore. There were not
many people in the club. A few couples, having dinner, some
children on the deck, Benny the organ player grinding out hits
from the '40s, "Chattanooga Choo Choo" and "Tuxedo Junction." I felt alienated, even there, even where I had worked for
a full year among people I knew very well. I liked them and
their calm, workaday lives, their good common sense and easy
warmth. I'd even had an affair with one of the waitresses one
night, back in the bungalow, the two of us desperately lonely,
going at each other with an awkwardness we couldn't over-

come. She was ten years older than I was, clearly trapped in her life. There had been more sadness than pleasure in our love-making, and the following day we found ways to avoid each other, though neither of us felt particularly aggrieved. I was thinking of the journey I was about to take, where it would lead me, who I'd meet. After my last drink, I walked back in the moonlight, determined to finish my project quickly and then get lost in the distances between where I was and where I wanted to be. The mesquite trees along the way were packed with cicadas, and their incessant, electric ratchetings made quite a ruckus under the full moon. In those cycles and pulsations of sound, I thought I detected a coded message, a sniggering din of voices from which I wished to escape.

"You don't need us," I said out loud, in the middle of the night, to no one.

The cicadas roared louder, as if in mockery.

* * *

It would take another week for me to connect all the wires, tighten everything down, check the gauges, and finalize my plans. With the help of a friend, I slid into the driver's seat one muggy afternoon in late May, inserted the key into the ignition, and gave it a twist.

Nothing.

My friend stood outside, under the hood, and called back.

"Wait a minute!"

My heart fluttered, then sank. A few agonized moments passed, while I dreamt of taking a bus at dawn if the truck would not start.

"Try it again," he called.

This time the engine turned over with a heavy groan, but

would not start. A bus wouldn't be the same, I reasoned. I would spend days in an ecstasy of half sleep, while the countryside rolled by and I sat there, completely at the mercy of the driver and his immutable schedule. My friend was at the window. "It's the timing, I think. Let me check it out while you turn the engine over. I can see if it's set right, and if not, I can set it correctly myself."

We connected jumper cables from the battery in his car, which we kept running, to the one in my truck. I turned the engine over and over again until he called out.

"What a minute!" Then: "Go on! Try it now!"

The engine turned over once, twice, then sputtered triumphantly into life. It was purring. It sounded powerful, and smooth, all eight new cylinders firing impeccably in perfect order. I was giddy. The following morning I would pack the last of my things into the back, say goodbye to my parents, and edge carefully down the driveway, out onto Arkansas Lane. Yanking the transmission into gear, I would disappear over the crest of the hill and head toward the interstate highway and the Pacific ocean. I was filled with anticipation and dread. Would the engine hold up? Had I really put it all together properly? What if I broke down in the middle of nowhere and was left with a ton of useless metal, and all my belongings in the back, and nothing but my feet to take me where I wanted to go? West Texas was daunting, I knew, a scorched landscape, arid and uninhabitable. It was early. The sun had yet to break over the horizon.

I was twenty-six years old, and already well on my way to nowhere.

On the Road Again

Just outside of Amarillo, I stopped by the side of the road. I had been driving all day, pausing only for lunch and gas. It was early afternoon when I saw the two of them standing there with a guitar case, two rucksacks, and a cat on a leash. They were young—two hippies dressed in linen blouses and bell-bottom pants—and they looked harmless and a bit forlorn, the desert stretching out behind them with nothing but cactus and sand. In the split second it took to see them, windblown and obviously as homeless as I was, I decided to pick them up. Maybe it would be more interesting to have someone with me on the trip, rather than pushing on with nothing but the radio and my anxious thoughts to keep me company. They were part of the same *volkswanderung* to which I now belonged, to which my generation seemed particularly prone. "All come to look for America," as Paul Simon had sung. In my newly forged idealism, I thought I owed it to them to bring them along.

Hours before, I had left Arlington and passed through Fort Worth, heading west on a highway built out of millions and millions of red bricks, a WPA project that began in the city and stretched for miles under the withering sun, a bright ruddy turnpike seemingly baked out of the landscape itself. The day was clear, with a few high clouds building on the horizon already shimmering in the mounting heat. I had no air conditioning, but my windows were open and I happily sped along in my customized truck. Now and then the radio would pick up some country preacher who howled about God and damnation, or the exuberance of a local car dealer hawking his cut-rate bargains—*The sweetest little deals in West Texas!*—and always, everywhere, the billowing, elastic chords of steel guitars and some country singer's weeping over betrayal and lost love. I kept one ear cocked to my engine, in case the slightest irregularity occurred—the chattering of a loose tappet, or a soft knocking that might develop into something critical that could leave me stranded among dry snake-infested arroyos. But the engine hummed and the truck felt solid under my touch as I rolled through Wichita Falls, and Vernon, and Childress, skirting the border of Oklahoma on my way to the high, cracked windswept plains of the panhandle.

In Amarillo, I left the main road and started off through some of the seediest parts of Texas, towns so parched and barren it didn't seem possible anyone could survive. That's when I saw them huddled together in that desolate landscape, and I skidded to a halt. In a moment, he appeared at my window.

"Hey man, thanks for stopping!"

"Where are you going?" I asked.

"We're headed west. California. Just about anywhere."

"I'm on my way to Colorado. I can take you that far."

His eyes widened with excitement.

"Bodacious!" he said. He called to the girl who was making her way toward us on the apron of the highway, struggling with her rucksack and cat: "He's going to Colorado!"

"Hop in," I said. "There's plenty of room. You can put your stuff in the back."

Egan and Florence were from Tennessee. They had hitchhiked south to Dallas to see Egan's mother, a divorcée who lived alone with three cats and an Irish Wolfhound and worked in real estate.

"She's got her own office," Egan announced proudly. They had gotten the kitten from Egan's mother. After a brief visit, the two of them had hit the road again and I was the fourth ride they had flagged down that day. He was younger than me by about five years. She might have been even younger, eighteen or nineteen, and they regarded me at first with a mixture of suspicion and respect. Egan had long brown hair and a scraggly mustache. He was slight, with thin shoulders and almost no hips. She was thin, with limp blonde hair and watery blue eyes. Egan called her *Flo* and sometimes *Florida* when he was being affectionate or making a big pronouncement of some kind.

"Well, Florida, we did good, didn't we?" he said, meaning the ride I was giving them. I could see her again in the rearview mirror as she tried to give some water to the cat in a seashell she had plucked out of her rucksack.

"Where'd you get that shell?" I asked.

"My mom had it in her bathroom," Egan said. "She got it down on the coast near Corpus Christi." Then, as if I suspected him of theft, he added: "She said I could take it."

We swapped stories for the next fifty miles, and by the time we got up near Hartley, we were already friends. Egan felt comfortable enough to pull out a joint and light it up, and Flo loosened up a bit, but was congenitally shy and never com-

pletely relaxed around me. She spent most of the trip fussing
with the cat or packing and repacking their gear, while Egan
sat up front, his bare feet on the dashboard, chattering away
about their trip and their plans once they got to California. I
thought they might be married, but it became clear they were
a couple, sharing a hometown and a brief past, more like brother and sister than lovers. They were good company, and easy
enough to be around.

"This is a bodacious truck," said Egan finishing his joint
and squinting at me through the lingering smoke. "Bodacious"
was his favorite word. He used it to describe anything that
piqued his interest or that he found gratifying. I told him the
story of how I'd overhauled the truck and fitted it out for habi-
tation. "Wow!" he'd say when he was duly impressed, enough
to encourage me to keep telling my story. He was a good lis-
tener, or maybe he was just floating along on my words in a
drugged reverie, happy to listen to the drone of my voice.

The landscape grew lonelier by the mile, acres of dry wash
and a tumbleweed or two occasionally bouncing across the
road in front of us. In Dalhart, we stopped for coffee and gas
while Florence walked the cat and used the rest room at a
truck stop on the north end of town. I studied the map, decid-
ing it would be best to stop for the night somewhere across
the border in New Mexico. It had been a long drive, and I was
tired. I didn't ask Egan to drive, though he offered, as I was still
leery about the truck, and if anything happened to it, I wanted
to be the one at the wheel. About an hour later we hit Texline,
on the edge of the Kiowa grasslands, and bid Texas goodbye.

"And good riddance!" Egan smiled, though the countryside
didn't really get any prettier as we made the crossing.

We camped in New Mexico, then crossed the border into

Colorado the following day. We found our way to I-70 and began to climb, up to the very foot of the Great Divide, then turned off onto Highway 6 toward Loveland Pass, swinging up a narrow two-lane road that meandered up the flanks of the Gore Range, which gave us a breathtaking view of the country below. The slopes were clad in velvety skeins of grass and tufts of wildflowers poking up through fractures in bare rock. The sky glimmered a vitreous blue with some low lying clouds that seemed to scrape themselves on nearby peaks as they passed eastward. We were glued to the windows, breathless at the sight of the great spine of the continent emerging around us, tundra dotted here and there with small, opaque tarns, until a few final bends in the road brought us to the summit. I pulled to the side of the road, then threw open the doors in the back to let the truck fill up with that cold, rarified air. Next to the road were banks of pristine snow that had survived into June. Our heads swam with the altitude, and we laughed and gamboled about like children, tossing snowballs, shading our eyes and looking westward across the Arkansas River to the even higher peaks of the Sawatch Range, beyond which lay our destination in the far valleys of the Western Slope. The sun stood directly above us.

We were on top of the world.

Across the Great Divide

I arrived in Aspen in June, 1970. It was still a sleepy ski town just beginning to wake up from the long slumber caused by the silver bust of the late nineteenth century, when America shifted to the gold standard and the mines in Aspen were closed. In 1970, many of Aspen's secondary roads and almost all of the alleys downtown were still unpaved, and you could walk along them on a summer day kicking up dust. After the orgiastic climax of Woodstock, the so-called hippie generation was beginning to break up, losing its focus—if it ever had one—and coming apart in subtle but definitive ways. We were drifting around the country looking for something else to do after the revolutionary excitement of the 1960s and the terrible punctuation point Kent State had put on the whole sad story. We had to get away from middle-America, which seemed to have won the day by gobbling up our art, our ideas and culture, marketing it so that tie-dyed T-shirts were sold in fashionable stores everywhere, and where even Sonny and Cher had their own television show. Who needed it? Many of us were seeking Shangri-La outside of mainstream culture, where we could carry on with whatever ideas of paradise captured our imaginations.

* * *

When I pulled into Aspen that bright spring afternoon, it was meant to be a temporary stop on a much longer journey, spiritually and geographically. I had planned to move on from Colorado to join whatever remnant was left of Haight-Ashbury in San Francisco. I didn't know at the time that the famous but ephemeral bohemia had already begun to lose its peculiar character (and characters), who would migrate to another part of the city—the Tenderloin—much like the once-thriving artistic community of the West Village in New York shifted to the East Village in the 1970s and '80s, as every art community in the past has transplanted itself to another affordable location as soon as it was "discovered" and thereafter colonized by dilettantes, entrepreneurs, aesthetes, art dealers, imitators, hangers-on, and upstarts of every stripe in search of vicarious thrills and reflected glamour.

* * *

Sailing into Ute City (Aspen's original name), I was unimpressed at first—the town had yet to undergo the Victorian gentrification that would take place shortly, a transformation that would turn it into a gingerbread heaven for the wealthy. The dark stone of the downtown buildings expressed the town's depression, having fallen apart after the country's conversion to the gold standard. The streets were still relatively empty, and Ajax Mountain retained dirty wads of snow on its highest reaches above Ruthie's Run. There were scores of shops that hadn't yet been renovated and turned into Rocky

Mountain boutiques—a reflection of Rodeo Drive there on the Western Slope above the Roaring Fork Valley. But there was something compelling about the town. It was boxed in on three sides by mountains. All winter, there was only one way into or out of town, west down Highway 82, a two-lane country road that dropped slowly between high ridges to Carbondale and finally Glenwood Springs, where the interstate highway provided the first contact again with regular civilization. Aspen had a funky, faded glory. Time swept into the Roaring Fork valley from the west and eddied there in a great circle, never leaving and never changing, a circle on which the streets, the houses, the very people swirled like wood chips in a mountain pool. I had the impression that whatever happened in the rest of the world—war, demonstrations, violence, hunger—would never find me or touch me in Aspen. I couldn't have been happier or felt more at home.

Perhaps I hadn't known until that day that I was looking for such a place, a hideout. I'm sure this was true of the many others who showed up at that time, certainly for Hunter Thompson, who'd set up shop outside of town in Woody Creek, even more remote than Aspen itself. He'd lived in Key West and Big Sur, but even those towns were relatively well-staked-out places compared to Aspen in the 1970s. Of course, realtors and developers, speculators and their wealthy clients would soon follow, as they always did, from Montparnasse to Greenwich Village, from Key West to Haight-Ashbury. "Bill Greed," as we called him, a generic, legendary figure like Paul Bunyan, would soon buy up the town. But for the time being Aspen was a fairly pristine place to set up a new bohemia, no matter how temporary and superficial. And that's pretty much what happened during the '70s before the West Coast *nouveau riche* got wind of the place a decade later and filled up Red Mountain, Starwood, Snowmass, and Aspen Grove with palatial cabins meant to signify how woodsy they were—log mansions with jaccuzzis, hot tubs, steam rooms, trout ponds, massive picture windows, guest quarters, multiple bedrooms, marble floors, corrals for the horses, servants' quarters, three jeeps, a town car, a snowmobile, and a sleek new truck in case they ever had to haul something and so they'd look Western when their family and friends showed up. It's an old story. Paradise always disappears when the angel with the flaming checkbook arrives.

But on my first day in Aspen, most of the brick or local sandstone buildings showed signs of weathering. Little had happened in the intervening eighty years since the bust, save for the paving of downtown streets and the cutting, in the '40s and '50s, of ski slopes on Ajax, Highland, and Buttermilk peaks, as well as on the ridge of Snowmass mountain a few scant miles west, down valley. As we drove slowly along Main Street and back again looking for a good place to park, we felt let down, a palpable disappointment at its ramshackle, abandoned air. This surely wasn't the Shangri-la we were expecting. Only once did Egan breathe his customary epithet of wonder: "Bodacious," as we passed Paepcke Park with its little wooden gazebo evocative of a bygone era of picnics and parades, summer concerts and secret assignations under the Colorado stars. We turned off Galena Street and found a place to park on East Hyman, which was ordinary asphalt in those days, open to traffic. Not much later, a short stretch of East Hyman from Galena to South Mill Street would be paved over with antique bricks imported from St. Louis, and turned into a walking mall, as would E. Cooper Avenue a block away. Ornate streetlamps, wooden benches, and narrow streams fringed with grass and

young aspen trees were installed to complete the illusion of
Belle Epoque elegance and security. It would be one of the first
marks of gentrification. But for now, Aspen was more or less
an authentic nineteenth century mining town, perched on the
western flank of the Great Divide, pondering its better days.

* * *

We got out of the truck and stood on the pavement breathing
the fresh mountain air.

"I'm gonna walk the cat," Flo announced. "There's a park
down there at the end of the street. She needs some exercise."

"Hold on," said Egan," I'm comin' too." I watched as they
shuffled down Hyman Street, Egan with his odd off-kilter
gait, and Flo with her unbound sheaf of blonde hair, leading
the cat on a leash like a tamed, premature infant crawling on
all fours. I walked back toward Mill Street to a grocery store
I had glimpsed. I was hungry, and wanted to buy more supplies. Tom's Market was located on the ground floor of what I
would come to know as the old Elk's building—an imposing
three-story stone building with high-ceilings, tall rows of windows, topped by a decorative cornice and cupola from which
an American flag flapped gaily in the wind. A sign that identified the Elk's Lodge—B.P.O.E.—jutted out over the sidewalk
on Galena Street. Tom's itself was gloomy, wooden floors and
rows of rickety shelves stocked with produce. The scent of
fresh-cut meat from the butcher's block wafted down the aisles
to mingle with the scent of carrots, cereal, bread, turpentine,
and the sawdust they used to sprinkle on the floor every night
and sweep up every morning to keep the place clean. I bought
a loaf of bread, some baloney and cheese, a few cans of soda,
and paid the cashier.

* * *

A few years later, I would venture upstairs. No one I knew had ever been upstairs in the Elks Building. Through the intercession of a mutual friend, I had been invited to speak to Lorenzo Semple, Jr. I entered the building through a door off Galena Street, then climbed two wide sets of stairs. The hallway was dim and cavernous, a long corridor with rows of closed doors, boxes, and various clutter: a roll top desk, a floor lamp. I ended up at the back of the building, where I was let into a light-filled office. In this room, Lorenzo worked with little more than a desk, typewriter, chair, phone, and some stacks of paper here and there in piles on the floor.

"Come on in!" Lorenzo said affably, holding the door open for me and gesturing toward a folding metal chair. "Have a seat." Lorenzo was Dino De Laurentiis's chief screenwriter at the time, and he was working on a remake of *King Kong,* starring Jeff Bridges and Jessica Lange. I was an editor at a literary magazine we'd founded, and we wanted to interview Lorenzo. He'd written some popular and intense films that included *Pretty Poison, Papillon, Parallax View,* and *Three Days of the Condor,* which I had seen the previous year and admired. Screenwriting ranked low on our totem of literary genres, but these films were serious and gripping and I wanted to ask the man who'd conceived them if he would submit to an interview for a special "Locals" issue of *Aspen Anthology.* Lorenzo had one squinty eye and one staring eye, which gave him an odd, fractured look, as though he was both bored and attentive at the same time. He punctuated many of his sentences with a terminal grunt that could come across as dismissive or self-satisfied, though I never knew him to be anything but straightforward and honest. It struck me as peculiar, a man in the Elks Building in Aspen, Colorado, high among evergreens and snow-capped peaks, typing away, his head filled with images of a gargantuan Hollywood beast resurrected among vats of hot mulled wine and condominium complexes, après ski outfits, and imported French wine.

When the interview was conducted by our fiction editor, Hancel McCord, Lorenzo was forthcoming and direct. "In all honesty, I usually love terrible reviews of things I write, because I think they richly deserve it." Coming from anyone else, this might sound like false modesty. But Lorenzo was frank and self-aware, even self-critical, for someone who made his living in Hollywood. Later in the interview, McCord asked: How does a young writer start in the movies? Lorenzo's answer was tart, and to the point: "It's about as reasonable to imagine that you could write a script and mail it in and have it done as to imagine that you could sketch a terrific car and mail it to General Motors, and they would say, 'Wow! Here's our next year's Buick!' I find people, particularly here in Aspen, perfectly well-meaning people pumping gas who say 'I've written a script, where do I send it?'"

Much later, while teaching screenwriting at the Aspen Writers' Conference, Lorenzo would impart these sentiments to his eager students, who in turn were understandably disappointed. The chances of having success in the movie business were nil. During the final days of the conference, these same students wore T-shirts that said FUCK LORENZO printed brazenly across the front. One of the students wrote to me a decade later to proudly announce that she'd had her documentary accepted for production, though it was by a small company and never distributed widely.

And Lorenzo was not much more sanguine about the film

industry as a whole. He said, "I do not see much future for the art movie in America because they get more and more expensive...for every success there are a hundred catastrophes, and endless imitations before they realize that won't work...hundreds of millions of dollars over the years down the drain on imitations."

Then he mentioned *Rancho Deluxe,* which "was a catastrophe, except in Aspen, of course. The Aspen movie!" He was wrong about that: *Harold and Maude* was far more popular, while *King of Hearts* took the prize as the quintessential local flick, playing again and again to packed, enthusiastic houses. Set in France during World War I, *King of Hearts* is a psychological fantasy in which the lovable residents of a nearby loony bin take over a small town that has been evacuated and is due to be blown up. Filmed in 1966, the picture flopped in England and America, only to be revived in Aspen (and across the country in college town art houses) because of its wild, carnivalesque atmosphere and the notion that the film's odd characters could so easily substitute for the town's missing mayor, town council, shopkeepers, and citizens; this was an allegory for the way Aspen's residents viewed themselves. Aspen was a town of misfits and freaks, refugees from the cities and suburban malls of America, places they had repudiated in favor of this town where they could live out their dreams of creative independence and sexual liberation, and pursue other modes of consciousness via drugs, yoga, meditation, hiking, skiing, health fads, the I-Ching, and anti-capitalistic activities of all kinds.

Aspen, in those days, was no place for people with bourgeois ambitions, or the dewy-eyed Yuppies who would follow. It was a real-life village of idiots who planned to take over the place, and almost did. And here we had arrived at the very be-

ginning of it all, though of course we had no idea about any
of this. We just liked the lay of the land and we were happy
enough to be stopping by on our long journey to the coast.

* * *

I found Egan and Flo relaxing in the park, spread out in the
grass as the high-mountain sun soaked into their bones. The
cat crouched nearby, under the shadow of a butterfly's wings.
They looked so innocent, so lost, these two children of the
Aquarian Age in their scruffiness and languor that I almost pit-
ied them, and had a nagging sense that something awful might
happen. But I tried to brush my misgivings aside.

We sat in the penumbra of Shadow Mountain, munching
our sandwiches. I didn't know yet that Wagner Park would be
the scene of many local events, most notably weekend rugby
scrums and softball games that pitted the staff of one bar or
restaurant, one business or municipal department against another, part of the civic life of Aspen that made the town special
and authentic, with some customs and events even dating back
to mining days. This is what distinguished Aspen from other
Lincoln Log ski towns like Copper Mountain or Vail. Those
villages seemed pre-fabricated by some architectural firm in
Denver or Boston or New York, according to some Master Plan
of what a ski resort should look like. When President Gerald
Ford skied at Vail, someone on the press corps described the
place as "shake 'n' bake Tyrolean." Vail had been constructed in
the 1960s. To walk on its pre-conceived, blueprinted streets was
to feel a prevailing artifice. It was like the mockup for a film
about a Heidi-like village somewhere in the Swiss Alps, filled
with apple-cheeked villagers and milkmaids about to burst
into song. Aspen, by contrast, had a cultural life, a town gov-

ernment, and a history dating back to the nineteenth century. Its public buildings had been erected of stone that had been cut out of the local mountains and hauled into place block by block, meant to last centuries. Its houses dated from the Victorian era, no matter how many times they had been painted and primped up or how much gingerbread decorated their windows. Its streets, like the streets of any town with a long past, had accumulated over the years by the principles of slow and unpredictable growth. They had been set on a grid, but that grid shaped itself to the contours of the valley floor, bound and delimited by necessity, not design. Its parks and public spaces had evolved naturally over the years. Only the golf course, on the western edge of Aspen beyond Cemetery Lane seemed calculated and out-of-place.

It was this long-standing social and political reality that was the source of competition between Aspen and the newer resorts, and a good deal of snobbery on Aspen's part. Aspen was well aware of its past glory, and the glory of its present setting and charm. Vail was located in a valley too, and at the foot of a pass, but its physical features and panoramic views were not as dramatic. To enter Aspen by way of Independence Pass, descending the watershed of the Roaring Fork River past cliffs and spires and precipitous dropoffs on either hand, was to arrive filled with the majesty and ruggedness of its surroundings. Aspen was alluring in its rusticity, impressive in scale, larger than life.

* * *

Pamela McPherson, whom everyone called Mrs. Mac, was in her mid-sixties, with a crown of white hair and leathery brown skin toughened and creased by the sun over years of skiing and hiking. She owned a blue Victorian with white trim called Snow Chase Lodge, which sat directly under the shadow of one of the ski lifts on Ajax Mountain. It had a small front porch and peeling clapboard siding. She lived alone and loved to talk to her young visitors in order to find out all about them. Her tenants seemed like the children she'd never had and she treated them as such, cooking meals and letting them sneak off without paying the rent, making them coffee in the morning and sometimes stuffing a dollar or two into their pockets with a maternal wink. Everyone loved Mrs. Mac and protected her fiercely. Whatever few rules she had were taken seriously. She especially loved the girls and would spend hours chatting with them around her kitchen table. The girls were given the few available proper rooms upstairs, with brass beds and little vanity tables, while the boys would stay in the basement in a dormitory setting with bunk beds and a metal shower. After almost a week in the truck, this lodging suited me just fine. There were eight pairs of bunk beds, four on each side of a small aisle, and I chose one at the end of a row and stretched out on the bottom bunk to try it on for size.

That evening, with nothing to do, I wandered downtown with Egan and Flo to look for a cheap place to eat. The actual downtown area of Aspen in the 1970s was just eight or ten square blocks with shops and restaurants spread around a grid. From our perch at the edge of the ski slope, we strolled down South Galena to Cooper Street and found a dive called King George's Pizza and Ice Cream Parlor. King George himself was a lanky man with ruddy hair and green, wolfish eyes. He regarded everyone with benign suspicion. I ordered a beer, but King George's icy glance at Egan and Flo let them know that they'd better not try to order one themselves. Many people in town considered George a little crazy, but harmless. It was difficult to understand his intermittent tirades, and his sentences often seemed disjointed, not really adding up to anything. We didn't care. We were hungry and ordered a large pizza with as many toppings as we could afford. After warmed-over beans and cold slices of meat, the pizza tasted like heaven. The beer's cold, effervescent bite set off the spiciness of the pie and we ate it and ordered a second, smaller pie. George squinted. He knew we weren't locals. George was acquainted with everyone in town, and the wave of hippies that had begun passing through must have upset his sense of domestic tranquility.

After gorging ourselves with the King, we stood out on Cooper Street in the twilight thinking what we would do next. Egan took his guitar from its case and placed it on the sidewalk in front of him.

"Hey Flo," he said, "Make Minnie dance (they'd named their cat Minne). I'm gonna play and see if anyone will toss some money in."

Being a hippie was one thing, but begging on the street offended my middle-class upbringing. I stood off to one side to watch their little show as Egan sang and strummed out a song, and Florence happily made her cat dance, jerking it up on its leash like a puppet. A few people stopped to listen, then continued on their way. One or two threw coins. Egan scooped up the change, stowed his guitar back in its case, and the two of them walked up the hill to find my truck, where they would sleep for the night. I decided to stay in town to explore the streets and watch the last light fade against the taller buildings and the flank of Red Mountain, awash in a rosy tint that gave it its name. As the last light declined, it modulated from white to yellow to a rich bronze that plated the trunks of trees, the bricks and sandstone of the buildings, the roofs, the very streets with gold as the air swam with cottonwood seeds and the clouds reddened, then faded. I watched this from a little park on Monarch Street, across from the Crystal Palace, and was struck by the glory of it as the sky to the east over Independence Pass turned a deep oceanic blue. I had admired the natural beauty of New England, but this was different, less alien, less stark. A hush enveloped the town, a serenity that filled me with a sense of restfulness and immediate peace.

Then and there, I made a decision that would change my life.

The Silver Circuit

"I've decided to stay."

We were having breakfast at the Epicure, a little café on South Mill and Main, cattycorner to the Hotel Jerome. The Epicure featured crude, naïve paintings of birds, flowers, and mountains on the walls, giving it the festive air of a Paris bistro. It was a pleasant diner where you could order granola with blueberries or bananas, scrambled eggs with tofu and scallions, or big sticky bran muffins still warm from the oven. Tables had been set out in a small courtyard, screened off by a ten-foot hedge, which you entered through a door in the back.

"You're gonna stay for good?" Egan's eyes widened.

"Well, until September at least. I plan to move on to California in the fall. But I think I'll spend the summer here. It's a nice place, and I'm not in a hurry. You can stay too if you want."

Egan and Flo hadn't planned on this. When they climbed into my truck outside of Amarillo, they thought they'd hit the jackpot, a single ride all the way from west Texas directly to the Haight in San Francisco, with a few stops along the way.

Egan stirred his coffee listlessly while Flo stared at the table as though it might move.

"I think we'll go on to the coast," he said glancing at her. "Right, Florida?"

She lifted her head and smiled. "Yeah."

"Look," I said, "I'll drive you out to the edge of town when you're ready, and you can hitchhike from there. Somebody's bound to be going your way. It's a pretty straight shot all the way from here to California"

"Yeah," said Flo again.

"Yeah," said Egan.

* * *

Later that morning I drove them out of town on Highway 82, past the airport and the road up to Snowmass Village so they could catch cars leaving the valley both ways. After piling out with all their belongings, we said our goodbyes. I caught a glimpse of them diminishing in my rearview mirror, two forlorn people lost in a huge landscape that threatened to swallow them forever, and I had that feeling again, a premonition that something terrible might happen. I wonder, even as I write this, if they survived: Egan, dreamy-eyed, distracted, willing to give himself up entirely to fate, and Flo, a scrawny little blonde, not much more than a child, leashed to her cat. They were part of a massive dislocation, a utopian dream, a chimera of happiness in which only children could believe. *All you need is love*, we chanted, but then we became the computer geeks, soccer moms, day school teachers and stock brokers of the '80s and '90s, conservative homebodies only slightly more disillusioned than our parents. All dreams of escape die eventually in someone's living room among the fixtures of domesticity, cut-rate furniture, and subscription magazines.

When I looked back again, Flo and Egan were gone.

* * *

For the next few weeks I busied myself with finding a job and a place to live. From Mrs. Mac's place, I could stroll into Aspen and explore it in detail. There was a high percentage of young people standing on street corners, driving past, filling the little bistros and cafés at all hours. I kept to myself, intent upon my immediate task: finding a job before my small cache of money ran out. Eventually, I would find work in the next valley, Snowmass Village, which had been constructed a few years before my arrival and needed service workers of all kinds to keep up with the rapid expansion of the resort. Like Vail, Snowmass Village resembled a Swiss hamlet; it had a few wooden shops and houses that were huddled around a small central square. There was a fake clock tower with a pointed roof, and a modest fountain that hardly ever worked and froze over punctually in the winter. The small group of people I met and worked with there soon migrated back to Aspen to live. Though the skiing was fabulous, nothing much happened in Snowmass Village at night, and we found ourselves driving into Aspen four or five times a week to patronize the restaurants and bars, the cafés and clubs loud with music.

By the time autumn rolled around, I had a job waiting tables at the Leather Jug, a studio apartment just down the hill at Arbieterdorf (German for *worker's village*, a name I found ominous and distasteful), and a group of friends to keep me company. I felt at home. Any thoughts of moving on to San Francisco and the Haight had vanished. I stayed in Snowmass for the better part of a year, then moved back into Aspen for good.

* * *

The city of Aspen, formerly known as Ute City after the local Native Americans, is divided between two monuments,
two poles of importance that dominate the town. The Wheeler Opera House and the Jerome Hotel anchored Aspen's civic, cultural, and social life and still do more than a hundred
years later. They were built by Jerome B. Wheeler, owner of
Macy's department store in New York, who had traveled west
to attend to his wife's precarious health. People with pulmo-
nary problems in the nineteenth century—those who could
afford it—traveled to the southwest to take advantage of its
dry, salubrious climate. The lack of humidity and the warm,
high-mountain sunlight were often prescribed for those with
everything from asthma and bronchitis to full-blown "consumption," as tuberculosis was commonly called. Doc Holliday had arrived in Glenwood Springs, just down valley from
Aspen, in the summer of 1887 to take advantage of the pristine air and the town's famous hot springs. He died there in
November of that year, unable to bring his tuberculosis under
control.

In addition to being a doting husband, Jerome B. Wheeler was a financier who dabbled in businesses and mining.
His financial success allowed him to erect Aspen's two most
noteworthy buildings. Like other civic-minded Aspen entrepreneurs, Wheeler wanted to provide the hard-bitten, rough-
and-ready miners with recreational alternatives to the bars
and brothels that once thrived along Cooper Street. Bringing
a touch of culture to the barbarians was a fundamental pur-
suit of western philanthropists. The early, ramshackle towns of
the Rocky Mountains needed to be civilized. Establishing the
hegemony of the law was one way. Building great palaces of

art was another. There's an opera house in almost every nineteenth century mountain town of any repute, creating a chain of venues, what was called the Silver Circuit, for aspiring contraltos or coloraturas back east. These opera houses stipple the Rocky Mountain region like a string of pearls on the throat of a corpulent diva.

What must it have been like to step out onto one of those stages on a Saturday evening and start singing to the miners who had completed a long week's labor in the stifling mines? What had the miners looked like, barely scrubbed of mine dust, stuffed into unaccustomed suits, choked by ties, their faces red with constant exertion and heavy drinking? How did it feel when the town's more prominent citizens—the Cowenhovens, Wheelers, Hallams, and Browns—mingled with the rabble from the smelters and saloons, the slag heaps and shafts in which they slaved six days a week? The heyday of the Wheeler Opera House didn't last long. The Silver Crash in 1893 brought most touring to a halt, and many of the Silver Circuit's grand entertainment halls were boarded up and silent. In 1912, an arsonist's fire gutted the Wheeler's upper floor performance space, and it wasn't properly restored until the 1960s, a few years before I arrived. Even that renovation looked old and dreary by the 1970s. We thought of the Wheeler as a quaint wreck where we could see movies or hear a concert if we were lucky.

One day in 1972, mid-afternoon, I was passing the Opera House and noticed a line of people snaking around the building from the entrance on East Hyman, down S. Mill. This was an unusual sight. The Wheeler seldom filled for any event, and a long queue in the middle of the day was notable. I spied two friends of mine, Cathy and Tommy Crum, lined up with the rest.

"What's going on?"

"There's a free concert," said Cathy.

"Oh yeah? Who's playing?"

"The Nitty Gritty Dirt Band," she said. "They're appearing at the Aspen Inn tonight, so they're giving a free concert for the locals this afternoon."

"The Nitty Gritty Dirt Band?" The name sounded preposterous. Who would give themselves such a hokey name?

"Come on, get in line," said Tommy. "You'll love it."

The Opera House was packed, even the balcony, which swayed and shuddered as we tramped in and took our seats. Thick velvet curtains smothered the high windows, blocking all light, so it didn't seem that much different inside than it would at night. Still, it was the middle of the day and completely unplanned, which gave the event a festive, impromptu quality, and excitement was running high.

"There's a comedian, too," said Tommy as we took our seats on the left-hand side of the balcony. "He's the opening act."

This news heightened my skepticism, but I was happy to be with my friends. I expected nothing more than a local garage band, some group of half-assed troubadours who had finally earned a big break by giving a free concert for the masses. No one had ever heard of Steve Martin, and he looked gangly and out-of-place in his white suit and cowboy boots, a banjo slung over his shoulder. He stood alone in a cone of intense light and went through his shtick: funny, self-mocking songs like "Ramblin' Man"; jerky, exaggerated gestures and non sequiturs; an apparent arrow through his head projecting out of both ears; fake nose and eyeglasses; an absurd lack of self-awareness and sophistication, imbuing his stage-character with a sympathetic charm; and a balloon-tying act that should have been a disaster but wasn't. How he managed to make the tired trappings of an outmoded Vaudeville clown work was a mystery. By the time he left the stage wearing a twisted crown of balloons and his enormous plastic nose, gibbering as he walked up the center aisle and out the back door, he had won us over. Martin had a genius for letting you know that he knew that he was being ridiculous. In a way, he was making fun of comedy itself.

Steve Martin lived in Aspen for several years in the early 1970s. I used to serve him drinks at Ute City Banque. He'd come in and sit alone at the bar, waiting for a table for lunch with a wry grin. He left after only a few years, apparently sick of the smug, condescending Aspen attitude many residents adopted with respect to the "ordinary," outside world. Such pretension, rather than any supposed superiority, set us apart. It was one of the least attractive features of the place, along with pure-bred malamutes or huskies, pickup trucks with gun racks and brooms jutting out of the back, and ZG license plates. Martin wasn't pretentious, and he didn't like to be ignored. Many found him shy and unassuming. It was an undeclared law in Aspen at the time that you didn't speak to celebrities, or even ogle them. This supposedly honored their privacy, but it also aspired to put everyone in town on the same footing. If celebrities were nothing special, then our status as a new-age, egalitarian society would be complete. We were rudely democratic, if nothing else. Hierarchies were for the capitalistic, fallen world we'd left behind.

* * *

Back in the Wheeler Opera House, the Nitty Gritty Dirt Band took the stage. "Motley" is a word usually applied to sailors, but this crew of musicians was as miscellaneous as a handmade quilt, a pack of cavorting harlequins, singing and playing their instruments like a human calliope. They reminded me of the rollicking groups I had seen back east on Cape Cod, but the Dirt Band was tighter, more professional, and their lyrics, harmonies, and chord changes were more sophisticated. And they were amplified. They may have started out as a jug band, but their talent and ambition transcended the genre. Jimmy Fadden blew a mournful harp, while Les Thompson clowned on bass playing the slob, letting the back of his pants hang down. Jeff Hanna and Jimmy Ibbotson provided vocals, accompanying themselves on guitars. Their antics were part honky-tonk, part burlesque, part pop group, and they knew how to command an audience's attention. We stamped our feet, calling them back for half a dozen encores.

That afternoon is long gone. But what lingers is the memory of John McEuen in full buckskins and mountaineer's beard leaning savagely into his electric violin, and Jimmy Ibbotson leaping from the front apron of the stage into the empty orchestra pit to land on his knees with the melodramatic precision of a rock idol, while still playing his guitar.

Over the years, I saw many other musicians, actors, comedians, and dancers perform on the Opera House stage, and even produced a few shows myself for the benefit of the Aspen Literary Foundation. In the distant past, Sarah Bernhardt, Lily Pons, and Burl Ives stood upon those same boards and had given it their all, as had Lillian Gish and Thornton Wilder, who staged an early version of *Our Town*. Gish returned to the Opera House as an honored guest in the 1980s after the renovation. This is all part of the historical record, but we were aware of it as we went about our work at the Literary Foundation on the second floor.

Once, I stood backstage and looked at the charred web of beams that loomed above me, the result of a fire in 1912 that nearly gutted the building. At any period in its history, the building might have disappeared altogether were it not for its sturdy Peachblow sandstone exterior and the concerted efforts of a few civic-minded philanthropists who managed to swoop in at crucial times to restore the structure to something of its former glory. Like other buildings of its kind, echoes ripple and shadows flicker, the faces of lost patrons crowd the spot-lit air, vanishing as the curtain comes down.

*   *   *

Some of the streets in Aspen were named after prominent citizens—Hallam, Hopkins, Francis, Gibson, Garmisch, Puppy Smith, and perhaps Cooper—while others, like Galena, were named after mining activities. Galena Street, for instance, is named after the mineral form of lead sulfide—*galena*—which is found in many areas of the United States and around the world. There's a whole town—a mining community in Kansas—called Galena, as well as Galena, Illinois, known for its lead mines and as the home of Ulysses S. Grant before and after the Civil War. Most importantly for Aspen, large amounts of silver are often found in deposits of galena, ore which then has to be smelted in order to extract and purify the silver for use as currency or plating. So it's natural that a street in Aspen was named after this lead ore whose occurrence is crucial to mining. Then there's W. Smuggler Street, whose name is self-explanatory. Other streets were given generic names found in all American towns of any size: Main Street, Spring Street, 3rd Street, and so on. The grid in Aspen is an amalgam of history, vanity, whimsy, and plain old numerical practical-

ity. In the twenty years I lived there off and on, I never learned
where any of the streets were by name—with the exception of
Main Street. All other streets existed in relation to that main
thoroughfare. Like all cities, Aspen is a web of parks, byways,
buildings and footpaths that seem to have been contrived to
confound residents and visitors alike.

* * *

For hard-core Aspen locals, some of the more interesting activities occurred in the basement of the Opera House. Through
a door on the side of the building facing East Hyman Avenue,
you could step down into a catacomb of rooms sectioned off
by flimsy screens that marked the limits of different ventures.
One of these comprised the town's original thrift shop, racks of
faded shirts, frayed jeans, boots, hats, even old ski equipment,
and military surplus items. You could buy web belts, canteens,
tents, utility knives, tin utensils, and plastic containers of all
kinds, which pleased the hikers. Later, the thrift shop moved
upstairs to the sidewalk level on South Mill Street, and even
later, to a spot just past the fire house on the corner of East
Hopkins and South Galena.

One of the enterprises called itself a café, though I don't remember its exact name and there is no mention of it in the
public record. It was a soup kitchen that served cheap bowls
of gruel and simple salad with a hunk of heavy, multi-grain
bread. Someone had scattered a few tables and chairs around a
common central room, and you would pay for your meal, step
up to a large pot, ladle out your soup, stash some greens on the
other side of your plate, add a chunk of dark bread, and take a
seat. It was a community living room where people could sit
and enjoy a cheap lunch. An added attraction was music, on

Saturday afternoons, when the space turned into a subterranean café where aspiring folk musicians could perform unam-
plified. I recall seeing folksinger Jack Hardy there for the first
time, and Jimmy "Stray Dog" Dykann, who'd only recently arrived from southern California. Musicians would soon appear
at the plethora of local clubs and restaurants that existed in the
1970s, an extensive circuit of live music that stretched from Aspen to Snowmass to venues down valley in Basalt, Carbondale, and Glenwood Springs before disco almost destroyed live
music in Aspen and the country at large. Not long afterwards,
the central basement of the Wheeler Opera House returned
to a warren of narrow hallways, exposed pipes, and cramped
rooms, one of which housed the local radio station for brief
time before it moved on to the Hotel Jerome.

    A small segment of the basement was vital to the mental,
emotional, and social health of local residents. The Pub inhabited a narrow space under the big stone steps and main front door
of the Wheeler at the corner of Hyman and Mill Streets. Patrons
entered by descending a set of stairs under those front steps. A
dark, low-ceilinged, smoke-infested hole, The Pub served shots
of whiskey and mugs of beer, as well as decent hamburgers,
fries, and "fire-alarm" chili. You could go there any time of the
day or night to drink, buy drugs, and visit your friends. The idea
was to get as loud and drunk as possible without passing out.
No frills, no airs. Wooden booths lined the two street-side front
walls, partially illuminated during the day by deep window
wells that allowed light to spill in on the revelers below. The two
a.m. closings were a thing to behold: bartenders and waitresses
struggling to pry the last customers out of their seats, cajoling,
threatening, pleading, then shooing them towards the door until the last straggler staggered up the steps and disappeared. "We

called it the two o'clock shuffle," my friend Tipi Cheryl recalled. "You might go home with someone who just happened to be going up the stairs with you."

The Pub opened for business at about ten in the morning, and there was always someone sipping his first cool mug of beer, waiting to see who else would stumble down the steps and take a seat on the next stool along the bar. By noon, the lunch crowd filtered in, and by four-thirty, the first wranglers arrived after they'd parked their pickup trucks along South Mill Street. You could see them lined up there, a score of battered vehicles with brooms stuck in one of the holes along the side panels, and always a husky or a malamute sitting up in the empty bed, staring at you with wary eyes as you passed by on the sidewalk. There were no real wranglers, of course, only city kids who'd adopted the Colorado lifestyle and liked to wear cowboy boots and Stetsons and act like they'd been herding cattle all day. The wranglers mingled with the potheads, hippies, ski bums, and the local working clientele, those who stopped in for a drink before or after their shifts at other bars or restaurants in town.

* * *

The second floor of the Wheeler Opera House comprised a number of offices that had originally been used by the Aspen Mining & Smelting Company, the bank's offices, an attorney, and a dentist before being occupied during the latter part of the 1970s by some of the town's burgeoning artistic community. Attornies Buzzy Ware, Dwight Shellman, and Joe Edwards, as well as Mike Strang—rancher, investment banker, and one-term U.S. Representative to Congress—had offices there too. The service stairway to the second floor was at the rear of the building on S. Mill Street. A wide set of risers brought you up to a long hall with offices on either side, each door topped with a high transom that gave the place a turn-of-the-century look. This was heightened by cracked, darkly painted wainscoting and high walls papered with light-brown burlap. The carpeting was musty, the street-side windows tall and sun-gorged, the ceilings fifteen feet above the floors, and each office was configured according to the inhabitant's needs and the architectural anomalies of the Opera House. In our office that housed the Aspen Literary Foundation, a large room with a deep, twenty-foot bookshelf, an armchair, and a light-table for pasting up issues of *Aspen Anthology* led to the door of a tiny cubicle with a window and a severe, sloped ceiling under the stairway that connected to the third floor. Across from this cubicle, running parallel with the large reception area, was a supply room. Except for the Xerox business, the offices on the second floor had been donated to nonprofit organizations by the city, which had purchased the building in 1918 for unpaid back taxes.

The third floor performance space was and is the highlight of the building. The once-dazzling proscenium of Jerome B. Wheeler survived as a token of the theater's glorious past. The original seats had been upholstered in Moroccan leather, but were replaced in the 1940s by rude benches, followed by old movie house seats bolted to the floor in the 1960s. A never-ending procession of players had mounted the stage to gesticulate, sing, whirl, and vanish as various Shakespearean troupes, minstrel shows, Vaudeville acts, burlesque queens, concerts, lectures, and even boxing matches appeared in turn, according to Wheeler's web site. By the 1970s, movies were projected onto a flimsy screen that dropped down over the stage. Manager John Bush selected the best films, not Hollywood blockbusters, so the place exuded the air of an art house theater, a hushed, darkened space with small audiences for most showings. The sumptuous chandelier, a marvel of wire and cut glass, dangled over patrons like some gaudy Victorian hat. Herbert Bayer had brought it from Chicago during renovations in the late '40s. And in the summer months, the stage was borrowed by the Aspen Music School for smaller productions. The theater stood empty during the day, and I would sometimes mount the carpeted stairs at one end of our hall to breathe in the atmosphere of silence and elegant neglect. Inevitably, there was a story about a ghost that inhabited the theater once the lights went down for the night. Standing there in that dusty Victorian cavern, I could almost believe it, though I saw nothing but rows of empty seats and the heavy velvet curtain that swept the boards like the hem of some debutante's enormous gown.

A Grand Hotel

An opera house is one thing, a hotel another. No one sleeps in an opera house overnight. In bad times, the theater may remain vacant and silent for months, even years, before some exuberant cultural renaissance resurrects it. But a hotel remains busy twenty-four hours a day. If it ceases to be a hotel, it becomes something else—a catacomb of shops and apartments that continue to house people around the clock and thus remains a focal point of life. Construction on the Hotel Jerome on Main Street started just months after work commenced on the Wheeler Opera House, and both buildings stood ready for service by 1889. The town residents must have watched them go up with mounting excitement and anticipation that their crude, hardscrabble mining camp would soon become a city of culture and a destination for travelers on their way west.

The Hotel Jerome officially threw open its doors on Thanksgiving Eve, 1889. It was one of the first buildings west of the Mississippi to be fully lit by electricity. We can imagine crowds standing on the packed dirt of Main Street, gazing up admiringly at the three-story building with its impressive façade, arched windows, entrance columns, and waffled brick parapet. A number of changes ensued over the decades, including a renovation in 1946 by Walter Paepcke and Bauhaus artist Herbert Bayer, when the original brick of the exterior walls was covered with a thick layer of blue paint. According to my friend Tommy DiMaggio, a project to repaint the Jerome white in 1969 had been contracted out to Michael Solheim, who would later manage the bar during its heyday as a magnet for bohemian artists. Once it had been painted white, the hotel was provided with contrasting sets of "blue eyebrows" over those arched windows, giving the building an inquiring look, a supercilious air of hauteur and childish wonder.

* * *

This is the hotel into which I strode, one hot afternoon just days after my arrival, to order a cold glass of beer and read the *Aspen Times* in hopes of finding a job and a cheap apartment, and to pore over articles describing life in the town. In 1970, a newspaper was still an historical text, a weekly chronicle of the town's heart and soul, and there was no better way to get to know a place than to study the want-ads, photos, editorials, columns, announcements, political diatribes, and social events.

The entire hotel—lobby and bar, cavernous hallways and rooms—had been furnished in a style dubbed, in the late nineteenth century, "Eastlake Gothic." Some of the original chairs, tables, and beds remained, creaky but usable, and the entire edifice possessed an air of vanished celebration and faded grandeur. The hotel was known as a place of secrecy and assignation. Down-valley residents might sneak up to Aspen for furtive trysts, while Aspenites occasionally rented rooms to avoid scrutiny in their own apartment complexes or neighborhood houses where prying eyes kept watch. No one—at least among my friends—knew who owned the Jerome or who ran it. It seemed to pass from hand to hand, floating on nothing but Christmas reservations and raucous nights in the bar on the first floor. In fact it was owned and operated by the Elisha family, but we didn't know that then. The lobby's massive dome, like a giant Tiffany lampshade, glowed faintly over armchairs so deep that you could sink into them for an entire morning to read a newspaper or doze over a dull book. An elk's head or two adorned the walls, and threadbare Persian rugs completed the effect of a bygone era.

The Jerome's most interesting artistic development occurred when Cherie and David Hiser founded the Center for the Eye, a photographic studio and workshop in the hotel's basement. It was in full operation by the time I arrived in 1970. Jerry Eulsmann, Eugene Smith, Todd Walker, and Mason Lions taught there, as well as Doug Rhinehart, Robert Heinecken, and Robert Gilka, director of photography at *National Geographic*. The students and teachers who participated in the Center of the Eye and its programs were serious about art and exerted influence over modern American photography. Almost none of them were based in Aspen, but their presence in connection with the Center added a distinguished and noteworthy element to the town.

Once the Center closed up shop, the space was renovated and occupied by two artists, Carol Alpern and Nini Jennings, who presented their own work and the work of other artists in a gallery there. Carol was an abstract painter of primal, glowing canvases, while Nini worked with mosaics, chipping particolored stone into shapes and welding them together in large sturdy frames, the smell of stone dust and epoxy heavy in the air. In another part of the basement, just under the lobby, Aspen's first FM station, KSPN, began broadcasting a wide variety of programming, from country & western to talk radio to rock 'n' roll. I visited Ed Thorne many times during his jazz show to chat about Aspen and the Writers' Conference. Ed was a bearded, affable man who smoked a pipe and was curious about all forms of art, and I'd smuggle a mug of beer down with me from the bar upstairs in order to prime him so he'd expatiate about jazz or literature or whatever else he was engaged in at the time. His wife, Missy Thorne, was a painter and part of the lively local art scene, along with Dick Carter, Tom Benton, Gaarde Moses, Chris Cassett, and Paul Pascerella. It was nothing to walk into a studio during a show and chat with the host while drinking beer, snorting a line of coke, or smoking a joint as the long hours wore away. We were young and obscenely healthy, so it hardly made any difference what we did. There was a joke that, for years, involved death and self-immolation in Aspen: no one, we maintained, would have the bad taste to actually die in Aspen. The few who did die had at least had the courtesy to go off and do it in a Denver hospital, or suffered some tragedy in the back country never to be heard from again, or returned home to die among family and friends, receding discreetly into an announcement later posted in the *Times*. I don't mean to imply that there were *no* deaths in Aspen. There were. But the town was a place of vitality and youth. Pain was a broken ankle or wrist, proudly achieved during skiing and displayed in a white cast. Suffering was a bad cold, or a severe hangover, easily obtained and just as easily shed. The real damage would come later.

* * *

The Jerome's street-level bar, located on the building's southwest corner, was truly the heart of the hotel, the place where
locals and tourists rubbed elbows. The Jerome Bar exhibited a
number of features familiar in Victorian barrelhouse décor: a
hard tile floor set with repeating, abstract designs; a brass foot
rail; a high, coffered tin ceiling; glass transoms etched with
lacy patterns; antique lamps that aped old gas fixtures of the
period; and of course a mahogany bar, with an ornate back-
bar carved out of blond wood said to have been imported from
somewhere in the Orient. All of this was polished and largely preserved when the entire hotel was dolled-up to its original Victorian splendor in 1985. One ritual involved the conven-
ing, every Friday evening at five, of local artists to sip drinks,
smoke, see friends, and gabble about work, or argue about the
nature of art in general. The artists always occupied a large
oval table at the front of the room near the main door: Tom
Benton, Missy Thorne, Dick Carter, Michael Cleverly, Paul
Pascarella, sometimes cartoonist Chris Cassatt from the *Aspen
Times*, and Gaarde Moses who had a graphic business. They
were a cool bunch, a few still spattered with paint, command-
ing the room with their intense looks and high talk. Once in a
while novelist Jim Salter would come in wearing a sheepskin
coat to order a drink at the bar. Steve Wishart, soon to become
a city councilman, sat at the very back where the bar bent
around under the TV set on the corner of the wall. I preferred
the side room, which you entered through a high swinging
door, a dark Victorian parlor with heavy velvet drapes cover-
ing much of the front windows, flocked wallpaper, turn-of-
the-century sofas and chairs, antique lamps with tasseled cloth
shades like your grandmother owned. These stood on marble-

topped tables with ornately carved mahogany stands. There
was an enormous mirror on the back wall tilted over a red love
seat, which made the place feel a little like a bordello. A glossy
piano crowded the front corner of the room. No one ever sat
and played, but I first saw Jan and Vic Garret there, one of the
early folk duos, accompanying themselves on guitars, enter-
taining a small but appreciative audience.

What made the side room special was its privacy, and the
fact that you could close the door between it and the main
bar. Voices and music from the bar's sound system would filter in, but the din was muffled and distant, making it possible
to speak in a regular voice and hear what was said in response.
This was a room for collusion, for lovers and crooks, schemers,
dealers, anyone who wished to remain anonymous and alone.
High in one corner of the room, a massive buffalo's head jutted out, hoary with dust, where I once saw Jack Nicholson and
Jim Harrison calmly enjoying their drinks, Nicholson—even
in that dingy room—still wearing his sunglasses after a day of
skiing. I wanted to engage them in talk, but what do you say to
such celebrated people exposed like that in a public place? They
looked comfortable and at ease, and I left them alone.

* * *

One afternoon, back in the main bar, I saw a woman sitting
with Timothy Marquand. Timothy was the son of famed novelist, John P. Marquand, and owned a house in the west end
overlooking Hallam Lake. His companion had a cloud of auburn hair, which she had frizzed, and languid green eyes enhanced by false eyelashes. Timothy introduced her as Viva.
The attraction was instantaneous and mutual, though I was
nobody and she was already one of Andy Warhol's supermod-

els, having made several films with him in New York in the
'6os. We talked for a few minutes as I sipped my drink, and the
warmth radiating from her was unmistakable. Her smile betrayed a mixture of interest and insouciant disregard. Clearly, she could take it or leave it and it would be all the same to
her. Such encounters were nothing to get particularly excited
about. Soon I rushed off to a meeting and she left Aspen several days later, so nothing more happened. Still, chance encounters sometimes make powerful impressions. The riptide of sex
is immediate and deep.

Another noteworthy encounter took place while I was sipping beer on the corner of the bar nearest the front door, my
favorite spot to take in the interior of the bar and the street
outside at the same time. It was about three in the afternoon,
and the place was nearly empty, aside from the bartender, me,
someone in the side room, and a couple who was sitting about
ten feet away, just beyond the handles of the beer pumps, but
not obscured by them. The man had twisted in his chair with
his back to me. The woman's head was lowered, and he was
leaning toward her, so at first it appeared they were lovers
whispering endearments. Then I realized the woman was sobbing while the man's head bobbed slightly as he hissed, "You
fucking cunt!" he said. "You bitch . . ." though I couldn't follow any of what he might have said beyond this. She sank under the barrage of his insults, folding into herself like a small
animal. Whatever was happening between them was none of
my business, and there seemed to be no threat of imminent
violence. Only the man's harsh and insistent epithets—half au-
dible snarls—ugly and disparaging, and the woman, shoulders
trembling, compelled my attention. When he finally turned
back toward the bar, exposing his profile, I could see that it was

Lee Marvin, lips set in a grimace of anger, fingers clutching his beer. That face was unmistakable, his eyes dull and narrowed in rage, long patrician nose, elongated head, and lean squared-off jaw. Soon enough they left, and the bartender asked if I would like another drink.

"Jesus!" I said. *"That* was something!"

"Yeah, they've been staying here for days. Skiing on the mountain. I guess you just never know."

* * *

In the 1970s, the Jerome was the best place to be on Halloween. Bohemian Aspen turned out in droves to celebrate warlocks, goblins, witches, wizardry and monsters of every description. Taking his cue from 1920s' Paris, artist Robin Mols created the first Beaux Arts Ball. There was a remarkable effort put into designing costumes for the event. Those first costumes were original and inspired, though in later years, rented costumes predominated. Halloween in Aspen was an occasion for high jinx and tumultuous revelry. I recall catching a glimpse of Superman snorting coke with Little Bo Peep behind one of the enormous potted palms in a dark hallway upstairs, and one reveler, who called himself "ElectroMan," was dressed in a black body suit strung with tiny lights that blinked and rippled as he moved, powered by a battery pack strapped to his belt. A flashlight dangled where his privates would be. Entering the hotel during the Ball could be a chore.

Local regulations regarding the number of people permitted to occupy a public space were ignored as throngs of celebrants slithered, edged, and pushed their way into the lobby of the building and the bar next door, then into the ballroom in back where one local band or another labored to make themselves heard over the general ruckus. To be jostled, shoulder to shoulder, shoved, bumped, pushed around in the crowd was a heady experience. Eventually, a pattern of movement—a massive eddy or vortex—would establish itself, and it was possible to be carried along, slowly but forcibly, from the lobby, to the ballroom, to the bar, and back around again into the lobby in an endless circle. Anyone who wished to exit the hotel had to plan in advance, and make for the door by an exertion of sheer determination against the powerful current.

* * *

An exotic restaurant once occupied a room behind the bar off the main lobby, now called Jacob's Corner. In the '70s it was called Al Aban, a faux-Morrocan eatery complete with handwoven rugs, incense burners, low tables, scattered pillows, a polished brass hookah, and a gorgeous, white-skinned, strawberry blonde, blued-eyed belly dancer named Donna; she was draped in translucent scarves and undulated expertly between the tables, egging men to stuff cash into the waistband of her pantaloons as she whirled past. One summer evening in 1977, during the second annual Aspen Writers' Conference, William Matthews, Stephen Dunn, and I shared bowls of harira, couscous, lamb kabobs, grilled chicken, and baklava, then settled back to watch the show. Stephen wrote a poem about it later that captured the experience perfectly:

Belly Dancer At The Hotel Jerome

Disguised as an Arab, the bouzouki player
introduces her as Fatima, but she's blonde,
Midwestern, learned to move we suspect
in Continuing Education, Tuesdays, some hip
college town.

We're ready to laugh, this is Aspen
Colorado, cocaine and blue valium
the local hard liquor, and we
with snifters of Metaxa in our hands,
part of the incongruous
that passes for harmony here.
But she's good. When she lets her hair loose,
beautiful. So we revise:
summer vacations, perhaps, in Morocco
or an Egyptian lover, or both.
This much we know:
no Protestant has moved like this
since the flames stopped licking their ankles.
Men rise from dinner tables
to stick dollar bills where their eyes
have been. One slips a five
in her cleavage. When she gets to us
she's dangling money
with a carelessness so vast
it's art, something perfected, all her bones
floating in milk.
The fake Arabs on bongos and bouzouki are real
musicians, urging her, whispering
"Fatima, Fatima," into the mike
and it's true, she has danced the mockery out
of that wrong name in this unlikely place,
she's Fatima and the cheap, conspicuous dreams
are ours, rising now, as bravos.

All Around The Town

A number of outlying areas—like suburbs or boroughs—ring the central topography of Aspen and have to be taken into account in any true description of the town. To the east along Highway 82, leading to Independence Pass, lies Aspen Grove. The houses here, built mainly in the '6os and '7os, are largely invisible from the highway below as it wends its way up towards the pass, as they are hidden among trees. The real charm of Aspen Grove is this cloistered quality, a sense of privacy and seclusion broken only by the sharp cries of magpies and rustling aspen leaves. The roads that wind up into Aspen Grove are fringed with houses, but they are at comfortable distances from one another, maintaining a sense of rustic isolation. Halfway up McSkimming Road, on the lower flanks of Smuggler Mountain, lies the one hundred year-old Aspen Grove Cemetery, which includes the graves of Bauhaus architect Herbert Bayer, and his mother-in-law, the poet Mina Loy. Bayer designed the grounds and buildings of the Aspen Institute, site of many important cultural events including the Aspen Music Festival and the International Design Conference.

Mina Loy, an eccentric English beauty, won praise from Ezra Pound, T. S. Eliot, James Joyce, and William Carlos Williams for her work, which is collected in Roger Conover's well-researched book, *The Last Lunar Baedeker*. Now largely forgotten, she lies under a simple set of stones—two granite discs, a smaller one offset on a larger one—designed by Bayer.

Loy's title poem, "The Last Lunar Baedeker," was certainly not written about Aspen (perhaps Paris in the '20s), but I know of few poems that describe the ambience of the place any better, especially the first few lines:

> A silver Lucifer
> serves
> cocaine in cornucopia
> to some somnambulists
> of adolescent thighs
> draped
> in satirical draperies.

Anyone who might have stopped in for a drink amid the Victorian gaudiness of the Paragon Bar on Hyman Street would have witnessed just such barely-post-adolescent habitués sprawled across ornate velvet furniture, half-somnolent with alcohol and pot, dressed in the comical hippie regalia of the day.

For part of the 1950s and '60s, Mina lived in an upstairs apartment at the corner of E. Cooper and S. Hunter streets, across from what is now Boogie's Diner. I lived in that apartment myself for a few months, never knowing that Mina Loy had been a resident of the same space only a decade before. I never saw Mina's ghost walk at midnight or heard her poems whispered into the air. That would have been a benefit my paltry rent didn't cover. I leased it from a friend of mine, Irene Morrah (later Ingold) who lived in the large apartment in the back to which my sunny garret was attached.

Decidedly eccentric and multi-talented, Mina Loy had been celebrated in the highest artistic circles in Paris, London, and New York before following her two daughters, Joella Bayer and Fabi Benedict, to Aspen, where they had been living since the late 1940s. Painter and collagist (works that she called "constructions") as well as poet, Mina was the first to put tiny light bulbs inside real calla lilies, and so invented the calla lily lamp. One of her friends, Gordon Brown, described a typical scene to me:

"One time I was walking along with Mina, who was dressed in a feathery hat and a velvet dress with puffy sleeves, when she dragged me into an alley off Galena Street to study the reflections in a puddle after one of the valley's dazzling afternoon rain storms. She looked like an old nineteenth century bag lady, but very elegant. Another time she commandeered my help in foraging through dumpsters for items she might be able to use in making her constructions, including cardboard egg cartons which she lined up and pasted together side-by-side until she had a wall of identical gray pockets resembling the sound-proofing in modern recording studios."

* * *

Difficult Campground is farther east on Highway 82, past Aspen Grove, at the precise point where the highway begins its ascent to the summit of Independence Pass. The campground has been the site of many local gatherings and events, but was mostly a destination for people who were looking for a beautiful spot to pitch tents or park RVs. The Roaring Fork River flows past the encampment, purling among willows on a glittering bed of glacial till. But just before you reached Difficult Campground, an obscure dirt road on your right took you down to the old gravel pit where a rusty crane was parked, a quarter of a mile or so below the campgrounds. You could park there yourself, and a short walk through the trees would bring you to a small plot of land on the riverbank. Though it may be developed today, this particular recess among the poplars and saplings was peaceful, sheltered, and unoccupied, except for a conical, canvas structure—a modern tipi—erected and inhabited by Cheryl Burrows, a latter-day settler and back-to-the-land advocate who had permission from owner, Elsa Mitchell to occupy the plot. There were many young people living in tipis and abandoned cabins with dirt floors in the Roaring Fork Valley, but Cheryl was one of the first and most persistent, occupying hers for over four consecutive years. Most tried it for a season or two, then quit.

This was the era of communes and self-sustaining farms, experiments in rustic living of all kinds. The environmental movement was gaining real momentum, and the children of the Aquarian Age valued the bucolic life over the smoke and noise of over-crowded cities. Too much violence and crime, too many injustices and wars, drove them to search for whatever was left of pristine American wilderness. Wasn't there a less complicated way? Wasn't it possible to live off the land, with as few possessions as possible, and still enjoy a significant, dignified life rich in personal experiences and spiritual rewards? Cheryl would only laugh at this kind of analysis: "I wouldn't call myself a settler or anything. I was too busy chopping wood and boiling water and cooking to think of anything else, and I certainly didn't see myself as part of a social movement. It was enough just to stay cool in the summer and warm in the winter. There was always something else to do, and I had to do it. Living in a tipi can be a lot of work." Theories and philosophies have little to do with the practical tasks of subsistence level living. But *Walden* is a powerful symbol of one kind of American longing and aspiration, the counter-desire to our national obsession with money and property. *Walden* is in our blood, too, and manifests itself from time to time in Shaker communities, the Amish, the Quakers, Transcendentalism and Brooke Farm, New Harmony, Nashoba for freed slaves, utopian movements of all kinds that surface—sometimes in corrupt and destructive forms—throughout the history of our country. Egan and Flo were part of this tide of millennial hope and youthful idealism, which is why I worried about their welfare and what would happen to them when the crushing weight of industrial America reasserted itself in their lives, sooner or later.

* * *

On a beautiful autumn afternoon, Cheryl and I set about erecting her tipi according to specific directions tucked inside the tipi's shipping box. She had ordered it from the Sioux Indian Tipi Company, a pre-cut, pre-fit expanse of new canvas that would fit snugly over a skeletal cone of lodge poles, twenty foot lengths of pine, four inches at the bottom and two inches at the top, which her friends had cut up on the Pass and hauled down in her truck to the site. One of the hardest jobs, she told me, had been wielding a drawknife to strip each trunk of bark until it was smooth and white. The idea was to take three of the poles, place them next to one another on the ground, tie them securely at the top with a long rope, then prop them up to make a tall, standing tripod. The rope hung down from

the middle of the tripod, waiting for the next step in the process. Now we placed the other lodge poles at regular intervals
around the tripod by propping them up against the juncture of
the three original poles near the apex. I had to shinny up the
rope and tie all the poles together securely until we had the
skeleton of the tipi built. Even harder than peeling the trunks
was dragging the canvas "skin," which was heavy, up to the
top and wrapping it around all the poles, on every side. This
was done by tying a corner of the canvas to the last pole, and
walking it around the conical frame so that it draped snugly on
the wooden understructure. We had to do this three times to
get it perfectly smooth. Once this was accomplished, the tipi
was essentially finished. It could be "sewn" together by sticks
on its front side, where the entrance flap was located. These
sticks served to stitch the canvas shut through holes made in
the material for that purpose. Cheryl added a second inner
wall or liner, about four or five feet high, that she had measured and sewn to personalize her space. Then she tied it up
so that it circled the interior. Old scraps of insulation, rags, and
straw could be stuffed between it and the outer skin to provide
comfort at the living level. The floor was made of dry grass,
covered with colorful rugs. Cheryl cut a special pipe hole in
the canvas, which allowed her to install a wood burning stove
that kept the tipi toasty on cold winter days.

Later, she would upgrade to a twenty-two foot tipi and install two stoves for extra heat. She cooked on this stove, too.
She had some wooden crates for shelves, and a couple of sleeping bags accounted for the rest of the furnishings. Eventually,
she would add a Stickley chair and cut another hole in the canvas to add a stained-glass window, an innovation, no doubt,
that would have astonished the Indians. Her tipi was so unusu-

al that *National Geographic* wrote a feature about it in the December 1973 issue.

Life was good, especially in the warmer months when Cheryl could gather herbs and other plants from the surrounding woods to supplement the food she bought in town, prepare tea, and occasionally, to smoke. I recall one afternoon smoking mullein, a common American weed, which Cheryl called "Indian tobacco." It was awful, inducing dizziness and fits of spasmodic coughing. Cheryl then tried to steep mullein in hot water for tea, but the results were equally as repellent. Perhaps it had to be prepared in a certain way, about which we knew nothing. On the coldest winter nights, the fire in the stove would die out sometime between midnight and dawn, so the air inside the tipi would be frigid in the morning.

I stayed in the tipi a couple of these nights, and remember seeing ordinary red wine we had been drinking the night before frozen in its cup on the little table in the center of the room. It was necessary to leap out of our bedrolls, run to the stove, and light it as quickly as possible before diving back into bed to wait for the air to warm up. All summer Cheryl hauled water from the river for drinking and shared it with her dog, Xanadu, years before *giardia* infected Colorado's streams. She dug a latrine nearby in the woods, and took showers in town at her sister Anne's condominium. But generally, she stayed in the tipi whenever possible. Hardiness is an inherent blessing of youth, and we thought nothing of shivering and sweltering and living as lightly as possible off the land.

* * *

A bit further up the Pass, the grottoes drew us on hot summer afternoons like bathers to a beach. The grottoes are a collection of huge boulders left over from the Ice Age through which the Roaring Fork River flows, composed of flumes and spillways and waterfalls, as well as stone cavities, twilit and damp with spray. Woodstock had given us permission to be "children of god," to appear radiant and naked to each other without fear or shame. We felt, like Whitman—who had come back into vogue as the "the original hippie"—that we had to shun society and go back to the woods to acquire a better understanding of our primal natures, our animal appetites:

> I will go to the bank by the wood and become
> undisguised and naked,
> I am mad for it to be in contact with me.

So Whitman had written at the beginning of "Song of Myself," and whether we knew it or not, we were his disciples. This need for nudity and frank exposure wouldn't last long, but when you are twenty-one or twenty-two years old and vibrantly healthy, you are proud of your body and sure of your worth, your innate beauty, willing to share it openly. On the rocks of the grottoes we cavorted like characters out of Greek myth, sprawling on the rocks or diving into the clear pool under the waterfall filled with snowmelt from the Pass above.

Perhaps I am making too much of ordinary skinny dipping. But there was something ritualistic, erotic, and exhibitionistic about what we were doing. I have the clearest picture of a young woman, freckled and raw, her red hair flung across one shoulder, the soft flesh of her buttocks and hands against the rough, timeless stone, her casual posture—legs drawn up, arms propped behind—skin so white it was luminous, cleanlimbed, svelte, an alpine odalisque anyone would be happy to photograph or paint. I wish I had a photograph of her, a photograph of time itself, the photograph of an instant, an hour. A picture of human perfection, and what it means to be indolent, vain, and young. A portrait of all that is furtive and vanishing, even as we regard it through admiring eyes.

* * *

To the north of Aspen lies Red Mountain. As the sun sinks lower and light streams up the valley from the west, Red Mountain absorbs its rays, glowing first a pale gold, then bronze, then red as the star's beams draw out the natural color of the soil, suffused with rusty deposits of iron ore. It's the high concentration of iron ore in the soil of Colorado's mountains that gives the state its name. The earliest Spanish explorers noticed the red of Colorado's mountains and wrote "Sierra Amalgre" or "Red Range" clearly on their maps. Higher up, mountains are devoid of soil of any kind, as they are composed of loose shale and igneous rock thrust up from the earth's core to cool and harden over sixty million years ago. This bare rock, these peaks, glow purple in the evening light, immortalized in "America the Beautiful," which has several times been proposed as a replacement for "The Star-Spangled Banner" as our national anthem.

But on the base of Colorado's peaks, or on the many ranges of foothills and mountains not high enough to reach above tree line like Red Mountain, there is enough soil to support the growth of evergreens, poplars, aspens, and thickets of wiry, scrub oak. These varieties grow vigorously in the state's rocky alkaline loam. I remember landscaper Wes Cantrell telling me that aspens, the most prolific of all trees in the Roaring Fork Valley, were both the sturdiest of native inhabitants, and the frailest, a contradiction nature contrived to balance in ingenious ways. "There's 'orange' disease," Wes told me, "a kind of fungus or mold that attacks aspens and keeps them in check. Then there's the fact that the bark of an aspen is so delicate a cat scratching one might kill it and bring the whole tree down." Wes shook his head and grinned. "On the other hand, the seeds from a single aspen would be enough to reforest the entire valley, evidence of the tree's toughness and will to survive." But even the greenery Colorado's lower slopes provide is not enough to obscure the ruddy tint discernible on Red Mountain. Less than a mile west of Red Mountain, on the edge of the golf course built in the late '70s, is Red Mesa. And on the eastern slope, west of the town of Walsenburg, which Flo and Egan and I admired as we drove north into Colorado for the first time, is the Sangre de Cristo range, whose name evokes both its color and the Spanish heritage of the area, securely rooted in its history.

Red Mountain might just as well have been dubbed "Gold Mountain," for the amount of money it would take to buy property and live there. Accessible by a single road that rises above the site of the old hospital, Red Mountain was one of the first locations outside of downtown Aspen to be colonized and developed for private housing. Even on its lowest tier of streets, the view of Aspen and Ajax Mountain across the narrow valley, with its intricate crisscross of ski runs and broad slopes, is spectacular. Higher up, the view widens to encompass sights down valley and higher up still the wall of Ajax Mountain expands, as the town itself spreads out like a living map below. Who can live on Red Mountain? The privileged and the rich, their houses creeping higher, growing bigger by the year, perched on various ridges like aeries watching over the movements of life in the valley. From there, the residents of Red Mountain oversee the comings and goings of the seasons, the traffic of skiers, artists, scientists, musicians, and tourists who flow in and out of town. To descend into the dives and fleshpots and opium dens of Aspen and rise again each night to sleep in one's own private estate, like a duchess or a baron, that was something to be desired. But like the Upper East Side of New York, or Beverly Hills in Los Angeles, Red Mountain was not, and never could be, an enclave for artists. Most of the town's new or struggling artists lived in rented rooms, apartments, trailers, cabins, cottages, even shacks, if they were habitable and looked *up* at Red Mountain.

But successful, *established* artists might live on Red Mountain. Leon Uris was living there with his second wife, Margery Edwards, when I arrived in town. Uris's third wife, Jill, was a first-rate photographer and collaborated with Uris on two books—one about Ireland, the other about Jerusalem. And the abstract painter Yvonne Thomas had been recognized in New York City as a serious and accomplished artist before she ever arrived in Colorado and set up a studio in her modest brick Victorian cottage off Shady Lane. There might have been other artists living among the aspen groves and sprawling meadows on Red Mountain, but I did not know of them. For most of us, Red Mountain was a height we might never scale. Even the approach to Red Mountain was steep and precarious. A short stretch of road near the base of the mountain ramps up at such a steep angle that it turns into an icy slide during winter months and cars veer off into the woods at regular intervals. Even jeeps and four-wheel vehicles, heading up or down this chute, do so at their own peril. Once, forced to head back to town during a white-out, I inched my way along a narrow dirt lane halfway up the mountain and soon lost the road alto-

gether in my headlights. The snow simply swept in and erased
all visible traces of it. When I stopped and stepped out of my
car to see if I could determine where I was, I'd drifted off into
a field to one side and had to back up to find the track again,
peering out of my side window until I hit the main road again
a few hundred yards away.

* * *

The west end of Aspen is actually part of the town proper,
not a suburb. It represents what many cities describe as "old
town," that grid of streets near the central part of an urban
area from which all later growth radiated, and still the source
of its particular charm. The area north of Main Street and
west of the Hotel Jerome consists of a lattice of broad, poplar-
lined streets and two-story gingerbread Victorian houses with
large unfenced lawns, the very picture of small town American bourgeois domesticity. Though the houses were constructed around a general template for Victorian dwellings, each
home incorporated some feature peculiar to itself. One might
have a cupola on the corner of a projecting wall, another might
present a bay window, yet another a wrap-around porch with
a swing. A walk through the west end presents the observer
with an array of pastel colors, though some of the grandest and
oldest of the homes are constructed of the nineteenth century's favorite building material, brick. The Stallard House on
W. Bleecker Street (now the Aspen Historical Society) is a good
example. The Sardy House on the corner of Main Street and
South Aspen, originally a funeral home, is another example of
Victorian grandeur.

In addition, a number of professional organizations have
moved in over the years and erected modern buildings to

house their various activities. The Givens Institute provides conference facilities for the University of Colorado School of Medicine and might host discussions about anything from brain tumors to chiropractic. The Aspen Physics Institute has been a venue, in recent years, for hotly debated issues including the nature of black holes and the validity of string theory. And the Aspen Institute for Humanistic Studies was inaugurated in the late 1940s by Walter and Elizabeth Paepcke as a place for the meeting of minds from the worlds of philosophy, business, and the arts. The Institute is the core and source of Aspen's modern cultural life, and without it Aspen might have remained a plush but rather conventional ski resort. The Aspen Institute soon became the site of the city's renowned Music Festival, and from that first cultural landmark grew Aspen's cadre of other artistic programs: the International Design Conference (now defunct); Ballet West (from Salt Lake city), Aspen FilmFest, various local theatre groups from Aspen Community Theater to Aspen Theater-in-the-Park to Aspen Stage, the Aspen Art Museum, the Aspen Writers' Foundation, whichsponsors the Aspen Writers' Conference (now Aspen Summer Words), and the Food and Wine Classic to sate the appetites of connoisseurs and wine aficionados in the summers. Offspring of these, in Snowmass, include Anderson Ranch Arts Center and the Snowmass Jazz festival.

Occasionally, and in accordance with Walter Paepcke's desire that Aspen be a place where mind and body meet—business, science and the arts converge in surprising and fruitful ways. In the late '70s, Al Lyons, founder and director of Aspen Stage, mounted a production of Peter Shaffer's *Equus* in the main conference room at the Givens Institute. The audience sat in circular, ascending tiers of desks around a small ovular

floor below on which the action took place. I wasn't expecting
much when I took my seat, but it turned out to be one of the
best two hours of theater I ever experienced in Aspen. And later, in the 1980s, Lyons produced a version of Dylan Thomas's
Under Milkwood in the basement of the Hotel Jerome, a rousing
success that had audiences in stitches and moved by turns. I've
seen concerts in living rooms, ballet in bars, and once Ricky
Jay threw a playing card right over the top of the hotel, though
I wasn't there to witness it. I did, however, view a couple of
playing cards stuck to the ceiling of the Jerome Bar, which Jay
had tossed during a trick; they stayed pasted against the coffered tin for years.

To amble through the west end of Aspen on a warm summer evening with sunlight streaming through the poplars and
a few magpies bickering in the branches is to relive the Gilded
Age tranquility of pre-World War I America. In the 1970s, Aspen's Grande Dame, Elizabeth Paepcke, still lived in the west
end in a magnificent house with a garden overlooking the quiet beauty of Hallam Lake, which has since been established as
a nature preserve. On cool October mornings, it's still possible
to see Mallards splash down on their way south, or deer brows-
ing on the last greenery clinging to the low lying branches of
trees or the tender shoots of marsh grass growing on the mar-
gins of the lake. The larger houses are imposing, but tucked
behind them here and there are carriage houses converted into
comfortable dwellings, and gardens kept impeccably groomed
and neat. I witnessed a magpie lure a cat up the trunk of an old
poplar, then fly away at the last second leaving the cat stranded on a the thin tip of a branch, which dipped under the cat's
weight until it fell thirty feet and scampered away unhurt but
decidedly chagrined. No one can tell me animals are unable to

strategize or think. I was acutely aware of the magpie's devious-
ness, and the cat's shame.

Though unprotected by walls or fences, void of guardhouses
or special security patrols, the west end of Aspen exudes a sense
of safety and peace. If a marauding army were ever to make
its way up the Roaring Fork Valley from Glenwood Springs, I
have no doubt that Aspen and its tonier environs would prove
irresistible to the invaders' appetite for easy booty and treasure
of all kinds. But I have no trouble imagining that, once having
penetrated the quiet haven of the west end, the army's leaders
would pause and, detecting the unruffled mood of the place,
move on.

***

If Bill Greed stalked Aspen Grove, Red Mountain, and the west
end, he ballooned to Bunyon-esque proportions in the exclusive residential area known as Starwood. This name is something only real estate agents and new-age dreamers could have
invented. Real estate nomenclature, conjured up to denote new
housing projects, is almost always insipid. Each new development bears a lame, compound neologism like Pleasant View,
Shady Ridge, Green Acres, Oak Lane, or Pine Meadow. These
aren't the names of geographical places, but they do conjure
vague, idealized states of mind. Starwood, by comparison, is at
least moderately creative. It marries two of the Aquarian Age's
favorite natural phenomena, stars and forests, and suggests that
life in Starwood will be one long idyll of happiness, health, and
arboreal mystery. John Denver was perhaps the most famous of
Starwood's residents. What could the Starwood suggest but the
presence of hobbits, unicorns, and wizards guaranteed to make
your life inside its boundaries an epic fantasy?

As Aspen's first and only gated-community, Starwood occupies a forested ridge above a business park and across the valley from the diminutive airport, Sardy Field. It is accessed by a single road, which rises from McClain Flats, a scenic route connecting Red Butte on the western edge of Aspen to the wilds of Woody Creek. As Starwood itself isn't surrounded by a wall or a fence, it's a bit uncertain as to the utility of the gate and its one sleepy guard. The area might be accessed, day or night, by any of a thousand paths to anyone willing to hike up the hillside. That aside, abruptly encountering a guardhouse in the mountains of Colorado—especially those surrounding Aspen—is a curious experience.

The White River National Forest, in which Aspen is located, is mostly open to anyone who will strap on a backpack and enter it anywhere along the perimeter of its sprawling 2.3 million acre expanse. Apart from private ranches and public land controlled by the Department of the Interior, there's not a wall or a gate to be found anywhere, except at the entrance to Starwood. Rumor had it that each resident was initially required to buy a parcel of land large enough so that the house they built could not be seen by any other house anywhere in the community. In this way, a feeling that the hillside belonged to *them*, and *only* to them, was to be maintained. For the rich, this sense of singularity was worth the money. Elbow room, it seems, is an American aspiration that cuts across monetary considerations or class distinctions of any kind.

Surely Starwood's main feature, the quality that developers are *really* selling, is the view. From the ridge on which Starwood is located, it's possible to look south for many miles towards the Elk Range and its towering peaks—Mt. Sopris and McClure Pass to the west, Maroon Bells and Pyramid Peak dead south, Buttermilk and Highland ski areas to the east. Somewhere in that vista Mt. Daley and Capitol Peak loom and the trough of Castle Creek Valley, ploughed by glaciers, is also visible. One of the crucial aspects of selling any view is that the realtor can guarantee it won't change. And this panorama of peaks and valleys, lakes and trails is set in stone, not for years but eons. It's what inspired John Denver to write the lyrics of one of his signature songs, and it's one of the last things skiing champion and shooting victim Spider Sabich ever saw. Beneath this cyclorama of vaulting rock, planes land on the little strip of pavement known as Sardy Field. It's one of the peculiarities of the panoptic view from Starwood that you can look down on planes as they land, not up. And what's above Starwood? Nothing but sky, an immense blue-black cupola shimmering with stars which, at this altitude, are brilliant, free from pollution and city lights that obscure them in most every other sky.

* * *

Though Starwood may be the most exclusive of Aspen's residential areas, the others—Aspen Grove, Red Mountain, and the west end—are by no means inexpensive. For most of us, Aspen's condos and apartments, bunkhouses and rented rooms, funky hotels and B&Bs were sufficient and affordable. It was possible for a bohemian artist, a cultural vagabond, or a ski bum to find a place cheap enough to lay his or her head. That changed as the decades slipped past. As prices rose, the first wave of financial refugees moved into cabins, tipis, livable sheds, basement hovels, anywhere comfortable enough to make life bearable. Then we were driven down-valley to Snowmass, Basalt, El Jebel and Carbondale, some of us moving even as far as Glenwood Springs. Later, prices rose in many

of these down-valley communities, until no one but the al-
most-rich or decidedly wealthy could live in the center of Aspen or its sumptuous boroughs. The towns down-valley are today filled with Mexican immigrants, who perform the menial
tasks necessary to keep Aspen and its palatial estates running.
Ski bumming, by and large, is a thing of the past. As I have in-
dicated, the original name for Aspen was Ute City when the
area was first settled by miners prospecting for silver in the
surrounding hills. This was changed to Aspen in 1880, but a
hundred years later, in the 1970s, we were already calling it Fat
City, in keeping with the local lust for easy living and quick
wealth. Or, as my friend Joyce (whose mother was Mexican)
liked to call it: Cuidad Gordo. The first Spanish explorers,
searching for the fabled city of El Dorado, might have done
worse than to discover Starwood in Aspen—that "sweet Rocky
Mountain paradise."

Oh, Give Me a Home

I knew one thing.

I had to find a place to live in Aspen I could afford.

Once fall arrived, my plan was to sell my panel truck and use the money to put down for a few months' rent until I could find a suitable job. Parking in town was difficult and once there, I could walk easily from place to place. Letting the truck go was also a symbolic gesture. I was making a commitment to stay in Colorado and my plans to travel on to Haight-Ashbury evaporated.

Wherever I lived had to be in the core, because the Pitkin County Bus system had not yet been funded and deployed, and long out-of-town distances made walking impossible. You can't rely on hitchhiking, especially once you acquire a job and have to return home late at night. A high percentage of Aspen jobs for unskilled labor exist in the restaurant industry which—apart from skiing and camping—provide for the community's bread and butter. I'd quit sleeping in my truck as soon as I arrived in Aspen, staying in Mrs. Mack's dormitory for a week until I found employment at the Leather Jug in Snowmass. Having a steady income allowed me to quickly secure an apartment in the newly-built Arbeiterdorf at the bottom of the hill. The Leather Jug was a few steps away, up the hill, in the West Village. The situation, then, seemed ideal. I would work at the Jug, and live at the Arbieterdorf for the summer, leaving my truck parked in the lot until I needed it to drive into Aspen to shop or sample the night life.

* * *

One of the first places in Aspen I remember living was a basement apartment under a condominium complex halfway up Monarch Street at the bottom of Ajax Mountain. The tiny apartment had been meant to house a superintendent, but renting it out would bring in a little more money for the owner. The complex was owned by a German speculator named Hans Grammiger. He owned a number of buildings around town, but this one had been contrived to resemble a Swiss Chalet, with dark exposed beams and white stucco on the exterior. Hans was tall, with dark brown eyes, and a wide swath of skin down the middle of his head. He had an aquiline nose, and thin lips, and most of us thought he was crazy. Certainly, he had crazy ideas. One of them was particularly zany, and Hans had been fighting the City Council for years trying to implement it. He'd wanted to build a restaurant high up on the thin, rocky edge of Shadow Mountain, overlooking the town. There were no roads on Shadow Mountain, and it loomed over the ski runs on Ajax Mountain, so access would be difficult, if not impossible. To remedy this, Hans proposed to construct a single gondola, anchored somewhere near West Hopkins Avenue, that would take customers up to dine, then bring them back, sated and happy. What if a fire broke out, the City Council wanted to know? How would the Fire Department be able to get up there and put it out? How would an ambulance reach the restaurant in order to evacuate a patient? Poor Hans. He battled the authorities for years, to no avail. In the end, his dream remained just that—a dream—and all that was left of it was a melancholy cable he had strung halfway up the slope, guy wire to an old man's fantasy, which dangled for years.

After negotiating with Hans for the apartment, we came to an agreement quickly. "Ninety dollars a month," he said, then squinted as if to read my reaction to the sum he'd proposed.

"Ninety?"

"Ja," said Hans." Ninety dollars a month."

The place was a dump, and I suspect that it had been set aside for someone who could watch the furnace, inspect the pipes, and keep track of the electrical system of the complex in case a fuse blew and plunged the apartment above into darkness. My apartment could be reached off the alley by descending a set of stairs beneath the wooden deck of the building above, then crossing the dusty concrete floor of the basement under a maze of wires and pipes to a door in back which opened into a tiny room with a sink, a bathroom no bigger than a closet, a table, a chair, and a raised bed that sat atop a couple of bureaus that had been wedged there to prop it up. There were just three or four feet between the mattress and the ceiling. The bed had a short ladder that had been nailed onto the end. A sickly light filtered in through two windows, set at ground level, beneath the wooden deck. For the year I lived there, I felt more like a hibernating animal than a human being. Sometimes, the snow piled up in the alley outside until it eclipsed my light altogether and my apartment really *was* buried underground. But I could read undisturbed for hours, and wrote some of my first publishable poems there. I had no phone, no television, not even a radio. If I had to be thrown into a cell for some reason, I'd be ready. This was my initiation into literary monkhood.

We weren't proud of our poverty, but we embraced it as a way of expressing our anti-materialistic beliefs. *All you need is love.* At twenty-six and with my artistic and intellectual bent, the material world mattered not a whit. Like the Beats before us, experience was the all in all, not what we owned. Tipi Cheryl would eventually install herself in someone's backyard shed, with a sleeping loft and a workshop below where she could pursue a modest business sewing "Easy Hats" for ski shops and, later, Bloomingdale's, but before that, she lived in her tipi outside of town, driving back and forth in a 1942 Army Jeep. Other friends lived in cabins with dirt floors, or tiny A-frames in which you could hardly stand. Drinking water could be had by melting the snow outside. If you were hot, you could open the windows. We were robust, careless, and free. Security, we felt, was futile. We accepted death and change—and why not? They seemed so distant and implausible. "Be here now!" So my little burrow on Monarch Street was an anti-capitalistic castle. I lived in a world of books, of abstract ideals and utopian theories. What did it matter where I lived, so long as I had my priorities straight? In the end, however—and this is crucial—we all had jobs and worked forty hours a week like everyone else in America, never doubting that self-sufficiency was a virtue, and that taking care of ourselves was necessary if we were to claim any self-respect at all. Our middle-class backgrounds dictated this. We didn't intend to live impecunious lives *forever*, just until success found us and elevated us by virtue of our own efforts and talent—assuming that we had any. We were as ambitious for comfort or ease as anyone else and we longed for the day we could move up in the world propelled by our own undeniable accomplishments.

"Ninety dollars a month?" I asked.

"Ja," said Hans again, and we shook hands. I preferred to look on him as my patron, crazy or not, and he asked me whether I knew of a poet from Iowa named James Hearst.

"Hearst?" I shook my head. "No, I've never heard of him."

Hans explained that Hearst had visited Aspen in the summer for a number of years and had rented a room from him, so I was not the first or only poet to take advantage of his beneficence. As the author of ten books of poetry and two volumes of prose, and as a professor at the University of Northern Iowa, I doubt Hearst ever lived in a subterranean cubbyhole or washed dishes to pay the rent. Still, Hans knew more about art than I did about real estate, and this elevated him, in my eyes. For the time being, I could get by on ninety dollars a month— an unheard of rent, even then—and use the rest of my money for the basics. Life was tolerable, if a bit cramped.

* * *

Yet before my little fox-den in the basement of Hans Grammiger's apartment complex, I had the good fortune of finding the penniless, free-living poet's dream home and living in it for nearly two years. This time-honored method of avoiding rent is more prosaically called "house sitting." Unguarded and vulnerable while their owners gallivant across Europe or the far East, such getaways provide temporary shelter—and a beautiful if illusory dream of comfort and security—to artists of every stripe in need of living space. Most of these homes have guest apartments or outlying cottages or carriage hous-

es, which can easily harbor a person who's looking for a place
to finish a novel, compose poems, or research material for his
next volume of nonfiction dealing with the emotional life of
whales. In return, the artist-in-residence will watch over the
property and call the fire department if a frayed wire finally
crackles into flame. Implicit in these arrangements is the idea
that intruders will be dealt with vigorously as well. Such sce-
narios rarely occur, and the artist is left alone to pursue the
dictates of his or her imagination. It's a symbiotic relationship.
If the ancient concept of patronage still exists in the modern
world, perhaps this is the form it takes.

For years, the only other house visible from his picture
window was a rambling Swiss chalet owned by Keith Hefner, Hugh's affable, bearded brother. We'd see Keith around
town wearing a fringed buckskin tunic, a pretty blonde bunny perched on his arm. To the west, the steep walls of the ravine and some open public land that lay beyond it assured that
Bruce's view in that direction would remain unobstructed for
the foreseeable future. The lot next to Bruce's, fronting Main
Street, belonged to his sister, and it had a small horse corral,

    Bruce Berger wasn't a multi-millionaire, but his little "cab-
in," located off a loop on the end of West Main Street, offered
a haven from the clamor of downtown Aspen. Designed and
built in 1947 by architect Fritz Benedict, Bruce's cabin is a one-
bedroom log home perched on the edge of a ravine above Castle Creek, with a fabulous view facing Highlands and Buttermilk ski areas. The mountains rise up in Bruce's windows like
the legendary peaks of Middle Earth. Bruce let native trees,
grasses, and shrubs grow wild on his property—aspens, poplars, blue spruce—this created a sense of wilderness and privacy near the center of a bustling miniopolis.

which screened him to the east and kept the traffic at bay. But Yeats is the real genius loci of the place. I often thought of Innisfree while living there, though Bruce's cabin was built of more than clay and wattles. It was, and is, in fact a fine example of modern architecture inspired by the designs of Frank Lloyd Wright.

Fritz Benedict had studied at Wright's school, Taliesen, in Spring Green, Wisconsin before visiting Aspen the first time in 1941 to participate in the National Skiing Championships. Absorbing many of Wright's central ideas—a low-pitched roof, an emphasis on the horizontal rather than the vertical, mitered windows that meet seamlessly at the corners of a building, and the ambition to match, whenever possible, the shape and materials of a structure to the landscape in which it is set— Bruce's "cabin" is a prime example of Benedict's style of residential architecture. It is made entirely of stone, wood, and glass. Even the ceilings are wood, long flexible planks of white pine (stained brown) lapped on each other like the boards on the side of a rowboat, a style called lapstrake. The fireplace and chimney are made of Peachblow sandstone that was dredged up near the banks of the Frying Pan River. The floors are wood, as are the cabinets and shelves and doors. The exterior walls are constructed of long sections of lodge pole pine, sealed with chinks of mortar. A big leather armchair sits in one corner of the living room, near the fireplace, and bookshelves line the interior wall. In a separate room on the other side of the fireplace, a large wooden desk is set against the west wall, and a baby grand piano dominates the rest of the room. For most of the day, and in all seasons, sunlight pours through the expanse of glass in both rooms, which face south. The house soaks up heat, a natural solar dwelling without the need of industrial panels or messy skeins of conductive wire. On the coldest nights, the fireplace is sufficient to warm the place, augmented by a small furnace that forces hot air through grates in every room. From the outside, the house resembles a big lean-to, its back wall towards the street somewhat higher, pitching the roof towards Castle Creek and beyond.

Bruce Berger is a man of modest height, with blue eyes and a sheaf of thin blond hair. An impish smile animates his boyish face, which is round with pale delicate skin. He has sometimes been mistaken for John Denver, both men possessed of wholesome, choirboy looks, though Bruce is a bit older than John and anything but a choirboy. He is known for his outrageous puns—he calls his house "The Fritz Carlton"—and has an incisive intelligence which is sharp, but never cruel. He can apply it to any subject, at any time, gently skewering pretension and deflating the pompous with a wry chuckle. He is an accomplished writer, having written several books about Aspen, the American desert, and the Baja peninsula in Mexico, where he spends his winters since his mother died in 1989. He is a poet of great technical skill and formal dexterity. Having studied music with Edith Oppen, he can sit at the piano and play a haunting Chopin polonaise followed by a raucous, barrelhouse tune. As a man of great integrity, he will not venture to sing. For decades, he has attended the Aspen Music Festival and written many articles about it, as well as a definitive history of the event. He was briefly a contributing editor and wrote articles for *American Way*, American Airlines' popular onboard magazine. He is an expert bird watcher, not only in Colorado and Arizona, but on trips to Central American rainforests in Costa Rica, Oaxaca, and Chiapas. He documented the demise of Glen Canyon on the border between Utah and Arizona when a dam was built to inundate it. For over thirty years he battled the people in the community who would tear down his house and ruin his property to re-route highway 82 straight into downtown Aspen. And he won. Shortly after I met him and we'd established a friendship based on our mutual love of literature and writing, he offered to let me stay in his house while he traveled to Arizona in the winter to visit his mother, and I jumped at the chance.

I recall languorous evenings and afternoons sunk into the soft depths of Bruce's armchair, with a fire crackling in the grate, reading selectively through his library of books, all of which were by great authors, and some of which were rare first editions still relatively crisp and well-preserved. Sometimes I shared the house with others, as the bedroom was on one side of the house, and it was possible for someone else to sleep on a fold-out couch in the room with the piano on the other side of the building. One winter, I allowed a city councilman, Steve Wishart, to sleep in the piano room for a couple of weeks because a new apartment he had rented was not ready to be occupied. Steve wrote political diatribes, though I suspected he harbored a secret desire to write a novel. He had attended Yale, where he had participated in student demonstrations in the mid-1960s. Steve was a prodigious drinker. He would stagger in or out of the house in the middle of the night muttering to himself and stamping his feet. One evening, I was startled awake from a deep sleep by several gunshots outside that seemed to have come from somewhere close to the house. Leaping out of bed, I ran into the living room to see if Steve was there.

"Steve," I yelled. "Steve, are you okay?"

Silence.

Anxiously, I entered the piano room and peered around the corner. The bed's blankets were rumpled, and one of the pillows lay on the floor. The phone was off the hook and the door to the deck was wide open. Then Steve came stumbling into the room, a pistol in his right hand.

"Steve!" I said. "Are you all right?"

"My fren...," he said, the words sliding together and dissolving, "...my fren down Bisbee just died. I'm gonna see him off proper."

"What do you mean?" I asked. "And where did you get that gun?"

"I got some more ammo aroun' here," he replied.

"You can't shoot anymore," I said. "The cops'll be here any minute.

"Where's it...?"

It was impossible to reason with him, and I was terrified that he'd wind up shooting himself, or me. Worse, if the police showed up and arrested him for disturbing the peace, how would I explain to Bruce what had happened, that I had let a madman stay at his house, and that the whole neighborhood had been disturbed? What would I say if the entire scandal appeared splashed across the front page of the *Aspen Times* the following afternoon?

I retreated to my bedroom and prayed nothing more would happen. Two more shots rang out. I flinched each time. Should I go back to the piano room and wrestle Steve to the ground, disarming and holding him until the authorities arrived? I listened for sirens. Nothing. I crept back to the piano room to have another look at Steve. He was sitting on the edge of the couch, fiddling with his pistol. "That's the right salute," he said, his eyes drooping. But there was no menace in his expression. Just a heavy sadness, a man half slumped into himself, his head wobbling slightly as he breathed. I went over and shut the door.

"I think you sent him off the right way," I said, replacing the phone on its cradle. "Why don't you try to get some sleep now?"

"Sure," said Steve. "No more ammo anyhow."

He crawled into his bed, and I stepped out onto the porch to listen again for the sounds of approaching trouble. The trees were silent. There was a single light on in Keith Hefner's chalet. Then it went out. The sky was dark, but clear, riddled with the indifferent stars.

* * *

Most of my days passed tranquilly. Once Steve was gone, I settled back into a routine of reading and writing, then going out at night to work, and coming home after midnight to tumble into bed. In the evenings, I would watch the sun set beyond Bruce's deck, which dangled precariously above the Creek. In the mornings, I'd rise to the sound of jays or magpies wrangling in the poplars that walled the property off from his neighbors, and buffered the sound of traffic that flowed around the corner of West Main Street. I was halfway through Bruce's library, enriching my inner landscape while at the same time becoming a scholar of his view—the weather patterns, the texture of the sky at different times of day and in different seasons, shadows that played across banks of snow in his backyard, the dignity of his little stand of blue spruce, the Elk Mountain range tonsured in the foreground with ski trails, the lavender profile of peaks beyond. On limpid spring evenings, I'd watch hang gliders launched off the west ridge of Shadow

Mountain, first one, then several others, until the air thronged with them. They drifted above the house like dandelion floss, scattering westward as if to colonize down valley fields with the seeds of ideal, well-rounded Paepcke men.

One year I was sharing the place with a friend of mine, Irene Morrah, from Charleston, South Carolina. Irene was a lovely woman with a molasses drawl and a quick sense of humor. Merriment was part of her character. She had the kind of charm that only a fine southern upbringing could instill. Later, she would marry John Ingold and move to a modern house in Starwood. For the time being, we lived in harmony in Bruce's cabin, sharing the premises as friends. I lived in the bedroom on one side of the house, and Irene lived in the piano room, with access to a second bathroom on that side of the cabin. Irene was involved that year with some directors and producers who were in town attending one of the early programs of the Aspen Film Festival.

One day, Irene introduced me to a couple of her friends from the festival—a sexy, dolled-up fashonista named Rikki with green eyes and disturbingly blonde hair, and her boyfriend, Jöran, a dashing Nordic type who wore leather mukluks, a bulky ankle-length fur coat, and a scarf tossed negligently around his throat. Rikki exuded the cool indifference of a baroness. Jöran's jaw came to a dimpled point, shadowed with stubble, and his eyes burned wolfishly. Irene brought them to the house one day, just before lunch, and introduced them to me with a smile.

"Kurt, darling" she began, "These are my friends, Rikki and Jöran. They're in film!" she laughed. "I wonder if you would mind if they stopped by later today, between events at the festival, so they can rest. Their hotel is out of town."

I shrugged. "Fine with me." I hadn't planned to be home anyway, and they could sit out on the deck, or read.

"They won't be any trouble…will you?" Irene said, turning to them, her voice a caress. You couldn't deny Irene anything. She effused warmth and a civilized, southern style.

* * *

I had just taken a shower before heading back to town. As I was drying off, I heard the front door open accompanied by Rikki's fluttery shriek and Jöran's chuckle. They'd come back early, and there I was in my bedroom, naked, not four feet away behind a flimsy interior wall. Okay. I'd continue dressing, then wait until they were safely ensconced in the piano room. I planned to slip through the door as soon as I could determine they were out of sight. That was only neighborly, what any considerate host would do. I wondered where Irene was, why they had come alone and early. It had been only a little over two hours since Irene had brought them out to the house to meet me. I had heard nothing from them for a few minutes, so I assumed they were on the other end of the house, resting. I was putting on my shoes to go out when I heard Rikki's voice—a high rasping whine.

"Oh Jesus!" she intoned. "Oh God! …" Then some serious gasping. I thought I might have been mistaken, but it happened again.

"Baby…Oh…Ohh!"

What's going on in there, I thought. *A damned revival meeting?* I knew perfectly well, of course. Either they didn't know I was in the house or they didn't care. I thought they must have noticed my coat on the chair by the door, a half drained cup of coffee, evidence that someone might be present. But I don't think consideration for others was high on their list of priorities.

"Ohhhoo!" Rikki's voice rose in a plangent, ascending falsetto, almost keening. I wasn't against sex by any means, and Rikki was a piece of work. Maybe I was a bit jealous. But it angered me, too, that a couple of strangers whom I had only just met, and to whom I had extended the use of Bruce's house as a kind of back-stage blue room or lounge, were now blithely using it as a hideaway for a tryst. *This isn't a cheap hotel you can rent by the hour!* I wanted to shout. *Get a room!* But of course, I kept my mouth shut. I decided to wait until the crescendo of their desire would be loud enough to mask any noise I might make going out. It didn't take long.

"Ohmyygodd!" Rikki screamed.

I took a few steps across the living room, grabbed my coat off the back of the chair, and slipped out the door.

When I finally found Irene in town and told her the story, her eyes grew wide. Then she laughed.

"Darling, I had no idea! Did they *really?*

"It sounded like someone was getting murdered in there!" I hammed it up. I liked to make Irene laugh. There was nothing quite so charming, or so easy. "Should we call the police?" I joked. "What if we go home and find two dead bodies?"

"Dead?" she raised her eyebrows.

"Overexertion," I said, "It happens all the time at this altitude."

"Darling, I promise I will never, never, never bring anyone home again."

When I returned later that evening, I poked my head through the front door and called: "Hello?" When they didn't answer a second time, I strolled up to the piano room and called again: "Rikki?" There were some displaced cushions and Bruce's piano, its lid for once clapped shut, its silver strings silent.

* * *

It didn't take Bruce long to figure out that it would be more fi-
nancially beneficial if he rented his house each winter while
he visited Arizona, instead of handing it over to an itinerant
house-sitter like me. The dream, as John Lennon had sung,
was over. After two idyllic seasons, I was looking for a place to
rent year-round—or for someone who was looking for a roommate.

Tipi Cheryl had a friend, Dinah Kinsman, who eventually
became a real estate agent and who was renting a two-bed-
room trailer at the base of Smuggler Mountain. The Smuggler Trailer Court was small, and a bit bleak and dusty. But the
trailers were cheap and the court was within easy walking distance of downtown Aspen. A few of the residents owned vehicles, though more often, motorcycles stood parked on the
gravel near the edge of the weeds and, here and there, a bi-
cycle. Not all the trailers were in good shape, propped up on
cinder blocks, twenty feet from one another. Dinah's trailer
was perhaps twelve feet wide and sixty feet long, with a small
kitchen, living room, and a cramped hallway that led to a
small bedroom along one side (mine) and a slightly larger bedroom twelve feet wide in the very back. Some of the trailers
had "skirts," which meant that a metal sheet had been added
to extend from the base of the trailer to the ground to keep
the space under the floor sealed and airless. Other trailers, like
ours, were open, giving owners plenty of room to stow things
underneath. In the summer, this was fine. But in the winter
the wind swept in under the floors and chilled the rooms even
when we had the heat cranked up. Icicles clung to the eaves

and large slabs of ice plated the roof. In the spring, ice chunks would crack and slide off with a thud.

Smuggler wasn't the only trailer court in the valley, but it was the only one within the city limits of Aspen. Well hidden in a back corner of town, no tourist would ever have to suffer the shock of coming upon it among the regal façades and sprawling mansions that dignified Aspen's streets. Smuggler was a mole on the face of a meticulously made-up woman. Perhaps, for that, it added a touch of fallible human beauty, as on the cheek of an eighteenth century queen. Residents of the court during the 1970s worked as bartenders, waitresses, handymen, construction workers, and artists around town, and I would guess that all of them were renters. Dinah was companionable enough, with long blonde hair, blue eyes, and full lips. She was sturdy and strong-limbed, and seemed to have been born with a natural tan, though she was a skier and loved the outdoors, which accounted for her tawny complexion. She had come to Aspen to find the good life, and fell in love with the place. She had a boyfriend named Chip, and the two of them made a happy pair, sharing the trailer on winter nights, though Chip had an apartment of his own and was just a visitor. I had a girlfriend then, too, so during the most frigid weeks of the year, there were often four of us in our respective bedrooms hugging each other for warmth, buried under mounds of extra blankets. When the wind kicked up, the trailer would rock until morning, like a boat on high seas.

* * *

One winter, I lived in a tiny loft above Adrienne O'Donnell's leather shop on the second floor of the Brand Building on the corner of Hopkins and Galena. Adrienne was a lovely, generous woman with a broad smile. The loft was even smaller than the space I had rented in the basement of Hans Grammiger's apartment building, but it had everything I needed—a tiny living room with a couch, a bathroom with a shower stall, and a sleeping loft. No kitchen, not even a hotplate, but I was working next door at Jake's Abbey and could eat there. The shift from living in a basement to what was essentially an attic had a positive psychological effect. I was above ground, even if I didn't have a window to enjoy. Adrienne worked all day in the shop below, which I accessed by climbing down a short set of steps through an opening in the ceiling. I felt like Santa Claus, or a burglar, each time I descended and said hello to Adrienne. I was at my desk at the Aspen Literary Foundation for most of the day, and Adrienne left her shop before I came home to get ready for work at Jake's. We hardly crossed paths, and kept out of each other's way.

The Brand building had been erected in 1891 during Aspen's construction boom. Back then, it housed the First National Bank, but during the Depression, it was a drive-through gas station until it was condemned in 1971. The first time I saw it, the old drive-through gas station was a gloomy space that smelled of grease and gasoline vapors. A large oil spot lay in the center of the raw concrete floor, and a chain that had once yanked engines out of old cars still swung from the ceiling. This was prime real estate in the very heart of Aspen, and it wasn't long before the building was purchased by Harley Baldwin and renovated. Once more, the peacocks had driven out the rats, and I was out on the pavement looking for a new home. Today, the first floor houses exclusive boutiques by the likes of Gucci, Louis Vuitton, and a few transplants from Rodeo Drive in Los Angeles, while the second floor—which is where Adrienne had designed and constructed her leather goods—has been converted into luxury condos.

There were other temporary digs here and there. Kathy and Tommy Crum let me rent a spare bedroom in their house on Cemetery Lane for a month or so, before they bought a house of their own on South Ute Avenue behind The Gant. I house-sat for Michael and Nancy Iceberg in their panabode in Old Snowmass Valley. There, I watched cloud patterns stipple the flanks of Watson's Divide across the valley, and deer as they splashed daintily across Snowmass Creek at dawn. I had a car again, a decrepit Volkswagen bug that broke down once on my way home from work in the middle of the night, stranding me in a snowstorm—I almost died of hypothermia before a driver picked me up and dropped me at the foot of the hill below Iceberg's house. For a few strained weeks I lived with a woman I was dating, occupying a second bedroom in her house in the West End before it became obvious that our living arrangement and relationship were bad ideas. Perhaps there were other places, so ephemeral I have now forgotten. I was little more than a gypsy. But I worked steadily, never out of a job, and as I approached thirty, shame prevented me from house-sitting or sleeping on someone else's couch. The poor poet's persona was getting old. But this was after one final sharing arrangement—perhaps the best I had ever had.

* * *

Joyce McMullen had been a friend of mine almost from the moment I arrived in Aspen. She was younger than any of us, about Flo's age, but without any of Flo's fragility or shyness. Joyce had grown up on in Colorado Springs, and was the only native Coloradan among us. Her mother was Mexican, and

Joyce spoke fluent Spanish. Her skin was freckled and pale, and if it weren't for her dark eyes, you might not suspect she had any Mexican blood in her at all. She was both street-wise and gullible, a devastating combination. Everyone loved her. She was thin, even gawky, still in her late teens but already a citizen of the world. At least, *our* world. No one looked down on Joyce or pandered to her because of her age. She had already traveled and experienced life, and was a great believer in romantic theories. For Joyce, the world was invested with an abiding mystery, and ordinary, mundane reality was only a veil thrown over a deeper enigma, one that special individuals had penetrated and tried to explain to the rest of us living our humdrum lives.

She wasn't exactly an orphan, or even a runaway, but she must have felt disaffected or lost in one way or another; she sought answers in unorthodox bodies of thought from the likes of Velikovsky, Castenada, and the mysteries of Machu Pichu. Creating a counter-culture involved more than dressing in strange clothes and letting your hair grow long, more than constructing alternative economies and political systems. It meant re-exploring the psyche, researching new spiritual and religious truths to fit the altered vision of things. We often laughed at Joyce when she voiced some of her more preposterous ideas. But we weren't much different; we tried to make sense of the madness that surrounded us, trying to find a new world in the rubble of the old.

Joyce's boyfriend—let's call him Wally—was a drug dealer. That appellation, however, is entirely misleading. There was nothing violent, rapacious, or greedy about Wally. He was a warm Italian with a ruddy beard, who walked around town in a full-length beaver coat, turquoise jewelry, and a cowboy hat. He was always smiling. He refused to deal in lethal drugs like heroine or meth, but instead relied on marijuana to make his living. The idea of Wally hanging around a schoolyard trying to lure kids into addiction is unthinkable. He and his small band of cohorts believed in the social utility of marijuana. They believed they were shamans of a new consciousness. Even if you didn't use drugs, you had to love Wally. He was a man of his word. But his profession still lay outside the bounds of respectable society, and the federal authorities had another view of him. Wally wasn't exactly a big-time dealer, but his activities managed to show up now and then on the DEA's radar. This kept Wally's eyes open, his nose to the wind.

Wally had set Joyce up in a fine split-level house at the end of Waters Avenue, a cul-de-sac. The house was tucked into a grove of aspen trees behind which lay nothing but woods. It was a perfect retreat for Joyce, where she could pursue her study of occult philosophies. Wally seemed to exist in the world like a ghost, appearing and disappearing at will. When Joyce decided the time had come for her to travel to Peru and scour the jungle for a legendary lost city she had been researching, she invited me to watch the place. For the first time since Bruce's cabin on Main Street, I would be able to live in relative luxury, to spend my days pursuing my own studies. I moved in with Joyce, occupying a room of my own filled with light and the dappled shadows of aspens that bent and seethed in the afternoons when the wind rose. After familiarizing me with the house, Joyce packed, boarded a plane at Sardy Field which took her to Denver, and from there to whatever adventures awaited her among the remote peaks and valleys of the Andes. Back at the house, I shut the door, sighed deeply, and settled into the couch to begin reading my stash of books.

That house was a blessing. I'd meet Wally now and then in town, where he'd nod his head and ask how it was going.

"Fine," I'd say. "What a great place!"

He'd nod again. "Okay," he'd say, smiling.

Wally was often absent from town for months at a time, and didn't seem to worry about me and what I might be doing in the house. I allowed some friends to stay with me for a few weeks while they searched for places of their own. I built fires in the winter, and threw the windows open in the spring, listening to the sound of jays and magpies bicker in the trees. I wrote stories and poems and essays which I later burnt in the fireplace and began again, always with the purpose of improving, always believing that I could. Some nights I'd walk home from work, exhausted, gazing up at the pale stream of the Milky Way lighting my path. In February, a winter storm knocked out all power in the valley and I had to burn most of the wood that had been stacked in the garage. From time to time a car would wander into the cul-de-sac, slowly, hesitantly, then round the circle and vanish again. Once a month or so, Joyce might call from some village in the jungle to tell me about her adventures and ask if all was well. I'd assure her it was, then go back to the line or paragraph or sentence I was composing. Not a single word I wrote in that house survives. *Say a prayer,* Jackson Browne wailed, *for the pretender.*

When Joyce finally returned, tanned and invigorated, my second idyllic housing situation in Aspen ended. Joyce recounted hacking her way through vines, careening down rapids in a canoe, and finding ruins so overgrown they had to be excavated to be examined. She allowed me to stay until I could find a place of my own. That's when I moved back in with Irene to share Mina Loy's old apartment on the corner of Cooper and

Hunter. But that was after a harrowing experience that left me shaken, and later, amused, that I had been part of something illicit and dangerous. One day about mid-afternoon when Joyce was in town, I answered the phone.

"Hello?"

"Hang up the phone and get out of the house right now!"

"What?" I said.

"Get out now," Joyce barked. "And don't come back until I tell you. Call Adrienne's later. Now get out."

Then she hung up.

I panicked. What should I take? I decided I'd better get out and worry about what I had left behind later. All the way back into town on Waters Avenue, I expected to hear the thrash of helicopters swinging in low over the valley. Or the sound of sirens drawing closer, whizzing past me as I walked along, trying to look as inconspicuous as possible. I recall wandering around town, one ear cocked to the sky, visiting friends. The first time I called Adrienne's phone I was told: "Don't go back yet." I had a drink at the Jerome Bar. Then another. The afternoon wasn't looking so bad after all. The artists came in at five, and took up their post at the front table near the window. At six, I went out into the lobby and called Adrienne again.

Joyce answered. "It's okay," she said. "False alarm."

"False alarm? What happened?"

"We thought something was comin' down. You can go back now."

"Jesus," I said, "You scared the shit out of me!"

She just laughed.

The Hills are Alive

Music was our chronicle, our Text. Words meant something, and we pondered the lyrics as though they were lines from epic poetry. The more sophisticated among us preferred classical or jazz. The complex, delicate, arcane patterns of jazz waited for most of us to catch up, the way sex waited when we were children, or the pleasures of great food. For the time being, we occupied our minds with images like "newspaper taxis" and "a highway of diamonds," or cryptic phrases like "'Scuse me while I kiss the sky." The psychic wing of the counter-cultural movement began with advanced lyrics, enhanced by drugs. Drugs were the Eucharist of the revolution, the body and blood of change. There were plenty of lyrics that still said little more than "Oh baby, I love you" but we heard our contemporaries singing, "We are but a moment's sunlight / fading in the grass," which was a far cry from "Keep your sunny side up" and "Ain't we got fun." Our parents hated these new songs, reeling in confusion. But we knew they meant something. They meant we were seeking a new vision of things, carried by the music.

The rest of the country had already begun to turn to the
vapid message and repetitive beat of Disco. But *that* particular revolution in music wouldn't reach the Roaring Fork Valley until the end of the decade. The popular music scene in Aspen during the 1970s was vibrant and diverse. Foremost among
them was The Gallery (often called The Center), that had once
been located in the basement of the building at the bottom of
Little Nell. It was a long, dark, low-ceilinged room with a stage
and small dance floor at one end, and a four-way rectangular
bar at the other. There was scant ventilation, and only a couple
of exits. Any incident, whether fire or panic or something else,
could have resulted in disaster. But there was always a queue at
the entrance to The Gallery. Once inside, it was difficult to find
a seat, or to navigate to the bathroom or the bar. Wally Burke,
one of the owners, was an expert at booking acts. I remember seeing the James Cotton Blues Band, and Clarence "Gate-
mouth" Brown, as well as Melissa Manchester, Cajun fiddler
Doug Kershaw, The Flying Burrito Brothers, and a very young
Jackson Browne performing with The Eagles, an up-and-com-
ing group from Los Angeles, and two of the band members,
Don Henley and Glenn Frey, later became part-time Aspen residents. The list of featured bands is long: Harvey Mandell and
Sugar Cane Harris, Freddie King, Tom Rush, New Riders of
the Purple Sage, Boz Scaggs, Joy of Cooking, John Hammond,
Jr., Linda Ronstadt and the Stone Ponies, Pablo Cruise, Hot
Tuna, Charlie Musselwhite, Jimmy Witherspoon, Uncle Vinty,
J. J. Cale, Leo Kottke, and The Average White Band. We often
referred to The Gallery as The Galaxy, for the many stars who
performed there.

    The house band consisted of a group of local musicians,
whom we often preferred to some of the traveling acts. Bob-

by Mason and Geoffrey Morris headed the group, called Black
Pearl. They exchanged riffs on their electric guitars in a clam-
orous competition that could whip the audience into a frenzy.
Standing shoulder to shoulder at the edge of the dance floor,
we'd watch the dancers leap and cavort while on stage Black
Pearl ground out a set of thundering rock 'n' roll. The com-
munication between band and audience, each feeding off the
energy of the other, was obvious. At the end, musicians and
dancers alike would be drenched with sweat. It was exactly
what we wanted: a release of turbulent energy strong enough
to exorcise our frustrations, leaving us ready to drift home
and sleep, spent. The Gallery was a catharsis. Its bar manager, James Kane, was billed as "the fastest bartender in the
world." He and fellow bartender John O'Donnell whipped up
drinks in a blur. As a bartender myself, I would sit on a stool
and watch them work. Bottles flew in and out of racks, beer
foamed, and fruit spun in the air like the ingredients of a salad.
It all worked somehow. Wally smiled, the waitresses counted
up their change, James never seemed to tire, and the customers—breathing deeply, steeped in sweat—filed out at two a.m.
into the cold night air.

* * *

One night, Tipi Cheryl and I were on our way to the Gallery
when we noticed a ragged hippie creeping along the pavement with a very peculiar gait. One of his hands was drawn
up strangely in front of him, like a wounded claw, and he was
dragging his right foot behind him. He looked like Dr. Franken-
stein's assistant, Igor. As we drew closer, Cheryl realized that she
knew him, that he was not a disabled person at all, but someone
she recognized, someone who had been otherwise healthy.

"John!" she said, in great dismay. "What happened to you?"
John looked up and smiled. "Oh," he said, "It's nothing. I ate
some magic mushrooms and forgot to scrape off all the strychnine." (This turned out to be a myth; magic mushrooms do
not contain strychnine, so whatever John ate to cripple his leg
had nothing to do with mushrooms).

"Oh!" Cheryl gasped. "Do you want us to take you to the
hospital?" We were well aware that the strychnine, if it reached
his heart, could paralyze it, killing him instantly.

"Nah," he said. "I'm going to The Gallery to dance it off."

And so it was. We saw him later, capering to the rhythms of
"Sympathy for the Devil," his stricken leg completely healed.
He had a bottle of beer in one hand, and his other arm around
a girl. The sweat illuminated his face like a saint.

Nothing could kill us in those days. We were beyond reason.

* * *

Another venue that catered to the rock 'n' roll crowd was Danny's, on Hyman Avenue, across from the old Paragon. The
owner, Danny Wardwell, relied on lesser-known groups to
draw a crowd, but had trouble competing with The Gallery.
Danny's soon closed when Danny went to prison for dealing
drugs and when Hyman Avenue was transformed into a shop-
ping mall. That required tearing up the concrete sidewalks
and the asphalt roadway, then repaving the block with antique
bricks imported from St. Louis, along with two meandering
streams in miniature grass berms, stylish wooden benches,
and Victorian streetlamps. But back when it was open, you'd
enter Danny's through a front door located directly on the
sidewalk. Two large plate glass windows allowed passersby

to peek inside. Perhaps such public access, in full view of the street, wasn't as mysterious to us as The Gallery, tucked safely out of sight in a cellar, without windows, accessed by a narrow door set into a small recess at the bottom of a building. We loved basements. Many coffeehouses and cafés in the '50s and '60s featured descending stairways, bare brick walls, hanging pipes, and smoke-filled dimly lit interiors furnished with tables and chairs. The idea had been borrowed from German cabarets and speakeasies in New York, subterranean nightclubs that offered the allure of illicit behavior in repressive regimes. Most other clubs were underground too, but those clubs offered acoustical music for listening, not dancing. The Blue Moose (later The Flying Dog Brewpub) on the corner of Cooper and Galena was a popular spot for folk, country, acoustical rock, and bluegrass. One night in a fit of political pique, I burnt my social security card over a glass candle at the Moose, watching my old life go up in smoke. It was an act of male solidarity with women all over America who were burning their bras. Years later I'd get a replacement, but the act made me feel good, a small rebellion against the juggernaut of America.

One of the best groups to appear on a fairly regular basis was Sandy Munro's bluegrass troupe known as Easy Pickin's. The group included his wife, Mary Lynn on banjo, Sandy on guitar, Cash Cashman on bass, and John Sommers on fiddle. Sommers would go on to work with John Denver, fiddling and writing songs for the next two decades. As I understand it, Sommers wrote the smash country hit, "Thank God I'm a Country Boy," in his car on the way from Aspen to Los Angeles for a recording session. He sang it later in the Blue Moose when John Denver was in the audience, and Denver told him he'd like to record it himself. Easy Pickin's played everywhere around town, but the Blue Moose was one of their favorites. As you might expect, the bar had a blue moose head projecting from the wall behind the stage, overseeing nightly revels with a tight-lipped, ironic smile.

Another group that frequented the Blue Moose was Liberty, an acoustic trio which included—once again—John Sommers, plus the husband and wife team of Jan and Vic Garrett, whose earliest gig in Aspen had been in the side room of the Hotel Jerome. Jan's voice was a smoky combination of jazz, blues, gospel, and folk, which she used to great effect. While Liberty had seemed poised on the edge of wider success—they made one album but then broke up. There's no room for rationality in music or love.

Jan Garrett also figured into the makeup of another group, Danny Wheetman and the Honky Tonk Swamis, as one of The Android Sisters, Wheetman's pulchritudinous trio of backup singers who dressed like vamps and sang like Greek Sirens. Their harmonies were tight, complex, and melodious, recalling the Andrews Sisters of the 1940s. Wheetman himself would appear in various guises, often as himself—a multi-talented one-man band—or in various combinations with others as lead singer, backup singer, fiddler, guitar player, harmonica player, mandolin aficionado, songwriter, even comedian dressed in the trappings of a 1930s' troubadour. Much later, after his career in Aspen, he would help write and perform in a Broadway hit, *It Ain't Nothin' but the Blues*, which ran for 284 performances at the Ambassador Theater. Before that, he'd been a cast member in *Lost Highways: The Music and Legend of Hank Williams*, which opened in Denver in 1987. For most of his career, however, he joined Sommers as part of John Denver's band and traveled the country playing huge venues, and even penned

a Christmas carol sung by Kermit the Frog. The Blue Moose
also hosted solo acts like Chris Cox and Glenda Griffith. Glenda was a beauty with flaming red hair and a voice that soared.
Her guitar work was nothing to sniff at, either. And her writing skills were considerable, if a bit unorthodox. She moved
to California later to pursue her musical career. I accompanied her once to the offices of Irving Azoff in Hollywood, and
watched her open at a small college venue north of Los Angeles for Richie Havens. Like other Aspen performers, more or
less talented, she might have made it big, she was that close.
But the stars align, then re-align, then pass on to other spheres.
The Blue Moose existed for a moment in time, offering a stage
to the many talented musicians who had found their way to
Aspen once the vitality of the '60s had run its course.

Just down the street from the Blue Moose was Werner
Kuster's Red Onion, one of the town's oldest continuously operating bars, one that had started in the height of the mining
era. The front bar, with original floor tiles and high windows
looking directly up at Aspen Mountain, was the home of Aspen's Rugby Club for most of the '70s. On any given day, members of the club could be found hauling overflowing mugs up
into the air and singing fight songs in what was affectionately
dubbed Beer Gulch, the small rectangular area to the left of
the front door. The place was chaotic and loud and fun. Pure
alpine sunlight cascaded into the high windows and bathed patrons in a beery, amber glow.

It is only fair to point out that Aspen had a vibrant live music scene even before the 1970s, and that many accomplished
musicians appeared in Aspen's music halls and bars. In the
Red Onion's back room, for instance, Billie Holliday once performed in the early '50s after being arrested for drug posses-

sion and losing her license to perform in New York City. She
was still allowed to tour, and so made her way to the state for
a number of dates in Denver and other Colorado towns. There
were others: Vince Guaraldi, Armando Perraza, Hazy Oster-
wald, Jimmy McKean, Ethel Ennis, Cal Tjader, Eddie and the
Pacesetters, Pete Barbutti, and Jack Jones. A duo called The
Hustlers was popular in the late '60s and featured Twirp Anderson and Jan Camp (later Jan Garrett) who made two albums
and packed the place for après ski with lines around the block.
But the Red Onion's main act was one Freddy "Schnickelfritz"
Fisher, whose name alone conjures up other comedic jazzmen
like Cab Calloway and Spike Jones. Fisher and his group—with
Walt Smith on Piano, King Fisher (the bandleader's son) on
cornet, Jim McCabe on drums, Les Gaylord on bass, and Fisher himself on clarinet—mixed comedy routines with jazz, and
tore up the place almost every night of the week. It was impossible to avoid Fisher's legacy in Aspen, even as late as the 1970s,
and there were people who still knew him and talked about
him after I'd arrived on the scene. There were many photographs of Fisher on the walls of bars around town where he
had performed. The one I recall vividly depicted Fisher, bare-
footed and playing his clarinet, stepping blissfully over a carpet of women's falsies, which he had spread out on the stage
at his feet. Su Lum and Barbara Lewis honored Fisher with a
full biography, *Fisher the Fixer*, a book that covers his life from
the time he lived in Hollywood, where he owned and operated a nightclub, to Aspen, where he lived until his death in the
1960s. His contribution to Aspen and its musical heritage, can't
be overstated.

   This can be said, too, of Fisher's son-in-law, Mead Metcal-
fe who married Fisher's daughter, Joan, and opened a famous

dinner theater, The Crystal Palace, in 1957 and for the next fifty-one years presented two shows a night to wildly appreciative audiences. His brand of satirical music, lifted directly from the headlines, was clever and on target. Full of martinis and roast beef, Metcalf's patrons would shuffle out flushed and satisfied as the next show's audience queued up around the block. Many nights as I walked by the front window—covered mostly by cut-glass panels so passersby couldn't easily see what was happening inside—I'd find a narrow gap between the panel and the window frame that offered me a sliver of the spotlit stage and a few seconds of whatever performance was happening at the time. It was perhaps the only time I've been a stage-door Johnny.

Just down the street from the Red Onion, across from Wagner Park on the corner of S. Mill and the Cooper Street Mall, was another jazz venue, The Zoo, later to become The Golden Horn, an upscale Swiss restaurant owned first by Hubert Erhardt and his wife, Trudy, before it was sold to Klaus Christ (rhymes with "mist"). As The Zoo, the club featured Rick Astor, Steve Knowlton, and Dean Billings, as well as Freddy Fisher and his bunch when they weren't headlining at The Red Onion down the street.

Other noteworthy acts that preceded the 1970s included John "Falling Rock" Locke, whom I never met nor saw perform (a poster figured him with a long, ragged beard and a banjo looking like a rustic mountain man), and Glenn Yarbrough and the Limeliters. Yarbrough and another band member, Alex Hassilev, bought and operated a club in Aspen called The Limelite (later The Limelite Lodge) in the late 1950s, after appearing there during a previous ski season. They brought a young singer named Judy Collins up to perform with them.

The Limelite was only half a block away from the Crystal Palace, on the west side of Wagner Park. In 1965, after the Limeliters moved to San Francisco to work at the Hungry i, they had several national hits, including "There's a Meetin' Here Tonight," "A Dollar Down," "Have Some Madeira M'Dear," and "Whisky in the Jar," and later on his own, Glenn Yarborough had a hit with "Baby the Rain Must Fall." I had heard many of these songs on the radio back east, and knew the lyrics by heart. By the time I reached Aspen, however, The Limeliters were long gone. Briefly in the late '70s and early '80s, a club called Paddy Bugatti's thrived under the main lobby of the Continental Inn. The room was really a three-sided box, with no back wall and no real stage—at least not an elevated stage. There was a wall behind the stage, but the opposite side of the room opened out into the lobby that led to a restaurant on the far side. By any measure, it should have been a poor space in which to hear music, but the intimacy of the room allowed musicians and audience to enjoy proximity and a shared experience that larger venues did not allow. Bobby Mason and Jimmy Ibbotson of the Nitty Gritty Dirt Band played there as a duo, and I recall seeing Glenn Frey of the Eagles sitting in one night with one group or another, tucked modestly into the background. Country-folk musician Wayne Stewart played Bugatti's, and would later record an album, *Aspen Skyline*, featuring Wayne and many of Aspen's most prominent musicians in cameo performances. Even later, his band—Area Code 303—would include, among others, John Sommers (yet again!) as musicians continued to shuffle and reshuffle the pack of talent that inhabited Aspen and the Roaring Fork Valley.

That shuffle included a number of ad hoc groups thrown together and ironically named, which might exist for a day or a week or even a particular gig, whose personnel might include anyone, whose repertoire was decidedly eclectic, and whose musical legacy vanished at the end of the gig. The ones I remember include: Lord Nose, Tyrone and the Bearded Apple, Meat Bubble, The Whistlepigs, Four Pound Ear, Bertha and the Turks, Spider Speedwell and the Spaceshakers, Lost in the Shuffle, Hogg Wilde, Crisco and the Greaser, Halfway Healthy and the Yellow People, Aloha Lou and the Wakiki Cowboys, Uranus, The Cheap Feel Blues Band, New Latin Crusaders, Lucky and the Ducks, The International Moisture Exchange, Poor Richard's Almanac, and Grown Men. But there were others.

Few of these venues charged a fee at the door, and when they did it was usually not more than a dollar. An exception was the Aspen Inn Club, which featured a heftier cover charge and a two-drink minimum. The idea was to pack people in and make money on the sale of drinks. It was common practice to catch the first set at one place, the second set at another, and perhaps a third late-night set somewhere else. It was challenging to see as many groups in one night as possible, and to run into as many people as you could along the way. Socializing might have been as important as the music, and being seen was as crucial then as it is now when you are young and desperate to fit in and be popular.

A much-anticipated annual event, the Deaf Camp Picnic, raised money each spring to bring deaf children from all over the country to spend a few weeks in the mountains at the Aspen Camp School for the Deaf. Luminaries such as John Denver, Jimmy Buffett, and the Nitty Gritty Dirt Band played for free, much to the delight of the huge crowd spread out on blankets in the grass enjoying barbecue, beer, and whatever drugs they might have brought while the sun dazzled the meadow and newly-sprouted dandelions everywhere dazzled back. Because it was a benefit for the Deaf Camp and some of the students would inevitably be in attendance, a pair of signers stood on opposite ends of the stage to relay lyrics to the crowd. Buffet's immortal line, "Why don't we get drunk and screw" was always a favorite. The interpreters smiled, but never dropped a sign as the band played on. Mary Travers, of Peter, Paul, and Mary, sang at the Brown Ice Palace one winter for the benefit of the Community School. John Denver appeared in Paepcke Auditorium at the Aspen Institute for the benefit of the Community School as well. The Middle School had its famous musical adherents too. Starwood, Jimmy Buffet, The Dirt Band, and many others helped raise money for them in various concerts over the years. There was a benefit in the Snowmass tent for Greenpeace, and one in the Ice Garden to "Save the Season Pass," which was enjoyable if ultimately ineffective.

Anything might trigger a benefit concert—some needy and deserving organization, a local character in financial trouble, one of the arts groups whose budget depended on outside sources of funding, even a leg broken in a ski accident might become an occasion for local musicians to exercise their largesse. Benefit concerts were an indication of how much community feeling existed in Aspen among the local population, regardless of the fact that tourism and skiing were its main industries and it was fundamentally a company town. Most of us who had no steady, high-paying jobs or substantial future prospects, stuck together and shared our woes and successes, cooked Thanksgiving dinners for each other if we weren't returning home to our families, exchanged Christmas presents, and generally considered our life in Aspen together to be a collective experience. The more attractive and admirable aspects of hippiedom, whatever else you might say about it, valued friendship, sharing, and an easy-going fellow-feeling that looks altogether childish today. Aspen in the 1970s may have been just another ship of fools, but it was our ship and we let it drift merrily where it may.

* * *

When Marilyn Hennig and her husband Lennie opened Le Cabaret, downstairs at the corner of South Galena and East Durant Streets, their ambition was to provide an alternative to Mead Metcalf's successful Crystal Palace across town. The rivalry didn't last long. Le Cabaret opened with a bang, faltered, caught itself, then finally fizzled out altogether. As bar manager, I watched it all unfold with a morbid fascination.

Marilyn and Lennie had built a state-of-the art dinner theater, complete with the best sound system ever installed in town, an overhead projector to flash slides onto the walls that flanked a semi-circular stage built on the bottom tier of a three-tiered room, with brass railings and tables draped with crisp linen that overlooked the performance area on three sides so there wasn't a bad seat in the house. A lobby with a parquet floor and an old mahogany back bar imported from Paris gave the place a veneer of class, along with Persian rugs, a sound booth, and a lighting system even the Wheeler Opera House couldn't match. The dinner show was spectacular, if a bit overambitious. Audiences flocked for a look, then thinned precariously as the year wore on. When Le Cabaret folded after little more than a season, the place was bought by David Moss, who quickly converted it into the Paradise Theater (later Rick's American Café), a nightclub equipped with a green room and an electronic curtain that masked the acts until they could set up and were ready to appear. The club was so chic, it could easily have existed in Los Angeles, New York, or Chicago: B. B. King, Ricky Nelson and the Stone Canyon Band, Poco, John Prine, Taj Mahal, Russell Smith and the Amazing Rhythm Aces, Hank Williams, Jr., New Riders of the Purple Sage, Asleep at the Wheel, and Commander Cody and The Lost Planet Airmen. Flash Cadillac provided a few raucous nights of 1950s rock 'n' roll, while Jack Casady and Jorma Kaukonen of Hot Tuna updated the earlier era's boogie woogie with some sizzling acid-inflected compositions from the 1960s that still felt relevant. And for those who loved to dance, The Freddy and Henchi Band cruised into town now and then to provide a powerful backbeat, always opening their show with the words: "Welcome to Freddy and Henchi's party!" In many respects, that's what Aspen resembled in the 1970s, a city-wide party that felt like it would never end.

One of the most exciting events to take place in The Paradise Theater in the late '70s was the triumphant return of a local group, Starwood, after it had recorded a self-titled album for a major record label. Starwood, named after the exclusive subdivision, was composed almost entirely of local musicians whose success for a brief period made everyone proud. The group included Bobby Mason on lead guitar and vocals, David James Holster on vocals and rhythm guitar, Haden Gregg on vocals and rhythm guitar, Bryan Savage on sax and flute, Bernie Mysior on bass, Bobby Carpenter on keyboards, and Michael Buono on drums. Their return to Aspen, after recording for RCA at the Caribou Ranch in Nederland and touring the country as an opening act for more famous, established groups, was nothing less than electrifying. The songs, which we knew by heart, had become tighter, bigger, more professionally arranged, and the appearance of the group on stage more theatrical. Holster wore a black sequin frock coat with a searing red rose on the back, while Bryan Savage appeared in a dapper, cream colored suit. The group had been refined by their experience, and we were seeing them with new eyes. But just as suddenly, they fell apart, victims of the high tension and stress rapid success often brings. Though as individual artists, they would go on to pursue musical careers, Starwood as a group would never record another album or appear together on a national stage. For a while, it felt like the town itself had failed, but the bubbling matrix that was live music in Aspen continued to draw musicians from around the country, and continued to produce talented, unique acts that would enjoy success, more or less, on a national level.

* * *

There is, of course, more. I have only scratched the surface of what was taking place musically during the formative and creatively turbulent years of the 1970s in Aspen. Additional venues included Alice's Alley, The Magic Pan, Trader Ed's, The Depot, Aspen Mine Company, Al Aban, Bandera (which became Michi's, then The Cheshire Cat, and finally, Columbine, in rapid succession), The Tippler, The Student Union, The Happy Hearth, The Brass Bed, Andre's Restaurant and Bar on Hyman Street, and one winter in the Pink Room behind the main lobby in the Hotel Jerome, I witnessed a performance by Victoria Garvey and the Moondog Medicine Show. I heard John Denver sing in a big room at Prince Bandar's mansion in Woody Creek Valley. He sang alone, accompanying himself on his guitar. For a while, Bill McEuen had a recording studio at his house in the Eastwood-Knollwood area up the Pass. Later, Gordon Wilder and Greg Simone opened Rainshadow Studios, with Chuck Witt as tech, down valley across the highway from the Old Snowmass General Store, and Ed Thorne built a 16-track studio on the corner of Hopkins and Hunter Streets in the center of town.

For a few years, I produced a Christmas show, *The Great Roaring Fork Valley Yuletide Extravaganza,* which took place at midnight on the eve of Christmas Eve in the Wheeler Opera House as a benefit for the Aspen Writers' Foundation. That first Christmas show was successful, though looking back on it I realize it was also labor-intensive and extracted a pound of flesh for every dollar it brought in—a little over $3,000, which was big money for us at the time. We hyped the evening on both radio stations, and tacked oversized posters on every available wall in the Valley, but I had no idea how many people would show up at midnight so close to a major holiday to attend a concert that would last into the small hours of the morning. We had to book the Opera House for midnight because the usual movie was showing earlier at nine. When we opened the doors at eleven-thirty, a line had formed around the block. Virtually every musician in the Valley was scheduled to play, as well as a group of scat-singers from Boulder called Rare Silk, who'd flown up for the show. Dan Sadowsky emceed the event, and I recall several highlights—Danny Wheetman and his band pounding out their rendition of "Sea Cruise" by Huey "Piano" Smith, and Patti Ehrlich sitting alone in a cone of light singing the sultry, erotic ballad "You Don't Know Me" while the audience breathed along dreamily. I was so galvanized— so thoroughly stoked with alcohol and drugs—that I couldn't sit still for long. I'd run up to sit in the very center of the front row of the balcony, then hustle back down to our office on the second floor under the theater, which served as a kind of green room for acts waiting to go on stage, then back up to the theater to catch another act. I was down in our office when Cathy Lee Crosby showed up with Cher and her boyfriend at the time, guitarist Les Dudek. In town for Christmas, Cathy Lee and Cher didn't stay long, disgusted no doubt at the frantic state of affairs both in our office and in the second floor hallway where scores of people were milling about. We stuffed Les's nose with cocaine and sent him upstairs to sit in with Bobby Mason and his band.

At some point, someone handed me the door receipts, in cold cash, and I rushed over to the Golden Horn with my pockets bulging to ask Klaus Christ if I might store them in his safe for the night. I don't know how many people we turned away, but the audience stayed put until almost dawn, drinking beer (we had acquired a special permit) and cheering each new act as it took the stage. We had to clean up and lock the doors as first light broke over the walls of Independence Pass. I trudged home wearily up Main Street, thankful for the audience, for the musicians, for the profits that would fund another issue or two of our literary magazine and keep our little enterprise afloat.

Let's Have a Party

Jake's Abbey had nothing to do with church. Its closest connections to monastic tradition were its Spartan furnishings and rough stone walls that formed its foundation when it was built during the mining era. It also had a large round stained glass window, five feet in diameter, behind the performance area. It was lit from within, and glowed steadily from six in the evening until closing time at two a.m., though often after the regular audience had filed out and the door was locked, the party would continue with staff and performers until sunrise or exhaustion finally set in to squelch our revels. I remember often stumbling up the back stairs groggily into the alley between Jake's and the Brand building in the grainy light of dawn. We could afford all-nighters because we weren't due back to work until six o'clock would roll around again later that day. We'd sleep all morning, rise at about two or three to shower, then go out for a hearty breakfast before returning to work. It was little different than working the night shift at a factory, if you didn't count the drugs and booze that raised our spirits and kept us going. At Jakes, we worshipped life. Our hymns were ballads, love songs were gospel, and we pondered lyrics as though they were scripture teaching us how to live.

Located in the Wheeler Block that was erected in 1891, the place was first called The Randy Tar (a chain with a maritime theme), then The Abbey Cellar, then Jake's Abbey. It occupied the space under Jake's steakhouse, a "Victorian Restaurant" as the sign above the swinging saloon doors proclaimed, complete with a rustic painting of Queen Victoria fading on the boards. The Abbey started out as a waiting area for people who were on the list to eat at Jake's. Bob Sproul paid little attention to The Abbey, but he thought it would be a good idea to entertain his dinner guests while they waited to be seated upstairs. Sproul was a businessman from New York, an accountant, and Jake's was a lark in which he had invested to get his family out of the city and bring them to Colorado for recreational skiing and fresh air. He must have purchased the building in the mid-'60s for a good price, with the intent of opening a restaurant—named after his son—where locals and tourists could order a cheap steak and a glass of wine for a reasonable price in an otherwise prohibitively expensive town. As long as the musicians played for a small cover charge and he didn't have to pay them out of his own pocket, he was happy and his problem was solved. And as long as musicians had a venue to present themselves and their music, they were happy, too. Sproul would offer them a free meal, drinks and then leave them to their own devices. As a patron-father figure, we all desired Sproul's approval, but he was oblivious to what was happening night after night beneath his steakhouse and, if anything, viewed our artistic efforts with a bemused air. On the few nights when he would come downstairs to sit in the back, his presence had an electrifying effect on the musicians. Did his visit mean that Sproul was taking an interest in the music scene he had spawned? Would he finally put some money into the Abbey to spruce it up—maybe a new sound and lighting system, maybe payment for musical services rendered over and above what was charged at the door, perhaps a budget for promotional endeavors, or a makeover of the entire place so the carpeting stopped smelling musty, and the walls stopped leaking dried ancient mortar, and the one, cramped toilet in the far corner stopped backing up? But of course, Sproul had no interest in doing anything to improve the lot of musicians, or to promote music. The Abbey was a practical necessity, nothing more. The only time I ever heard him express a preference for music, it was for the old-timey sing-along stuff one might hear at a tourist trap in New York, like Your Father's Mustache on Seventh Avenue, which harped back to *fin de siecle* parlor music and barbershop quartets. From a business perspective, this might have improved the ambience of his steak house and I wonder why he never instituted it as a feature of the place. But acoustic music, some of it bluegrass, must have satisfied his sense of quaintness and good old-fashioned fun, and saved him the expense of buying costly costumes.

I mean no disrespect. Bob Sproul was a kind-hearted, tolerant man and though he must have sensed that something more important was happening for us night after night in his dank, restaurant basement, he was content enough to let us go our own way, as long as the customers were happy and he didn't have to put any money or effort into supporting our activities. He once told me that if I were a real poet, I'd be living in New York on the Bowery where I might have the good fortune to suffer properly for my art, the way poets are supposed to do. He had a point. What was I doing in one of America's ritziest resorts, in a landscape so utterly breathtaking it lifted your spirits just to look at it, among other white middle-class youths all healthy as ancient Greeks, and as good -looking too? What, exactly, he was implying, was the source of my poetry? And why were many of the musicians who came to wail and lament in the depths of his building on Galena Street so serious, and sometimes even unhappy? Bob Sproul was the perfect foil for our youthful pretensions, our boundless passion and angst.

The Abbey had two entrances. An inner stairway led down from the restaurant directly above. Once downstairs, patrons could settle in, order a drink, and enjoy whatever act was on stage at the time. When a table was ready, I'd get a call from upstairs. Then I'd pass the message on to the waitress, who would deliver it to the stage. The name of the party would be called out over the sound system, who would then go upstairs to eat. Pat Flynn, while playing a solo, would often call out over the sound system: "Donner, party of five; Donner, party of five." A few seconds later, not missing a lick, he'd follow with: "Donner, party of four!" It always cracked us up, though customers often missed the joke.

The second entrance could be accessed directly from the street to the right of the restaurant's main entrance. People who came in this way were our *real* audience. They had come to hear the music, not to eat dinner. Sometimes, if an act was big enough or something special was happening, people would line up on these raw, concrete steps and wait to pay a small fee and be stamped on the back of the hand. A third set of stairs, which I have already mentioned—an emergency exit into the alley prescribed by the town's safety codes—was never used by the public. The Abbey bar was tiny, perhaps ten feet long, with four or five rickety stools. The distance between the front

bar and the back bar was a mere three or four feet, so the bartender had to swivel carefully to pluck a bottle of beer out of
the cooler behind him, then turn around again to set it down
carefully on the waitress station. The back bar had three tiers
of bottles of more expensive liquor, and a mirror that made the
room feel bigger than it was. There was a door at the far side
of the bar that led to the boiler room, in which hardly a single
person could fit. That's where we did our drugs, mostly, when
we had them. It was handy, private, and relatively hard to see
from where the audience sat listening.

Only the small staging area was splashed with light from
two simple spots mounted on central poles. A dim, indirect
row of fluorescent bulbs illuminated the back of the room over
the drinking shelves. Otherwise, the room was lit by candle-
light and customers ogled each other in the reflected light of
the stage. The ceiling was constructed of rough-hewn slats
of dark brown wood. Soloists, duos, and trios had no trouble
performing at Jake's Abbey. Any bigger, and a group had to
squeeze together, shoulder to shoulder, while trying to avoid
hitting each other with the necks of their instruments. The
sound was surprisingly good for such a cramped hole in the
ground, though a new sound system would have improved the
crispness and over-all quality of voices and instruments by a
detectable level.

* * *

I began working for Bob Sproul as a waiter, upstairs in the
steakhouse. I walked in one day in October when he was hiring and began work that evening, sliding platters of steak off
my tray and on to the table for hungry skiers. The tips were
never that big. I had waited on tables back east, and nearby in

Snowmass Village, so the job came easily to me and I had no trouble breaking in. But I had my sights set on bigger things. Bartending was a way to make twice the money for half the effort. I became a bartender upstairs by mid-season, leaving the steak and baked potatoes behind, proving myself reliable and efficient when it came to slinging drinks and working cordially with the rest of the staff. I wanted to move downstairs into the precincts of the nightclub, so I lobbied Sproul for a position in the Abbey should one become available. It was not long in coming.

By early the next spring the bar manager downstairs had quit and I leaped at the opportunity. "I can do it," I told Sproul. "I can take care of the whole thing." He looked at me with an appraising eye, and nodded. "Okay, let's see what you can do." Once downstairs, I was in charge of my own little kingdom. I was responsible for ordering supplies, hiring a second bartender to take over on the two nights of the week when I would be off, interviewing waitresses, and of course booking all the acts and making sure things ran smoothly, according to Sproul's wishes. It was the autonomy, and the music I loved. Sproul paid me a reasonable salary, and I got a cut of whatever the waitresses took in, and tips from anyone who sat at the bar; I was a happy monarch ruling with a benign but firm hand. It was my habit to book acts for two, sometimes three, but no more than four nights, which would include a weekend. Occasionally, I'd book an act for a single night if it was feasible, so acts rotated on an erratic schedule. No telling who might be playing on any given night without checking the papers or the posters I hung weekly around town. Still, there were acts I booked on a regular basis which provided a repertory of music that pleased locals and brought in a crowd.

At night, after Sproul would lock up and go home, the structure of the building changed. Not physically of course, but in terms of use, as musicians would push their way up from the crowded space in the Abbey and filter into the abandoned restaurant, which they used as a sort of green room, tuning instruments and preparing to take the Abbey stage. Lounging at tables or on stools at the bar, it was easy to help themselves to whatever alcohol lay within reach—which meant simply walking behind the bar and taking whatever they wanted. There was no way of locking either the upstairs bar or the Abbey bar. This was true of the kitchen as well, and sometimes during an especially long night—when the upstairs manager was around—he would generously unlock the walk-in cooler, light the grill, and offer steaks to anyone who might be hungry, which meant just about everyone as the night advanced and dinner receded into the distant past. Often, he'd leave the cooler open and the grill on and wander downstairs to watch the show, effectively making it a self-serve operation to the delight of all concerned. We wondered how Sproul never seemed to notice, and speculated on how it might be possible for him to make a profit when such pilfering was taking place on a nightly basis. But he never said a word.

Sproul was an accountant. How could an accountant fail to notice so much missing stock, unless of course he'd never bothered to inventory it, or compare it to his profits, in order to operate his business at a loss for tax purposes? I know almost nothing about the intricacies of finance, but this seemed the only likely scenario to me. I lived in terror that one day he would come charging down the steps to confront me with massive losses, pointing to irrefutable evidence that so much food and liquor had seemed to vanish into thin air. Was he simply a bad accountant? Can you be that bad and still make a living? Maybe Sproul had bought the building at an extremely low price—some fantastic bargain that presented itself years earlier when there were still bargains to be had in downtown Aspen—and it didn't matter to him whether he made money or lost it in the restaurant business because, in the end, he'd make a killing when he re-sold the whole thing when the commercial possibilities of the town increased over the decades. Had Jake's Abbey and The Steak House been just a real estate deal all along?

* * *

And then there were the waitresses. Affairs between bartenders and waitresses are inevitable. People who work together often form a bond, and the intimacy of a job—especially into the wee hours of the morning—leads to an even greater intimacy given the right conditions—time, mutual attraction, and opportunity. I hired Jan and her roommate as a pair, because they could trade shifts and cover each other on their nights off. Jan's roommate, Karen, didn't interest me, but Jan was pretty and vibrant and readily available. She was a good waitress, too, and would show up for work in a sleek black dress, open provocatively at the top in order to galvanize the male customers. "It's always a good idea to show a little flesh," she told me. "And you can lean over a table, which doesn't hurt tips any." I liked her brashness, her frank sensuality, and we often joked about customers, so a conspiratorial humor grew between us though we kept up a professional demeanor as much as possible during working hours. Still, it wasn't long before Jan was making eyes at me. Every trip to the waitress station became a subtle, erotic encounter. Jan smoldered, cracked jokes and winked,

and generally shed her warmth in my direction until the flirting became irresistible.

At the end of a long and arduous shift one evening, I suggested we go upstairs after the last customer staggered out and
the doors were locked. Jan smiled. "Sure," she said, then sa-
shayed off to clear some tables. I'd been drinking black beau-
ties that night, cognac with a float of Grand Marnier, in order
to improve my general outlook and calm my nerves. On the
second floor of the building, above the main restaurant and
overlooking the street, there was an old Victorian apartment
Sproul never used. It was in dire need of a cleaning, but it had
its charms: a marble fireplace, a musty couch, some other furniture, and a large unmade bed that looked like it hadn't been
slept in since the nineteenth century. It was a classic four-post-
er, with velvet drapes and a wooden frame on top flaunting
lacy edges. There was a broken coffee machine in one corner,
some boxes stowed behind the couch, a cracked table top, a
tray of glasses on a service stand. Jan and I made our way upstairs, through the dining room, up another set of stairs to the
balcony, and a final set to the second floor, then down a short
hall to the door of the apartment. At the end of that hall, not
far from the apartment, was Bob Sproul's office where each
morning he'd tally up profits from the previous night. Afraid
we might be noticed if we turned on the lights—anyone passing on the street could look up and see the windows illuminated—we lit two candles and placed them on a side table near the
bed. On top of a marble coffee table, I laid out two lines of coke
and we sniffed these before tumbling into bed to enjoy the
benefits that sometimes come when working closely together.

The following morning we were awakened by the sound of
an adding machine clicking and grinding away down the hall.

"Jesus, it's Sproul!" I whispered, "What time is it?" I glanced at my watch on the bed stand: nine a.m.! We'd overslept, and now we'd have to find a way to sneak out without being noticed, though that seemed impossible as the door to Sproul's office wasn't more than a few feet away. We sprang out of bed and got dressed as quietly as possible. "Careful," I whispered, "not a sound." The rug assured that a creaking floorboard wouldn't betray us. But how to open the door without the groan of wood or the scrape of a hinge? Somehow I managed it—it must have taken me five minutes—and we stole down the hall carrying our shoes. I glanced down the hall before exiting the apartment to see that his office door was open, even catching a glimpse of his arm as he worked the adding machine lever. We made our way through the restaurant and down into the Abbey, then through the rear emergency exit into the alley.

"Whew!" I exclaimed. "That was close!"

Jan smiled, looking hung over. We laughed, then, in that awkward way new lovers have when they're not sure of what has just happened, or how things might change. Our heads were throbbing as we kissed goodbye. Though our affair would last a few more months, Jan would find another boyfriend and a new job—cab driving—and I had to hire a new waitress. I was a little hurt, but feelings, especially deep ones were something to avoid in Aspen, if at all possible.

Hoot Night in the Hole

By the time I go up the cement steps and unlock the door, it has stopped snowing and there are already a couple of people shivering on the pavement, waiting to come inside. This isn't unusual, as Hoot Night is our most popular event. So popular that we need a door man, Joe Popper, whom everyone called Joe-the-Door. Every Monday evening for years, musicians have been lining up to strut their stuff on the cramped stage at Jake's Abbey, bringing their friends along. By the time Scott Myers arrives, there are already a few more waiting at the bar to sign up. Scott is the Hoot Master tonight, and it's up to him to schedule the acts and emcee the event. He is a musician himself, and will appear later in the evening with his partner, Pat Flynn, whipping the audience to a frenzy with an up-tempo rendition of Bob Dylan's "Highway 61" and instrumentals like "Blackberry Blossom" and "Stolen Boulders." For the time being, though, he has work to do.

"It's gonna be a busy night," Scott warns me, taking out a large paper tablet to write down the acts in proper order. "I've had a few calls from people wanting to sign up in advance.

We're pretty full already." This will be bad news for the late-
comers, who are sure to show up to find that the list for the
evening is complete. The Hoot Master and I have to take all
the guff when things go wrong. Scott is only the most recent
Hoot Master, but there have been others.

One of the first was Jack Hardy, a classic folksinger whose
bitter, politically-charged lyrics rallied some people while
alienating others. Jack wrote almost all of his own material, though he also sang old popular ballads. He usually performed alone with his guitar, though sometimes his girlfriend,
Jill Burke, would join him on banjo and a friend, Toby, might
thwack out rhythm on an upright bass taller than he was. Jack
also appeared with Larry Gottleib as a duo, known as Jack and
Jake. Jack would laugh and banter with the audience, but if he
thought they weren't being respectful or weren't taking the
subjects of his songs seriously enough, he'd chide them. Red-
faced and glowering, he'd leave the stage early, then try again
later when the audience had re-shuffled itself and might be
more attentive. Jack would appear in a railroad worker's cap,
a buckskin jacket with fringe on the sleeves, jeans, and cowboy boots. He had a ponytail and a droopy walrus mustache,
and he sang in a soft, slightly hoarse voice, insinuating his lyrics while he glared at his audience as if to say: "You know what
I mean, so what are you gonna do about it?" Once, he gave his
audience a history lesson, explaining how Thomas Jefferson
was a hypocrite who kept slaves and had children with Sally
Hemings, while I stood nervously behind the bar wondering if
the audience would rebel and leave.

For a brief period, Chris Cox ran the show. Chris wrote
some of his own material but mostly covered other artists'
songs: Brewer and Shipley, James Taylor, and the Allman

Brothers. He would pound his guitar strings and sing at the top of his lungs. He was handsome, with blue eyes, sharp features, a dapper mustache, and long shoulder-length brown hair which he kept well-groomed, with an almost girlish luster. Chris always seemed a little frustrated to me, as though he wished to break through to stardom but somehow audiences didn't appreciate him enough, or didn't understand what he was trying to do. Like Jack Hardy, Chris was often irked by those who didn't respond properly to his music, or responded feebly. I never saw a musician work so hard to win his listeners over, or sink to such depths if he didn't.

By eight o'clock the place is packed. The phone has been ringing off the wall, and I am pumping out drinks as fast as I can. But after the initial rush, things calm down, especially once the music begins. Scott is already on stage, announcing the first act.

"Ladies and gentlemen, Mr. Alan Garber."

Alan has a landscaping business. There is something clean-cut and collegiate about him, compared to the scruffier, hipper musicians who have all been influenced by the sounds and fashions of the '60s. But Alan seems to have emerged straight out of the '50s. On the nights he's booked, he works all day, then comes in to serenade us with songs from the American folklore tradition, or English versions of the songs of Jacques Brel. He stands onstage now, leaning into the microphone, breathing the first guttural verses of "The Port of Amsterdam":

> In the port of Amsterdam
> There's a sailor who sings
> Of the dreams that he brings
> From the wide open sea . . .

By the time he gets to the final stanza he's straining to hit the high notes, face flushed, the veins on his forehead standing out as the song crescendos and Alan's pounding his guitar like he wants to beat it to death in sorrow and desperation. He's nearly sobbing as the applause begins.

* * *

Ginny has arrived. I am sweet on Ginny, and she likes me well enough, but never responds to my advances. She is a poet, too, and we work together at the literary foundation, but it's all business and I haven't been able to interest her in more. She sits at the bar and orders a drink. I make something special and place it in front of her. Drinks are on the house for Ginny. We chat for a few minutes before Scott mounts the stage again to announce the next act.

"Ladies and gentlemen, you know him, you love him, maybe you've fed him from time to time. Please welcome Mr. Jimmy Dykann!"

Jimmy "Stray Dog" Dykann had honed his act in the clubs and cafés of southern California before arriving in Aspen in 1972. He looks like a surfer, but sings like a cowboy whose voice had been rasped raw by the desert wind. He wears silk Hawaiian shirts, even in winter, and has wavy blond hair that makes him look like a character out of 77 *Sunset Strip* or *Hawaii Five-O*. I don't know where he acquired the nickname "Stray Dog," but it seems to fit. He belts out one of his own compositions, "Road Damage," which refers to travel of course, but to the abuse of alcohol and cocaine as well:

Road damage, road damage
Buddy you've gone too far
And now you're gonna have to live with the scars . . .

Once, he was arrested for drunk driving and had to spend
the night in the Pitkin County Jail. The judge, knowing about
Jimmy's talent as a musician, sentenced him to writing a number of original songs about the history of Colorado, and the
Aspen area in particular. The resulting book, *Old Houses and
Whores*, includes Dykann's lyrics and chronicles the lives of
gamblers, ramblers, settlers, and colorful characters of the
Rocky Mountain west, including Doc Holliday and a particularly salty old hermit lady called the Widow Collins. Later, he
recorded an album, *Colorado History in Song*.

* * *

I run upstairs to the main bar to get more coffee, cream, and
vodka. I chat for a moment with Russ Carter, general manager of Jake's, who's about to lock up for the night. The last
customer has stumbled out into the cold, and Russ is about to
come down for a nightcap. "You can let the musicians come up
when you're ready," he tells me. "It's probably getting a little
claustrophobic down there." It is. On crowded nights, there's
scant room for the musicians themselves and they have to
hang around the bar area near the main door, waiting to go
on. Sometimes they line the inner stairs that lead up to the restaurant, tuning their instruments and generally trying to stay
out of the way.

When I return to the Abbey, Dan and Kim Forde are singing "Creaky Old Gate," a local favorite Dan wrote; it quickly
transforms itself into a metaphor for a long-term relationship.
Dan wears a ten gallon dome-topped Calgary hat. He and his
wife, Kim, often play the Abbey, with Kim providing harmony
to Dan's original melodies. Tall and lanky, he takes the stage
and Kim sits on a stool beside him; they charm audiences with

affability and an easy-going style. Dan is an avid reader, and is forever pressing Robert Graves' *The White Goddess* on me, a book about the origins of poetic myth. He respects and honors his fellow musicians, and they enjoy having him sit in with them whenever possible.

* * *

"Come on back here."

Ginny smiles. I'd often invite her to step behind the bar and watch the show from there. It's the best way to see the room, and she'll be closer, which suits me just fine. Sometimes she even serves drinks if it gets too busy.

The audience has recycled itself a number of times and there are still people on the stairway outside waiting to get in. It must be snowing again, because new arrivals step into the room dusting big flakes off their shoulders. Now Scott is at the microphone announcing another act:

"Some call him genius, others call him demented. Some call him Pastor Mustard, others Dr. Sadistic. Me? I just call him the dude who owes me twenty bucks and a bottle of Boone's Farm Apple Blossom malt liquor. Please, a warm welcome for Dan Sadowsky!"

Dan bounces up to the stage in the guise of himself, having shed his many alter-egos and checked them at the door. Dan plays guitar and mandolin, and nothing he says, on or off stage, can be taken at face value. During his set, a beautiful woman gets up from a table in front of the stage and threads her way among the tables to the toilet in the back of the room. This is an opportunity he can't resist.

"Listen everybody," he whispers into the mic. "Everybody hush for a minute." When the room quiets, he tells the audience to listen for the flush. "Now, don't let on that we heard when she comes back, okay?" People are tittering as she returns to her seat, unaware that she's been the object of one of Dr. Sadistic's jokes. Non sequitors, conspiratorial winks, and bizarre pranks are Sadowsky's stock in trade, and not everyone appreciates his drollery. Sometimes he performs with a sidekick, Washboard Chaz, who adds a bit of extra rhythm to his act. For Dan, music is meant to entertain and divert. The funnier the better. Puncturing pretension is one of his favorite pastimes. He hates musicians like Dan Fogelberg or Jackson Browne, whom he thinks are sentimental and take themselves too seriously.

When Russ comes downstairs, I ask him to watch the place for a minute. "Come on," I say to Ginny, and lead her into the tiny furnace room behind the bar. We are sealed off from the main room, and I lay a couple of lines of coke on one of the heating ducts. We're both feeling loose, and the cognac we've been sipping has warmed our bodies and made us a little dreamy. The coke snaps us awake again, and we return to the club ready for the next round.

It's a group called Chicken Skin, consisting of brothers Bo and Dave Hale, together with Tim Dipietro (and sometimes Tony Grigsby on bass). Chicken Skin excels at choreographing their music, though much of it is parody of other groups and singers. They can ape a Neil Sedaka tune, or cover Presley's "Return to Sender," or even play it straight with Dylan, Beatles, or Crosby, Stills, Nash and Young. Often, they'll sing a capella, three or four part harmony, while they fill the stage with their antics. Once, in Snowmass, chef Tom DiMaggio presented them with "The Chicken Skin Award," a real piece of chicken skin stretched out on a piece of cardboard and baked in the oven.

Then it's time for Jessie Goldberg. I don't know exactly when Jessie showed up to perform at Jake's Abbey, but I suspect he appeared one night during an open mic session and, given the audience's hilarious response, decided to stay in town for a while. A doleful-eyed, disheveled, somewhat phlegmatic song-writer, Jessie writes outlandish lyrics that contradict his other-wise morose appearance, the way comedian Steven Wright's low-key demeanor seems decidedly at odds with his intellectu-al wit. It's this imbalance, this contrast between Jessie's physi-cal appearance and his light-hearted, preposterous lyrics that make what he sings even more funny. He sits at his Hammond electric piano with a straight-faced, almost resigned, expres-sion, and sings about the dehumanizing effects of conformity in the modern world:

> Ants, ants, everywhere ants
> Ants in short dresses, ants in long pants . . .

He follows this with a cracked ballad about human sexual-ity, whose refrain makes us howl with laughter:

> In and out and out and in and squirt, squirt, squirt . . .

Jessie never laughs, himself. It's hard to tell whether he knows he is being funny or not. The most he can muster is a lugubrious smile, something like Peter Lorre in *Casablanca* try-ing to ingratiate himself to Rick and avoid arrest

Another time, according to Pat Flynn, Jessie noticed one of Aspen's well-endowed dowagers heading for the bathroom in Jake's Abbey and stopped her to remark:

"Don't go in there now."

"Why?" she wanted to know.

"Because," said Jessie, "we've run out of film."

* * *

Musicians like Dan Sadowsky, Chicken Skin, and Jessie Goldberg know how to play their instruments and are thoroughly grounded in the musical traditions from whence they have
sprung. Straight comedy was another matter, and had a tenu-
ous tradition in the Abbey. In his autobiography, *Born Standing
Up*, Steve Martin reveals that one of his first professional gigs
was in Aspen, at The Abbey Cellar, when he was twenty-one.
Martin, too, was a first-rate musician—he knew how to play
the banjo and write lyrics that people enjoyed—but the core of
his act was definitely comedy, and he was brilliant at it. Arriving in Aspen in March, 1967 for a two week gig, he estimates
that he was paid three hundred dollars for his services, a large
sum for anyone who appeared at the Abbey at that time. His
act included jokes, banjo, and magic but it was all hilarious, all
meant to tickle and amuse. The English comedian, Jonathan
Moore, performed in the Abbey as well and was still working
in Aspen in the early '70s, as well as Ron Maranian, "The Ar-
menian Comedian," whom some of us got to know quite well
before he disappeared from the scene.

By the time Jessie has finished his set, the audience has recycled itself again and new customers fill the tables. This is the
moment in the evening when everyone takes a deep breath.
The mood seems to change as the early hours have passed and
the night moves into high gear; this is when some of the bigger acts will perform. The Romance Jazz Band, now crowding
onto the stage, features Bob Funk on trombone, Bill Street-
er on clarinet, Tom Paxton on bass, Bill Rollins on piano, and
Gordon Forbes on trumpet. Bob Funk would later go to New

York to found the Uptown Horns. New Orleans style jazz is a natural for Aspen. Now they are swinging their instruments and almost knocking each other off-stage. I've got my arm around Ginny, leaning against the back bar, and she doesn't seem to mind. Now and then I jump into action, filling orders or re-stocking the cooler, then return to Ginny and the show. Russ has gone home and musicians mill about upstairs, talking, rehearsing, trading licks on their instruments as the night whirls on.

"Hoot Night" is like a vast audition, a reality show before reality shows became popular, during which rank beginners perform alongside more polished musicians. There are people who are shudderingly bad, and those who have something more to offer. A string of acts follow one another: Your Relatives, with Cara Burgarella, Jim Sheehan, and Steve Cole; Lee Satterfield (who later left Aspen to join Nancy Griffith's band) and Price Berryman; Kristi Kranz and Kim Kuda; Steve Stapenhorst and his sister, Ellen; Patty Ehrlich; Kenny Thomas; and Steve Weisberg who would go on to join John Denver's band. Photographer Bob Kreuger picks out traditional tunes on his banjo. If Egan had stayed in town, I'm sure he would have shown up for Hoot Night, guitar in hand, ready to play. And then there is Bronco Newcomb, who wrote a song about the great Olympic ping-pong duel that was taking place at that time between the United States and China:

Ping pong for peace, pretty people, ping pong for peace!

* * *

We've reached the apex of the evening, prime time for musicians, and the audience is primed too, growing more and more

animated with each act. A group called Homebrew is one of
my favorites, and I whisper to Ginny: "Listen to this!" Homebrew includes Bobby Carpenter, Bobby Mason, David James
Holster, Bernie Mysior, and Michael Buono, and for a brief
time Glenda Griffith and Paul Wilcox. Homebrew proved to
be the incubator for the larger, more successful group, Starwood. By the time Starwood recorded an album with Colum-
bia Records, Griffith and Wilcox had moved on. To replace
them, Bryan Savage was added to the group for his exciting sax
solos, and Haden Gregg was brought on board to fill out high-
end harmonies. Starwood, then, was born out of the old husk
of Homebrew before dissolving due to internal conflicts and
the stresses of rapid success.

Individuals and groups who were already famous and successful play the Abbey from time to time. Russ Carter arranged for Steppenwolf to appear, but not the original group,
which had dissolved by then. In the 1970s, a number of groups
calling themselves Steppenwolf, with various original members, toured North America. None of them included the band's
most popular member, lead singer John Kay. Only the original bass player, Nick St. Nicholas, appeared in the group that
played The Abbey. Still, the place was packed, though some
felt misled and left early. St. Nicholas's girlfriend, a wild-haired
brassy blonde, accompanied him while wearing a black leather
jacket, spiked heels, and leopard skin spandex leotards. A noteworthy incident turned the evening into something of an un-
intended farce. The manager of Steppenwolf wanted to make
sure that there would be a drum set on the premises for the
band's use, as they were traveling without their own set. Russ
Carter assured them a set would be available, and ended up
borrowing drums from the Aspen Music School. It was a stu-

dent kit, however. When Steppenwolf showed up, they were furious. Imagine a burly, full-grown, long-haired rock percussionist sitting down at these diminutive drums trying to look cool while beating out the rhythm for "Born to be Wild." Carter had to make himself scarce for the rest of the night.

Even the whisper of a rumor is enough to produce hordes of fans, many of whom we have to turn away at the door. Rumors can be useful promotional tools. If someone calls on the phone and says, "I hear Jackson Browne is going to appear at the Abbey tonight!" I won't squelch the rumor. I simply say, "I don't know, it's possible." And it always is. Once, Clint Eastwood showed up, bending down to enter the door (his tall lanky frame and chiseled features were unmistakable), and novelist James Salter brought friends in to hear Myers & O'Flynn knock out their version of Chuck Berry's "No Money Down." Aspen was full of celebrities, from Cher to members of the group Chicago to Jimmy Buffet to Australian singer-songwriter Peter Allen. The atmosphere was charged, ripe with possibility.

* * *

One of the bartenders from upstairs is in the crowd, so I ask him to watch the place for a minute. "Come on," I say to Ginny, squeezing her hand and leading her back again into the furnace room. We're both of us in a pleasant mood, lulled by the music and the cognac and the general exhilaration of the night. It's stuffy but cozy in the little room, and I lay out a few more lines of coke on a small plate. While Ginny is leaning down to snort a line, I nuzzle her hair and begin kissing her neck. This too, seems to go unnoticed, until I begin to unbutton her blouse and her eyes snap open and she looks directly at me.

"What are you doing?"

"How come you don't want to make love to me," I blurt, a question that ought to contain its own answer.

Ginny's eyes are spinning. She looks confused, and half wild. "I don't know," she says, as though the possibility has never occurred to her. There's hardly any room to maneuver in the narrow space, and we're standing very close. The harsh light from the naked bulb above our heads, the concrete floor, the close walls contrive to give the place the feeling of a cell. Hardly romantic, but I persist.

"Let's make love." I put my arms around her and draw her in.

"Here?" she looks aghast. We can hear the music, someone strumming a guitar, the sound of applause. I lean back and try to unbutton her blouse. She squints at me.

"What is it…this?" she asks. "*This?*" Then crazily, impulsively, she rips her own blouse open and stands there as I gawk at her naked shoulders, her bra, the smooth skin of her belly and waist. The gesture has been so sudden and unexpected that it takes us both by surprise. We burst into laughter at the absurdity of the situation. Outside, not twenty feet away, the audience claps enthusiastically, someone whistles and yells "More!" I'm grinning at Ginny, but she's still giving me that intense, manic look. I feel powerless, chagrined, and all thought of sex dissipates like smoke. "No," I say, "okay. I just . . ." anything I say will sound stupid. My feelings for Ginny haven't changed, but I am unable to act and the moment has turned comic. Then it's gone. My head swims, and all at once the furnace heaves on with a great sigh. Ginny pulls herself together, elbows bumping against pipes and exposed joists as I try to collect myself. Nothing will ever happen between us. She will eventually fall in love with a young painter and I'll pursue my brief affair with Jan, then move on. All of this happens in the tiniest flicker of time. Then we are back behind the bar, still shaking our heads, applauding with everyone else as Dan Sadowsky takes the stage to introduce the next act.

"Thank you lovers of live and local music. You would think by listening to them, that this next act is a talented twosome who can write, sing, and pick with spectacular talent and ability. But that just shows how wrong a tourist can be, okay? Joe-the-Door just hipped me to the news that *one* of these performers is also *well* known among baby Harp seal hunters as the finest gay acid salesmen, not just in the Castro district, but anywhere. Be sure to ask them about it while they're trying to play. Boys and girls, please make welcome: Meyers and O'Flynn!"

One of the more exciting local groups to appear in the Abbey, Myers & O'Flynn are crowd pleasers and know how to manage an audience. Even as a teenager, Flynn was making a name for himself as a studio musician in Los Angeles. By the time he arrived in Aspen, Flynn was a full-fledged guitar phenomenon, a singer, songwriter, and formidable arranger of both his own material and that of others. Scott Myers is a young minister from Virginia who had attended Yale Divinity School and began his work in Aspen at the Community Church. But even at Yale, he was singing and playing guitar. I never hear Scott sing a word of dogma, or proselytize anyone. He has a clear, powerful voice and plays solid rhythm guitar. The two make a potent duo, and their harmonies are flawless. Whether they launch into covers of Neil Young's "Love is a Rose" or Huddie Ledbetter's "Titanic," or present arrangements of their own original material—"Ingram's Island" or "Continental Highway"—they bring the audience to a fever-

ish pitch. And Myers and O'Flynn are funny. When Scott Myers finally leaves Aspen for the West Coast, he will transform
himself again, first into the comic singer "Scott California" and
then into a successful screenwriter, with his first film, *K9*, released in 1989. Pat Flynn will go on to become an integral part
of New Grass Revival, then a sought-after studio musician in
Nashville. Jake's Abbey is an incubator, a cradle, but it won't
hold the immense talent of these two for long.

* * *

Judy and Jerry Fletcher, Penny Wheetman, Dave Shappert,
Mark Moriva, Paul Valentine, Terry Bannon, Mark Ross—no
telling who might show up as the night lengthens towards
midnight and beyond. After the main acts have appeared, the
audience thins. I always find the dregs of the evening as en-
tertaining as the high spots: would-be musicians who haven't
yet mastered their instruments, croaking out rustic songs
they'd like to premier. One young man, high on drugs, thrash-
es around the stage growling something unintelligible while
thumping dissonant chords on his guitar. He's followed by
a mountain girl decked out in a skirt that looks like it's been
fashioned out of a bed quilt. She strums a zither and warbles
ballads about flowers and baby deer. Her blonde hair falls, like
Rapunzel's, around her shoulders. The few customers who remain nod their heads and order a last drink. One or two have
already fallen asleep in their seats. Ginny has disappeared,
drifted out into the night with the rest of the audience, and
when I finally mount the stairs again to lock the outer door,
Scott and I—and a few other musicians—sit around and talk
for hours. I get into a harangue with Scott about spirituality.
He's not trying to convert me, just make a point about St. Paul.

My hero is Walt Whitman, a "simple-minded humanist," according to Scott, but we respect each other and wind up joking about religion and literature both. Exhaustion finally defeats us all. We shuffle up the back steps into the alley and disperse. It has stopped snowing. The first stars twinkle through gaps in the clouds, promising a dazzling morning.

Bark, Root, and Leaf

Ajax Mountain doesn't look much like Parnassus, but it has a Greek name. In most ways—size, strength, primitive vigor and physical courage—Ajax is an apt name for a mountain located in a resort dedicated to the physical life and the rugged natural environment that surrounds it. Beautiful young men and women fill the streets, tanned, fit, ageless. To walk through Aspen in the 1970s would have given anyone the impression that somewhere in the nearby mountains, not in Florida, lies the Fountain of Youth—fern-fringed, ready to be imbibed. Yet Walter Paepcke's dream of a place for the whole person, a concept that came to be known as "The Aspen Idea," included more than a dedication to strenuous outdoor activities. A rich industrialist, Paepcke was the CEO of the Container Corporation of America, based in Chicago, and his visit to this somnolent mountain hamlet in the mid-1940s marked a turning point in the town's history, awakening it from its long, post-mining-boom sleep. The story is so well known in Aspen, and repeated *ad nauseam* in every local newspaper, brochure and magazine, that there is little need to recount it in detail here. But it

is true that Paepcke started both the Aspen Ski Corporation
for benefit of the body, and the Aspen Institute for Humanistic
Studies—when he brought Albert Schweitzer to town in 1949
during the Goethe bicentennial—for the benefit of the mind.
It is true that his vision of attending to "the whole person" in
body, mind, and spirit has been somewhat realized in Aspen
during the fifty years since his death in 1960. For the small part
I played in bringing the literary arts to Aspen during the 1970s,
I often felt I was living in Walter Paepcke's dream. I would never have been able to convince anyone anywhere else to support
me in running a writers' foundation, starting a conference, expanding a bi-annual literary magazine, and managing various
reading series and other literary events had it not been for the
open-mindedness of Aspenites. I hadn't published anything, I
was unknown in the literary world, I had no money, and no experience. Yet somehow, unbelievably, it all came to pass. Aspen
was a hotbed of dreams, and I was one of its dreamers.

Why anyone listened to me I'll never know.

One of the first persons who *did* listen was a young Indian woman, Indira Singh. It was Indira's dream to add a literary dimension to the town's thriving summer cultural scene.
The Aspen Music Festival, Design Conference, Aspen Institute for Humanistic Studies, Ballet West, FilmFest, Aspen Art
Museum, and other organizations were already in full swing,
or emerging. A vital literary component was largely missing.
However, literary figures were associated with Aspen both before and after the 1970s began. Harold Ross, founding editor of
The New Yorker was born in Aspen in 1892—only three years
after the Wheeler Opera House and the Hotel Jerome opened
for business. A year later, silver was demonetized and the mining industry collapsed. His parents stayed in Aspen until Ross

was nine. By the time Ross published the first issue of the *New Yorker* on February 21, 1925, Aspen for him must have been a dim memory.

Though I don't know when famous Western novelist Luke Short arrived, he was actively writing until his death in Aspen in 1975 (where his ashes are scattered, along with those of Harold Ross). He had adopted his *nom de plume* from a real-life western gunslinger, probably at his publisher's urging. It is hard to imagine the red-blooded American male readers of his fifty-two cowboy novels being drawn to books like *Savage Range* or *The Marshal of Vengeance,* written by someone named Frederick Dilley Glidden.

The novelist James Salter began life as James A. Horowitz; he graduated from West Point, flew combat missions during the Korean war, and wound up in Aspen sometime in the 1960s, where he still lives part-time today. During the summer he lives and works on Long Island, but winter brings him back to Colorado for the skiing. A few evenings around Jim's table in his modest house in the west end is an education in the simple pleasures of conversation and good food.

In the late '60s and early '70s, Saul Bellow spent his summers in town as a guest of the Aspen Institute. According to Peggy Clifford, he referred to Aspen as a "pleasure slum," a description both prescient and accurate. Though he never wrote a word about Aspen, his presence in the town must have galvanized the literati.

Leon Uris lived on Red Mountain in the 1970s, working on various projects and once appearing at the Aspen Writers' Conference in the 1980s to counsel aspiring writers on the rewards and agonies of being a successful novelist. His wife, Jill, was a member of our board for many years.

Andy Stone, who published a fantasy novel, *Song of the Kingdom*, with Doubleday in 1979 has worked for the *Aspen Times* for years, where he contributes a popular column, "A Stone's Throw," about politics and social mores, writing which is always calculated to raise the hackles on some of his more thin-skinned readers. And I have already mentioned, Bruce Berger, who was the first writer I met when I arrived in town.

Those were the luminaries. The rest of us formed writers' groups and began to publish a bi-annual literary magazine—first called *aspen leaves*, and later, *Aspen Anthology*. This began with Indira Singh's founding of the first nonprofit organization in town dedicated solely to writing and the literary arts: aspen leaves, inc. As long as Indira's tenure lasted, aspen leaves, inc. existed almost exclusively to publish its magazine, *aspen leaves* (no caps, pun intended), a title we almost unanimously disliked. When Indira retired in 1975, the new editor, John Stafford, wrote an editorial note at the front of the very next issue of the magazine explaining what a trial it had been to jettison the old name and come up with a new one. Of the name *aspen leaves*, Stafford wrote: "We knew it was amateurish and sentimental, knew it embodied the antithesis of what we had in mind. It was a grave error, a millstone around our necks." We considered *Aspen Review*, which was an obvious choice, but were blocked by another magazine of the same name whose editor threatened to sue us if we didn't desist. We tried *Roaring Fork Review*, which we all loved, but were legally prohibited again because the name was owned by a newspaper down valley. I pushed hard for *Aspen Anthology*, though I knew it wasn't the best name. I had *Spoon River Anthology* in the back of my mind, the infamous fictional town that was filled with odd, outspoken, salty characters made immortal by death and Edgar Lee Masters. *Aspen Anthology*, I felt, was better than *aspen leaves*, with its precious reference to pages and the green outgrowth of the area's most prominent tree. And we wouldn't have to endure the same cover every issue—the blown-up imprint of an actual aspen leaf, which changed colors but not shape or size with each successive issue. With a less restrictive name, we could put anything on the cover, and each new number of the magazine would have its own particular character, though the interior design would remain consistent. We could distance ourselves from the far-fetched, tortured vegetal metaphor Indira printed on the very first page of Volume 1, Number 1 directly across from the masthead: the word "Cambium" appeared in thirty point type, which she intended to be the title of a running editorial at the beginning of each issue. First order of business, then, was to edify our readers by proceeding to tease out all of the various levels of meaning inherent in likening a magazine to a tree, beginning with a definition:

Cambium: (cam be-em) n. A layer of cells in the stems and roots of vascular plants that give rise to all secondary growth in plants, responsible for the annual rings of wood. (New Latin, exchange, from Latin cambiare, to exchange)."

In the rich loam of such a definition, an extended metaphor quickly took root:

> Layer—*aspen leaves* is...a non-profit educational
> corporation...working with writers...putting out a
> quality magazine twice a year...setting up writers'
> workshops...cooperating with educational institutions
> to enhance creative writing...providing a library for
> writers...establishing grants and scholarships...sending
> over five hundred copies of each issue at no charge to
> libraries and educational institutions.

Surprisingly, most of this ambitious agenda eventually came to pass. "Corporation" is perhaps legally accurate, but far too inflated to describe what we actually were: a small tribe of unknown writers struggling to establish ourselves among the other artists and arts organizations in Aspen. But the metaphor, unfortunately, did not stop there:

> Cells—*aspen leaves* is...15 people working together for two years...each manuscript of the 500 submitted for the first issue critiqued with a page of comments and suggestions sent to the authors of those not accepted.

This was followed by an admission—though it sounds like a boast—"Staff all under thirty years old." I was not among the original fifteen "cells" who worked so hard, as I had joined the staff after the first issue of *aspen leaves* went to press, but in my youthful arrogance, I shared the founders' relish for setting myself up as an authority. At once, I began reading submissions and scribbling my opinions on rejections slips to return to the unhappy authors who in any case had not asked for comments, nor expected them. This practice would end abruptly when a professor at the University of Nebraska—whose work I had dismissed with a few wayward and unwanted "suggestions"—wrote back to say that our magazine was no better than toilet paper and that we would be lucky if all we were remembered for was that we had rejected him. His brusque, professorial arrogance put a damper on my own presumptions. Soon I was returning material with a pre-printed slip that offered nothing but: "Thank you, we enjoyed reading your work, but . . ." This seemed safer and, in the long run, more honest.

But Indira's arboreal metaphor wasn't quite complete. There was still that tantalizing word, "exchange," and in one way or another it would have to be worked into the leafy comparison to which the magazine had committed itself:

> Exchange—*aspen leaves* welcomes you to join in a creation. If you write or know writers, be in touch. Leaves need water...contributions are tax-deductible.

"Leaves need water." Some of us shuddered at the pastoral analog that evoked. But we all understood the final brief sentence: the eternal cry for donations!

The first staff—those initial fifteen cells—included some interesting people. Besides Indira and her partner, Mary Guthrie (who owned and operated what was then the only bookstore in town), there was Adele Dusenbury, a reporter for the *Aspen Times*, David Bentley and Joan Nice, both former editors at *Climbing Magazine*, Julie Klevin, head librarian at the Pitkin County Library, Sue Michael, program director at KSNO Radio, Chris Cassatt, cartoonist and photographer for the *Aspen Times*, Bonnie Stretch, a former associate editor at *Saturday Review*, Bryant Ricker, production manager at the *Aspen Times*, and Sandra Stuller, city attorney for Aspen. This was an accomplished bunch, and generous, all of them donating their time by stealing it away from their regular jobs (and their time off) to see that first issue into print. Unlike other arts organizations which *begin* with public and private financial support, literary activity in any town across America is likely to start with a group of devoted individuals working *pro bono* to insure that the community is exposed to good writing, and *then* they seek funding. The little magazine movement in this country has been amply documented. Having begun in the 1920s, it was still thriving in the 1970s, and continues to this day. Nothing seems to be able to stop it—not cultural indifference, lack of

funds, a poor educational system, or even rising illiteracy rates.
For the past hundred years or so, literature has been a poor
cousin to the other arts, surviving mostly by its own craftiness
and sheer will.

* * *

That first issue, and subsequent issues, featured work by well-
known and established figures whose careers would continue
to flourish and whose work would become part of American
literature as it was being published. An unlikely contribu-
tor to that first issue was former Minnesota senator and 1968
presidential candidate Eugene J. McCarthy. In that very year
(1968), he wrote: "If any of you are secret poets, the best way
to break into print is to run for the presidency." There can be
little doubt that the luster of his name—especially on the cover of Volume 1, Number 1—was taken into account while con-
sidering the work he submitted. But McCarthy had obviously
read a lot of poetry, and knew what was going on in contem-
porary verse. He was not untalented, and deserved to be published. A few lines describing an old school near a gloomy park
show his ability:

> Beyond it stood the public school
> sealed summer sepulcher of heresy . . .

Quickly, he moves inside the empty building to observe its
abandoned contents:

> pale blackboards, books,
> lying like poisoned pigeons
> on the floor, husks of flies
> sucked dry by spiders,
> and bees with pollen laden thighs,

their myriad eyes deceived by glass,
dead or dying on the windowsills.

This is quite a bit better than the verse of other politicians
and celebrities I have seen who tried to break into print on the
strength of their names alone. Later, when I joined the staff,
we would reject work by actor Vincent Price, whose poetry
was neither naïve nor unaccomplished, but we found it a bit
too overwrought and Gothic for our tastes.

* * *

I don't know how my name was brought to Indra's attention or
why she invited me to be a poetry editor for *aspen leaves*. I suspect Bruce Berger might have nominated me, or perhaps Mary
Guthrie, whose bookstore in the Little Nell complex I haunted
regularly. But I recall walking to Indra's apartment in the east
end of Aspen beyond Herron Park on one of those sun-washed
evenings that make you feel like you're living in Yeats's Byz-
antium. Perhaps it was the summer of 1973, and I was ready to
meet the other editors and take up my task of receiving, sorting, reading, selecting, and rejecting work that increasingly
clogged our mailboxes—both at the Post Office, and later in
our office on the second floor of the Wheeler Opera House.
That day I met John Stafford and Hancel McCord, fiction editors, and Ki Davis, an extraordinary artist—sculpture and collage, as well as charcoal—who was turning her attention to
writing after a lifetime of accomplishment in the visual arts.

In her early fifties, Ki was a natural poet; her work seemed
to emanate from a depth of memory and emotion—images she
might otherwise have drawn, now described in words of un-
varnished power. I remember her excitement when, during a
workshop with Larry Levis, her poem was read and discussed

and Levis pronounced it "a real poem." Ki was the real thing. Later, she would bring poems to me to ask for my advice. I always felt inadequate, embarrassed somehow: the master asking the student for advice. Ki was humble, and never self-defensive when it came to her art. Only the work mattered. Still, she was anything but timid or easily discouraged. Ki was never on our staff, but her presence at our meetings and events— her stature in a town that immediately recognized her talent (she'd arrived in 1973)—was unquestioned and made all of us better as artists. Perhaps it was the seriousness and unwavering commitment of her example. She began drawing on paper and painting on canvas, then moved to collage, and on to sculpture, which she mastered as well. Her piece, "Interplay," stands at the head of the Hyman Street Mall—abstract, erotic, elegant—in contrast to many of the other installments that adorn public places: kitschy, avuncular bronze bears or stereotypical American characters, golfers and fishermen, molded quickly out of cheap materials for the popular market. Ki's talent transcended all of that. Sometimes we would gather at her house for an informal salon to read our poems to each other.

When she died prematurely of cancer at fifty-seven, we felt the loss deeply and knew that someone extraordinary had been taken from us. Later, we would publish a collection of her powerfully original, mysterious poems. In the introduction to that volume, John Frederick Nims, who had known her in Chicago, wrote: "My memories of Ki are all of a kind of celebration, a kind of radiance...She was a bright spirit among us."

*   *   *

I can't recall exactly where the first issue of *aspen leaves* was produced. It might have been in the offices of the *Aspen Times* itself. But I do recall that for a brief period all papers and files were stored in bureau drawers under my bed in the basement of Hans Grammiger's chalet on Monarch Street. We owned little or no equipment, but soon acquired a homemade light table, which I recollect setting up in Bruce Berger's house where, for another brief period, the magazine kept its office. All printed material in those pre-internet, digitally-free times, was produced on light tables. Computers had advanced only to the point of word-processing, spewing out long scrolls of text on special light-sensitive paper. We'd proof the copy, marking errors with blue pens, then return them to the typesetter for correction. Then we'd cut the corrected proofs into page-length pieces. We'd spread hot paste on the back of each page with a metal roller, and carefully position the page on translucent grid paper, which we'd taped to the light table. We'd line the left-hand margin of type up against a pre-determined line on the grid paper, smoothing it down. It was a tedious process, and took a toll on our eyes. Any subsequent errors we might discover during the paste-up process—a word, or a punctuation mark, sometimes even a single letter—had to be removed, with the precision of a surgeon, using an X-Acto knife. These second corrections would be reset, then cut to size (often tiny), touched with a dab of paste, and repositioned using the tip of the X-Acto blade. We became maestros of the light table, celebrating each miniscule correction, each replaced semi-colon or errant letter, with a cheer.

We did this twice a year for almost ten years, until our eyes blurred and our heads pounded with the strain of bending over a table that cast light up into our faces as we worked. Once all the grid sheets had been pasted up with the pages of the new issue, we would proof them again, then ship them off to Edwards Brothers in Ann Arbor, Michigan. I had discovered Edwards Brothers by some process of research and elimination, finding them to be the best and cheapest printers of perfect-bound books and literary magazines in America. A month or two later, back would come six or seven cases of the newest number of the magazine, and we would distribute them: first to subscribers, then to bookstores, and finally, free to libraries and educational institutions as we'd promised in our very first issue. We'd take a deep breath, drink some wine, grab some sleep, and begin the process all over again for the next issue six months down the road. None of this would have been possible without the support and generosity of Marge Brenner of Aspen Typesetting, who took a liking to us and provided excellent typesetting at a very reasonable cost. We called her "magic fingers" because she made the job of proofing, cutting, and pasting much easier than it otherwise would have been.

Our final office, our *real* office, was located on the second floor of the Wheeler Opera House once the city donated space to the growing number of arts organizations that had no real offices of their own. The building had been languishing for a decade or two, since its last renovation mid-century, so it might have appeared a bit dilapidated. To us, it looked like paradise. At last, we had a public address and no longer had to operate out of someone's living room. We were now an actual foundation, and the quaint ambiance of the building added to our luster. It might suggest that we had been there forever, that we had always been an institution in a town whose history stretched back to the previous century. When we first entered our office, it had one stuffed chair, a moveable wooden bookcase that had seen better days, and a long wide shelf built into the back wall on which we could work. We built a set of

cubbyholes out of raw lumber, which we labeled IN, OUT, UN-
DECIDED, and with various editors' names, then placed the unit
at one end of the shelf. We filed all our papers and other paraphernalia in the narrow supply room to one side of the main
room, and installed a phone in the tiny, closet-sized private office in the back corner of the reception area, which had our
only window. The private office contained a creaky chair and
the bottom half of a roll top desk, stuffed under the slope of a
stairway that led above us to the third floor. From this perch,
I could look out over the corner of South Mill and Hyman, including the west end of the Hyman Street Mall. Over the roof-
tops to the east, I could see the high ridge of Smuggler Mountain, and watch the weather sweep in—rain, snow, and the late
hallowed light. We had no electricity bills. Heat was provided. There was a bathroom just down the gloomy hall to the
right. We set our light table up at the end of the work-shelf
along the back wall. We hung a few prints that no one wanted.
We filled the shelves with books about literature and poetry.
Then we opened a bottle of champagne and drank to the city,
to the Muses, to the gods of artistic patronage and public charity. Nothing would make us budge until the building was again
completely renovated in the mid-1980s and we had to move to
the Red Brick Schoolhouse on East Bleecker Street in the west
end. Before that, however, the Wheeler Opera House served
for many years as Aspen's center for the arts.

Surrounding us on the second floor of the Opera House
were several other arts organizations—Judy Royer and Film-
Fest, The Music Associates of Aspen, Ballet West directed
by Mary Apple, Phillip Yenawine and The Aspen Center for
the Visual Arts (before it became The Aspen Art Museum
and moved into permanent quarters at the bottom of S. Mill

Street), a group dedicated to the study and preservation of the culture of the American Indian—and next to us, the law office of J. D. Muller, who became one of our fiction editors and served as our legal adviser. At the very front of the building facing Ajax Mountain was Heather Tharp's Xerox business and phone answering service—complete with an old-fashioned switchboard. On the third floor, up a narrow set of stairs in the back of the building, were the offices of Aspen Repertory Theater, directed by Bill Shore and Tom Ward, as well as John and Katy Smith of Grassroots TV, which had earlier kept some of its equipment and filmed some of its programs downstairs in the basement. Taken together, we were a happy but otherwise homeless bunch, and I proposed that we all gather in the literary office on Friday afternoons, just after office hours, to celebrate the end of each week by drinking wine and beer together and sharing stories of our individual struggles to uphold art in the little Rocky Mountain enclave we served. Those Friday afternoon soirees were a time of relaxed tension and laughter, and the beginning of community feeling.

* * *

The adoption of a new name for the magazine coincided roughly with our move into the Wheeler Opera House in the winter of 1975-76. We were officially *Aspen Anthology*, and a new staff addressed the task of collecting, reading, accepting and editing material for each issue. The great ongoing shuffle in personnel had begun, never to let up over the years. Rosemary Thompson became a fiction editor. I became editor-in-chief, while Donna Disch joined Bruce Berger as a poetry editor. Later in the decade, Tierney Whipp, Gita Goner, Virginia Slachman, Rosie Ligget, June Rosenfeld, Robert Crum, Barbara Lewis, Susie Iceberg, Jonathan Sherrill, Don Child, and David Rothman would join our crew, each contributing his or her time and talent to insure that the quality and vitality of the magazine would not lapse. Nancy Thomson was in charge of layout and design, the only one among us who knew anything about the arcane rituals of pasting up a print magazine. Cherie Cancellerie handled circulation, which was much too big a word to describe the actual situation with regard to readership and paying customers.

The Fall 1976 issue of *Aspen Anthology* included interviews with author Tom Wolfe and *New Yorker* staff writer Brendan Gill. We included a poem by Donald Hall, who was already an established writer and would go on to publish twenty books of poetry, as well as biographies, plays, short stories, children's books, and two memoirs on his way to becoming Poet Laureate of the United States in 2006. As one critic put it, Donald Hall was the closest thing to a "Man of Letters" our country would produce in the second-half of the twentieth century. We may have been green around the gills, but we had acquired a bit of savvy and literary taste during our formative years. We took pride in knowing that the magazine was well-edited, and that assiduous proofreading assured that each new issue would be relatively error-free.

I don't know why I took it into my head to produce a special "Local's Issue" of the magazine. *aspen leaves*, and later *Aspen Anthology*, had been conceived as national journals, and though they didn't really have a wide readership, they drew on a national pool of writers to fill their pages. The editors had determined at the very outset that we would not publish ourselves. But, as we were all practicing writers, and seeing as so many first-rate poets and novelists had chosen Aspen as their home over the years, we felt that an exception to our rule was warranted. We would produce a collection of local writing once, and once only. Then we would return to our mission of publishing the finest writing we could find, from whatever quarter, around the country. A call went out up and down the valley for submissions to this special issue and we hoped that—together with material from Aspen's already renowned writers—we might fill an issue and demonstrate the scope and vitality of work being produced in town. If readers—and especially prospective donors—might see what fine writers, not just in the past but even in the present, walked among them, they might be persuaded to become subscribers, or even better, part with some serious money to help underwrite our activities as a foundation. Such was the nature of our naiveté. We expected accolades, or at least an unusual level of interest, and we received neither. We had not anticipated that some people in the valley would interpret our call for submissions as an open invitation to be published without consideration for our editorial policy of selecting work we felt was of a high enough quality. Feelings were hurt, hopes dashed, residual resentment created that festered for years. But in the end, we produced what we thought was an accurate and compelling picture of the literary arts in Aspen, a snapshot of the era as far as writing was concerned.

In the spring of 1977, *Aspen Anthology #3*, a "Special Locals Issue," was published with a black-and-white photo of Hunter S. Thompson on the cover, which had been taken by Tommy DiMaggio in Thompson's campaign headquarters in the Hotel Jerome on election night, when Thompson was running for Sheriff of Pitkin County. Thompson looks haggard and glassy-eyed from his long campaign, and from the epic consumption of stimulants that kept him going. Clenched in his teeth, his trademark cigarette holder. Draped around his neck, an American flag. And on his head, a fiberglass wig he had donned in order to look like Thomas Jefferson. A few weeks earlier, he had shaved his head so his opponent—the incumbent sheriff, Carol Whitmire—would not have occasion to call him an unwashed, long-haired hippie. There are bags under Thompson's eyes, and a hangdog expression on his face. But there was good reason to feature him on the cover of our local issue, as he was one of the most famous locals writing at that time and perhaps truer to the spirit of the place than anyone else. With the calculating fervor of fledgling but ambitious editors we felt, too, that Thompson's appearance on our cover might help to sell more magazines.

In an editorial note that precedes the contents of the issue, I laid out the history of literary activity in the Roaring Fork Valley as well as I could determine. I made a number of reasonable observations, like ("Aspen is not a metropolitan area with a well-founded literary community, but a small resort town whose residents are, and remain, more interested in recreational than cultural activities") and a few preposterous ones ("*Aspen Anthology* is distributed throughout the Unites States and Canada"). That last assertion, with all its youthful inaccuracy and brio, makes me smile. As Bruce Berger writes in *The Complete Half-Aspenite*, *Aspen Anthology* was "a ruthlessly nonprofit literary magazine with a token national circulation." When we finally ceased publication after more than five years, we had somewhere in the neighborhood of one hundred actual subscribers. Other programs the foundation offered were more successful and therefore made more sense. The prospect of producing a bi-annual literary magazine for few more than a hundred people made its absurdity felt. "Maybe we ought quit," I said to J. D. Muller, who had come in from his office next door.

He nodded. "I think that might be a good idea."

Every year across America, editors of small magazines and presses come to this same conclusion with heavy hearts, having to finally admit that publishing with little more than idealism is a fool's game. For a beginning writer, publishing a literary magazine is an education, a rite of passage. During the years we published *Aspen Anthology*, I felt I knew more about writing and publishing—and literary activity in the country in general—than I have ever felt since. I imagined that we had our collective finger on the pulse of what was being written in America. I learned, too, how text was set up and produced, what "perfect bound" meant, what "offset" denoted in comparison to other forms of printing, how to gather and position graphics on a page, tactful and effective ways to deal with authors and printers, the lessons of raising money in any way possible to assure the next issue would appear, the difficulties of accounting and keeping records, how to manage a staff and hold their noses to the grindstone, how to promote each issue and find ways to keep the public's interest engaged, as miniscule as that public might be. These and a hundred other considerations and tasks involved in producing a small magazine absorbed us completely and we were grateful for what we learned, though we were weary of learning it over and over again with so little to show for our efforts.

Merely circulating an issue once we had produced it was a major problem. I could walk around Aspen, consigning a few copies to Carl's Pharmacy, Explore Books, the Aspen Book Store, and a few generous but only tangentially related businesses—a stationary store, a magazine stand—and I could drive down the valley to drop a few copies off at bookstores in Snowmass, Basalt, Carbondale, and Glenwood Springs. We held special "mailing parties" to address envelopes, lick stamps, stuff packets and sort them by zip code for our subscribers, hauling them to the post office the following day to be shipped out to who we hoped were eager readers.

One year I devised a plan to circulate the magazine around the state, hoping that this might widen our audience and strengthen our subscriber base. I drew up a map of the major cities and towns in Colorado and set out in borrowed car one beautiful spring day to bring the word to every Middlesex, village, and farm. It took several days of constant driving to locate likely bookstores and convince them to accept a few issues on consignment until, six months later, we'd bill them for what they had sold, plus send another consignment of our newest issue. I have hazy memories of driving to every corner of Colorado, hours alone in my car, meeting agreeable bookstore owners, and some not so agreeable, sleeping in cheap motels, then dragging myself out of bed the next morning to try again. I did this for two years, and finally gave up. I felt like Willy Loman on the road, and it was beginning to erode my enthusiasm. Then, too, the preponderance of so much bad work, in comparison to good, must have eaten away at our spirits until we could take no more. We kept an "unforgettable submissions list" to which we would add our favorite lines and phrases from the poems and stories we received. I remember one from a poem by an older Midwestern woman:" You have peeled the nail from the finger of my heart." I felt her pain. I felt my own pain. We'd had a good run, but it was time to admit the folly of our task, and direct our energy into other channels.

Poetry and Porn Stars

"Aspen was no place for poetry readings," writes Steve Martin in his autobiography, *Born Standing Up*. During his first visit to Colorado in the late 1960s, this was undoubtedly true, though poet and teacher Robert Vas Dias had founded The Aspen Writers' Workshop in 1964 and conducted it successfully for a few years. Another noteworthy poet, James Hearst, had been summering in Aspen since the 1950s, and gave a few readings at various venues, on his own. We meant to change things, with a vengeance.

Once we had established the publication of *Aspen Anthology*, the foundation began to branch out. By the mid-'70s we were presenting a full spectrum of literary events, year in and year out, in both winter and summer, with a constancy that surprises me even now. Besides readings, we established a lecture series kicked off in July, 1974 by poet and novelist Joyce Carol Oates, who packed Papecke auditorium with fans curious to know what she had to say about "Art, Experience, and Transformation." Bruce Berger, who was at that lecture, claims he remembers nothing of what was said on the subject (a claim I can corroborate with my own experience), but quite deftly describes the Q&A that followed in his essay "The Last Lecture," which he wrote in 1984. The essay recalls that Oates's "somnambulist delivery veiled the sharpness of her remarks," and goes on to record a number of actual questions and replies.

"You're so prolific," a woman commented. "How do you use your time so well?"

"I don't use my time well," Oates replied dreamily. "I spend most of it staring into the Detroit River."

And again: "I'm just an ordinary laborer," said a scruffy young man. "I've never had much of an education but I want to write. Is there any hope?"

"What kind of work do you do," asked Oates.

"I'm a carpenter."

There was a good answer to this and Oates found it. "I know of one carpenter who made it big."

A steady stream of lecturers passed through Aspen, holding forth on various literary subjects as part of our ongoing lecture series. In August, 1977, poet Michael Dennis Browne delivered a lecture entitled "Gods Beyond My God," about the poetry of D. H. Lawrence, a lecture I *do* recall for the clarity of its presentation and the passion of Browne's voice as he delivered lines from some of Lawrence's most famous poems. We were recording the readings and lectures, and I could listen to them again if I thought they were worthy of revisiting. In the late 1990s, I donated hundreds of recordings made over a twenty year period to the Woodbury Poetry Room at Harvard University, to be included as part of its permanent audio collection. I like to think of all those voices, all those words and ideas from so many years ago, stowed in the archives of the Poetry Room, waiting for someone to switch on a machine and bring them back to life.

We also offered workshops, from poetry to journalism, as well as a week-long seminar on the martial art of Tai Chi conducted by Gai-Fu Feng, translator of the Chinese Classics *Tao Te Ching* and *Chuang Tsu*. We screened films about various poets (James Dickey, e.e. cummings, Robinson Jeffers), and arranged for a benefit showing of Kurt Vonnegut's little-known television play, *Between Time and Timbuktu*, at Paepcke Auditorium in August, 1975. We adapted and produced a version of Conrad Aiken's short story, "Silent Snow, Secret Snow," for KSNO Radio as a special Christmas presentation in 1976, as well as various other radio programs. And we opened a Small Press Book Corner in the Aspen Bookshop, which we stocked with literary magazines and volumes from small presses we thought worthy of representation. In the meantime, we published eight more issues of our literary magazine, and began what would replace *Aspen Anthology* as the biggest and most important program on which the foundation would embark— The Aspen Writers' Conference.

Most of our programs had been designed to interest and serve local audiences. *Aspen Anthology*, in a modest way, had reached out beyond the ramparts of the Roaring Fork Valley to find a wider audience across the country. In June, 1975, I had attended the Boulder Writers' Conference, sponsored by the University of Colorado, at one of the larger motels near campus. William Burroughs, Richard Hugo, W. S. Merwin, William Matthews, and a host of other novelists and poets convened for a week of readings and workshops, and I drove home hatching a plan to replicate such an event in Aspen. We were still a very small organization, with a paltry operating budget. Everyone on the staff, including me, was a volunteer. The City of Aspen provided office space, so we didn't have to pay rent. Readings and lectures were free and took place in various spots—mostly galleries—kindly donated by the civic-minded. Almost every penny we took in went to producing our magazine. I knew that it would take more money than we had ever dreamed of spending to fly four poets to Aspen, pay them a working salary, and put them up somewhere in a city that offered almost exclusively high-end lodging. I calculated that I would need exactly one thousand dollars right away to place ads in high-profile national literary magazines to attract enough people to make it all possible. Their tuition fees would finance the whole thing, if I could convince enough aspiring writers to commit to two weeks in Aspen.

By the time I reached the top of Independence Pass on my way back to Aspen after the Boulder conference, I had it all worked out. The math was simple: I wanted four poets to teach classes of twelve students each, for a total of forty-eight conference participants. I decided in advance that I wanted to pay each poet five hundred dollars for his or her two-week stay (a figure that astounds me now for being so ridiculously low), and myself five hundred dollars for the year it would take me to organize it all. I had a day job bartending at Ute City Banque—which would support me while I planned and implemented the conference's events, venues, and other details. If forty-eight people paid $125 apiece to attend, I'd take in six thousand dollars. If $2500 of this total went to salaries, I'd have $3500 left over for plane tickets, food, and lodging. But I'd have to subtract a thousand for advertising, so the total of dispensable income would drop to $2500. What would happen if it all went bust? I had no money of my own, and once I had taken in the tuition, I wouldn't be able to cover the difference if the conference for some reason had to be cancelled. Ah, I thought:

I'll schedule the event for mid-June. That way, I'd be able to take advantage of the lower, off-season rates most lodges in Aspen offered. And I'd pick a deadline prior to the conference, say April 15th, at which time I could decide whether to cancel or not, dependent upon signing up forty-eight people. Before spending any of their money, I could return it, notify the poets that there would be no conference (thereby saving airfare and salary), and be free and clear, with a loss of nothing but my effort and time—and that bedeviling $1,000 that I would have to raise and spend by December in order to get our ads in for the following summer. That was the rub. When I arrived back at our office in the Wheeler Opera House, I was breathing heavily. One thousand dollars! I talked to the other staff members as they filtered into the office. Everyone liked the idea, but no one had any more money than I did. Finally, Nancy Thomson, a volunteer, furrowed her brow, pursed her lips, and said, "Wait a minute, I'll be right back."

Twenty minutes later she returned with a check for one thousand dollars, made out to the Aspen Literary Foundation.

"Where did you get it?" We were beside ourselves with curiosity and joy.

"That's easy," said Nancy. "I went downstairs to talk to Janet Landry." Janet was the director of Colorado Mountain College. "She'll front you the money, and you can pay it back once tuitions start to come in."

We were in business. I kissed Nancy, danced her around the office, and went directly to my desk to begin writing letters and making phone calls. By mid-April, forty-eight people had signed up to come to Aspen to be part of the first annual writers' conference. Each participant would pay $125 to stay at a lodge on Waters Avenue, if they were willing to share a room with another participant. But would these strangers get along, sharing such close quarters? A nightmare scenario presented itself to my overwrought imagination: two weeks of shuffling and re-shuffling people until everyone had found the perfect roommate, someone whose habits and behavior they could readily endure.

And what about me? Would all the plans, the schedule, the structure I had so carefully prepared, actually work once real people were involved? Plans are abstract, but people have problems and needs that can't be anticipated easily.

One such problem involved a poet from San Francisco, named Christopher. I had accepted him on the basis of the work he had submitted—since acceptance was dependent upon work submitted to our staff—and we had spoken briefly on the phone. I heard something peculiar but not alarming in his voice, an inflection that would make sense once he arrived in Aspen and I was able to greet him on that first day. Chris wanted to know if there was wheelchair access in Aspen, and though there really wasn't much at the time, I assured him that we would be able to assist him whenever that might be necessary. Chris was talented, bright, and almost totally functional in every way, but he hadn't informed me that he suffered from Dwarfism, a condition that often includes joint disease, nerve compression, and disproportionate organs. Chris's spine was radically disfigured, and it put extraordinary pressure on his internal organs. His lungs, especially, were slightly displaced, so any further stress on his breathing might prove fatal. At an altitude of 8,500 feet, there is far less usable oxygen than at sea level, and Chris's lungs began to fill up with fluid. One of his friends from San Francisco, Mona Simpson, (who would later become a novelist), cornered me near the end of our first week of activity.

"Chris is having trouble breathing," she said, her expression clouded with anxiety and concern. "We need to get him to a hospital right away."

My mind reeled with the most horrific possibilities: a death, lawsuits, total ruin. I collared Bruce Berger and pressed him into service. We carried Chris out of his room at the Snowflake Inn, placed him in Bruce's jeep, and whisked him to Aspen Valley Hospital where we deposited him in the Emergency Room and sat down to await a diagnosis. In no time, a doctor appeared and urged us to make arrangements to fly Christopher back to San Francisco as soon as possible. We had about six hours or so until his lungs would fill up completely and he would stop breathing. Bruce returned to the Inn to gather up Chris's belongings. What ensued was a wild, nerve-wracking trip down through the Roaring Fork Valley, onto the interstate at Glenwood Springs, then to Grand Junction over eighty miles away, with Chris in the back seat looking better with each mile as we descended the Western Slope into a more oxygen-rich atmosphere. At the airport, we drove out onto the tarmac directly to the plane. I remember picking Christopher up and transferring him from the back seat of Bruce's jeep to his wheelchair and steering him to the bottom of the stairs, where flight attendants took over. It was like picking up a half-filled sack of potatoes. Chris smiled wryly when we said goodbye. In the future, I would attend to the problem of participants who might suffer from various physical ailments, the effects of high-altitude on the human body, and the legal liabilities to which we might be subjected. Christopher went on to become a fine poet. I saw a few of his poems in literary magazines a few years later. The relief we all felt upon hearing that he had landed safely in San Francisco and was happily ensconced in his apartment was palpable, and the conference continued as planned.

* * *

People, places, and incidents over the more than thirty-year
span of the Aspen Writers' Conference flash into my memory
and as quickly disappear. Other directors came and went, but
my memories of the 1970s are the most vivid. People met, con-
joined, occasionally got married. I used to say that I felt more
like a madam than the director of a literary program. And I
joked that as director, I had the same powers traditionally invested in a ship's captain: I could marry people in an emergency. No one took me up on this, though it would have been fun
to see if such a makeshift union could hold up in a court of law.
One year, under the influence of too much wine at the opening celebration, I returned home to the house I was living in
at the end of Waters Avenue to find that I had locked myself
out. Bruce Berger and the poet Karen Swenson begged me not
to climb up through the transom over the front door, but I ignored their good advice. The transom ripped off its hinges under my weight and fell to the floor inside, where it smashed to
pieces. I fell on top of it, somewhat head-first. When I opened
the door, I was bleeding profusely over my right eye. The next
day, I greeted the conference participants with a bandaged
brow, which I had to brush off as a minor injury.

If it sounds like we did nothing but carry on and abuse ourselves, it's only because I've chosen to recall some of the more
colorful episodes here. Most years passed without incident, and
we were devoted to literature and serious about our art. The
workshops, lectures, and readings were first-rate and a virtu-
al parade of Nobel Laureates, Pulitzer Prize winners, and National Book Award recipients trooped through town adding

their luster to our program. I recall Joseph Brodsky at a reception we arranged for him at the Aspen Historical Society telling the crowd that when he had been in prison in Russia, he dreamed of such a place as Aspen, where people cared about art, and beauty surrounded them on all sides, a place of inspiration and lasting peace. Allen Ginsberg, Jane Smiley, Miroslav Holub, Derek Walcott, Grace Paley, Margaret Atwood, Geoffrey Wolfe, James Tate—I kept a list once that has since disappeared. Mostly, there was work to be done, and the quiet contemplation of art. The poet William Matthews captured the ethos of the time and place deftly in a poem. He was staying in a large, mostly empty Victorian home in the west end, which I had borrowed from one of our generous patrons who wasn't living in it at the time.

A Small Room in Aspen

Stains on the casements,
dustmotes, spiderless webs.
No chairs and a man waking up,
or he's falling asleep.

Many first novels begin
with the hero waking up,
which saves their authors
from writing well about sleep.

His life is the only novel
about him. Mornings
he walks past the park:
Tai Ch'i students practicing

like slow lorises.
A room on the second floor.
He'd dreamed of a ground floor
room, an insistent cat

at the door, its mouth pink
with wrath he couldn't salve
and grew to hate. All afternoon
he's a cloud that can't rain.

There's no ordinary life
in a resort town, he thinks,
though he's wrong: it laces
through the silt of tourists

like worm life. At dusk
the light rises in his room.
A beautiful day, all laziness
and surface, true without

translation. Wherever I go
I'm at home, he thinks,
smug and scared both,
fierce as a secret,

8,000 feet above sea level.
The dark on its way down
has passed him, so he seems
to be rising, after the risen

light, as if he were to keep watch
while the dark sleeps,
as if he and it were each
other's future and children.

The park noted in the poem is Paepcke Park, with its anach-
ronistic gazebo, where Tai Ch'i was practiced in the 1970s because Wagner Park was reserved almost exclusively for rugby
and softball leagues. He's right about resort towns. Beneath

the bustle of tourism, ordinary local life persists—bartenders, waitresses, cooks, shop owners, clerks, ski bums, doctors, lawyers, cab drivers, bus drivers, landscapers, real estate agents, school teachers, maids—people go to work and save and dream and struggle to better themselves, while the bills pile up and the years pass and the froth of tourism blows away like spume from the top of a wave. The Aspen Writers' Conference (now called Aspen Summer Words) was part of that wave, and is still growing. In an *Aspen Times Weekly* article in 2006, Bruce Berger dubbed the conference "an exalted folly," especially with regard to the early programs. I'm glad I didn't know what I was doing. It might have robbed the conference of some of its funkiness and glamour.

* * *

The bugaboo was, of course, and has always been money. Small community arts programs, especially in remote towns far from the centers of official culture, struggle to keep themselves afloat. A piecemeal approach is usually best. We received grants from every level of government—though we received just one grant from the NEA for our writers' conference before the rules changed and we were forced back on our state Arts Council in Denver and the City of Aspen, which endowed a small stipend each year to keep us going. For many years, Aspen's Thrift Shop contributed five hundred dollars, and once we received a grant from a private foundation in Salt Lake City that had ties to the city of Aspen through a family member. Sometimes, we received money from the Coordinating Council of Literary Magazines to cover publishing costs for *Aspen Anthology*. Occasionally, a grant from Pitkin County would rescue us from oblivion. In-kind grants of equipment, services, or

space were made in one facility or another, and for years I ca-
joled Aspen's fine restaurant owners to comp meals for our visiting writers. Then there were smaller donations from people
in the community. These trickled in over any six-month period, like a faucet no one ever quite shut off, and we kept running lists of them in every issue of the magazine. Most donations arrived by mail, in the form of personal checks. Some
were solicited. This was the case, usually, with Aspen's more
noteworthy residents, who had money to burn and a name to
lend to our enterprise, giving us added luster. I was hoping for
such an outcome the night I met with Jill St. John in order to
make a pitch for our organization and prevail upon her generosity.

* * *

Jill was dating a friend of mine, a young hot-dog skier named
Rick Head, who worked with me at the Golden Horn when
I was a bartender there. Rick was handsome and affable and
would later become a successful Aspen real estate agent. Rick
approached me one evening to say that Jill might be a prospective donor for the Aspen Literary Foundation.

"She's is very intelligent," he said. "She has a very high I.Q.
Many people don't know that. And she loves the arts."

Rich, intelligent celebrities who loved the arts were fine
with me. But how would I go about approaching her? He offered to arrange a meeting. I saw myself waxing eloquently
about the value of literature while Jill sat enthralled, in all her
beauty, ready to hand over a big check with a radiant smile.
I had seen her movies, of course, and some of her TV work,
a real charmer who had starred as Tiffany Case in the James
Bond Film, *Diamonds are Forever*, and posed for *Playboy* in 1960.

I hoped I had enough charm of my own to entice her to become one of our patrons.

A few evenings later, I found myself in the Paragon Bar on Hyman Street in a deep chair with mahogany arms, seated across from a plush red Victorian sofa where Jill and Rick were sitting, a low marble-topped table between us. After Rick introduced us, we ordered drinks and I began my spiel, which included information about all our foundation activities, including the Aspen Writers' Conference, and I slid a few issues of *Aspen Anthology* across the table to Jill so she could have a look at them.

"How much money are you trying to raise?" she asked.

"Well," I began, "anything you could give would be greatly appreciated." I hadn't given it the slightest thought. I believed that literature was its own excuse, needing no further explanation as to how it should be supported. The mere words *poetry* or *the arts* ought to cause educated and informed people to dig generously into their pockets and hand over whatever they could afford.

While she leafed through the pages of *Aspen Anthology*, reading a few lines here and there, Rick and I chatted about work, mutual friends, anything to pass the time. Jill seemed absorbed by what she was reading. After a few minutes, Jill looked up at me, a slight frown marring the luminous skin between her eyebrows.

"Tell me, Kurt," she said, "why is all poetry so sad?"

My heart sank. I knew I was lost. I launched into an impromptu defense, an apologia for poetry. I sputtered something about the comic effects in e. e. cummings. I mentioned the great farcical scenes in Shakespeare. I think I even brought up Odgen Nash, and spoke of wit in Pope and Johnson. But it

was no use. The more I spoke of the comic element in literature, the more serious and stupid I sounded. And why should
anyone have to defend poetry anyhow? An intelligent person
should know that tragedy, from ancient times, is the highest
and fittest subject for the greatest novels, plays, and poems.
Wasn't life sad? Or was it a prolonged party full of good times
and careless laughter? Why shouldn't poetry reflect life, real
life, and not some sanitized TV version of it? All of this was on
my mind, but of course I didn't say it to Jill. Before long, we
were gathering our coats and making our goodbyes. Jill slipped
into a lustrous silver lamé ski jacket and shook my hand.

"A little advice," she said. "When you ask someone for money, have an exact sum in mind, and let them know what you're
going to use it for. People who give money like to know where
it's going."

This was, and is, good advice. In her world—a world of
fame, wealth, and high society—money was not only something with which to procure commodities, it was a commod-
ity itself and had to be negotiated for. In my world, it was bread
and butter. You don't ask a beggar on the street how he is going to spend the quarter you drop into his cup. But if I were
ever going to acquire the knack of raising funds by lobbying
wealthy patrons, I would have to take Jill's lesson to heart. I
could say she left me with nothing, but at least she left me with
this.

* * *

Benefit events called for skills more suitable to my personality.
They required energy and imagination, not tact. The problem
was that my temperament ran to more extravagant activities—
like my Yuletide concert in the Wheeler Opera House—which

required huge amounts of labor for a minimum amount of income. It would never have occurred to me to throw an intimate dinner party for a few prospective patrons. I imagined banquets, festivals, mass community feasts. Michi Blake, who suggested asking Elizabeth Paepcke if she would agree to throw a garden party in her backyard for the benefit of the Aspen Writers' Foundation, proposed one such feast to me. Michi had catered several affairs at Elizabeth's house and knew how to move among the higher levels of local society. Elizabeth Paepcke represented the pinnacle of that society, having helped her husband, Walter, almost single-handedly revive the town in the 1940s. In a 1995 *New York Times Magazine* article Ted Conover wrote of Elizabeth "Pussy" Paepcke: "Her beauty—she had cobalt blue eyes and a dazzling smile—was the first thing people noticed about Elizabeth, but references to it vexed her."

I had seen Elizabeth Paepcke here and there, but from a distance. I am glad I did not have to deal with her directly. I would have withered under the intensity of that blue gaze. Michi was the perfect intermediary, and her vision was less populist than mine. She proposed formal invitations, and a handpicked crowd skimmed from the cream of Aspen's social order. We could ask the owners of Aspen's finest restaurants to donate food, each platter identified by a small flag stuck into one of the hors d'oeuvres, heralding that restaurant's sense of civic responsibility and culinary expertise. It would be a gala affair, one for which Aspen had been known during Jerome B. Wheeler's tenure at the top of Aspen's social ladder.

An invitation from "Pussy" Paepcke was not to be ignored. Aspen's plutocracy showed up in droves. But as the fated hour approached, a rain squall blew into the valley from the west and the whole operation had to be moved from Mrs. Paepcke's garden to the Paragon Ballroom on Hyman Street. This changed the tenor of the event from a light-spangled outdoor soirée to a Victorian bash under elegant, stained-glass domes imported from a turn-of-the-century bank in Paris that decorated the ceiling of the Paragon ballroom, so it hardly made a difference. Proceeds for the night remained firm, as we had sold tickets for it in advance. In an unusual display of formality for a town accustomed to the most casual attire, ladies and gentlemen circulated—drinks and hors d'oeuvres in hand— dressed properly in tailored suits and evening gowns. Elizabeth Paepcke, looking every inch the Grande Dame, greeted people in a receiving line while Michi oversaw the presentation and serving of the food. I had invited the faculty of that year's Writers' Conference to attend, and can still conjure up images of poets Bill Matthews in a cream-colored suit and panama hat, Jane Shore in a fetching summer dress, Gwen Head in a skirt and cotton blouse, and Stephen Dunn in a brightly patterned orange-and-black dashiki passing through the crowd like ambassadors from the foreign country of art. Art and culture, Aspen's "second economy," was reserved for the summer months of dandelions and clear skies, except on the night of the gala. But the rain passed, and people stepped out into a burst of evening light while the last tray of canapés shriveled under the Paragon's ornate lamps.

* * *

On the other end of the spectrum, we sometimes raised money by unconventional—even questionable—means. When a board member came to me with the proposition of screening the premier of a soft-core porn movie, *Alice in Wonder-*

land, I hesitated. She had met one of the film's backers and broached the subject with him. We needed money for an upcoming project. Time was of the essence. What would our dignified patrons on Red Mountain say? Would the good people who attended Elizabeth Paepcke's garden party at the Paragon walk out, never to be wooed into making another donation? A few days later, I found myself having afternoon tea with Dan Davis, one of the film's producers, who arrived fresh from the slopes in a flashy ski outfit, a serious man with a shock of black hair and a leathery tan. He said he would be willing to bring the unreleased film to Aspen, along with the entire cast, for a premier showing for the benefit of the Aspen Literary Foundation. Aspen, he must have figured, would be a perfect place to premier a soft-core adult film. The town was already showing signs of the Hollywood playground it would become in the 1980s and '90s. Still. How could I justify raising money for the literary arts by partnering with the burgeoning adult film industry?

I went back to my office in the Wheeler Opera House to agonize over my decision. Money was money; why shouldn't a shady business supply funds for a legitimate enterprise like literature? Robbing from the sleazy to give to the sublime? In the end, no one on Red Mountain or in Starwood noticed. Not a peep was heard from our trustworthy patrons. *Alice in Wonderland*, as it turned out, really was soft-core, more silly than salacious. An article written for the Aspen-Snowmass Guide by one of our editors, Nancy Thomson, captures the essence of the evening in a few wry paragraphs, and I welcomed it with the conviction that any publicity is good publicity.

"Through the Looking Glass," had a subtitle quoted directly from Lewis Carroll: "'Curiouser and curiouser,' cried Alice.":

Poetry and pornography are strange bedfellows. But money will make them lie down together. The Aspen Literary Foundation, publisher of a bi-annual literary magazine called *Aspen Anthology* devoted to the exposure of fine writing, pulled down its pants for art's sake and arranged a benefit showing of Bill Osco's soft-core porn version of *Alice in Wonderland*. A stranger symbiotic tradeoff would be hard to find.

Kurt Brown, the president of the Foundation and editor of the literary magazine, was nervous. To date, benefactors had been largely composed of Aspen's somnolent upper crust. Nobody wanted to shock or offend them. The newspaper ad obliquely mentioned a "Special Benefit Performance" but didn't say for whom. Dan Davis, co-producer of Alice, felt snubbed. So the pre-screening party got off to a shaky start.

Independently wealthy, part-time Aspen resident Frank Butler had agreed to entertain the cast and a handful of poets and writers before the movie. The poets arrived first. Nobody knew anybody. Frank, resplendent in a three-piece, all white suit, creamy shirt and ragweed colored tie, graciously greeted everybody at the door of his panabode in Mountain Valley. Frank's roommate, Rick, mixed drinks. The bartender got lost and never showed up.

Conversation lagged, sputtered and finally came to a halt. The poets sat on Frank's wall-to-wall, all-white sofa and watched a video cassette of *Gone With the Wind* on an enormous Zenith Chromacolor TV. In front of the couch, two red candles burned at either end of a marble coffee table that was, in fact, a sarcophagus. Carved into the surface was the host's name. His dog, Frodo, an all-white husky type, played quietly with his matching all-white toy dog whose name is Rick.

At the last moment the guests of honor arrived. The mirrored doors to the dining room swung open. Everyone scrambled to meet Kristine DeBell, starlet, who plays the lead, and sample the caviar, prawns and baked ham on the candle-laden table. Kristine is a former Playboy cover girl who has a fresh-scrubbed face that Seventeen could have made famous if she hadn't already outgrown them. She loves publicity, Producer Davis said. A roomful of poets must have been a disappointment. She's very, very pretty. Her eyes are blue and enormous. When she smiles, the rubber bands on her braces stretch in the corners of her pouty mouth.

Kristine, who was a model with the Eileen Ford Agency in New York before her acting debut, said *Alice* was her first movie. Evidently her acting talents are up to snuff. Osco's next feature, a porn version of *The Wizard of Oz*, will also star Kristine. *Oz* will be a disco porn movie. *Alice* was a musical.

Kristine said both movies are soft-core (sex scenes are simulated). At the moment of climax, the screen becomes a montage of double and triple images superimposed on each other until it's hard, if not impossible, to tell what you're supposed to be seeing. Kristine tilts her head prettily to the side, closes her eyes, opens her lips, and the music swells.

Kristine's parents, who live in upstate New York, have seen the movie, she said. They thought it was cute.

The Playhouse Theater was disappointingly half-filled. It was hard to tell whether the audience had paid $4 to support a literary magazine or take in a porno movie. Probably the latter. And, if that's the case, $4 was a rip-off. Alice isn't the kind of movie that will satisfy the raincoat crowd. It got an "R" rating. The producers decided to advertise it as an "X" anyway.

Editor Brown introduced actress DeBelle. She came bounding down the aisle in her brown velour pant suit and Frye boots and sprang up onto the stage to accept the microphone like an Academy Award. "Hi, I'm Kris De-Belle and you're not," she said. The audience waited. She politely mentioned the literary magazine and even did a little promotion for the upcoming, all-local-writers issue. She made a few more jokes, then bounced back up the aisle to her seat accompanied by a spattering of applause.

After the movie one poet was heard to shout "Bravo!" Another guest of the literary magazine had to be woken up.

The cast went off to the Arya Restaurant for an after-theater supper party, hosted again by Frank Butler and his roommate Rick. The poets were not invited but sent two bottles of champagne.

The opposite ends of the arts had met and passed briefly in the night. Not much money was made. Nobody seemed to have much fun. Kristine DeBelle took the first plane back to Los Angeles the next morning to begin work on *The Wizard of Oz*. Kurt Brown went back to poetry.

The Kiddie's Pal

If the asylum was being run by the inmates, it might be a good idea to take a look at some of them. 1970s Aspen was composed of runaways, refugees, and malcontents like me. Then there were people who had some money, who had chosen Aspen as a hiding place. The very rich chose Aspen because of its top-notch skiing and scenic beauty. There were the part-time transients and a small contingent of native-born Aspenites. But after 1970, a large influx of hippies arrived to change the social and political complexion of the town—though "hippie" is a rangy term and people who have been described as such by the older, conservative citizens would probably have disagreed with that word being applied to them. Let's call them ex-hippies on the lam from the political wreckage of the 1960s looking for a place to regroup and lick their wounds.

For whatever reason, more young people arrived every year, skewing the town's age demographics downward. Aspen in the '70s was no place for the elderly. Nor was it a place for non-Anglos. Even as late as the turn of the century, according to the 2000 census, ninety-one percent of the population

was white. Sixty-five percent of the population was under forty. There were almost an equal percentage of men to women.
It was a paradise for healthy young white people who liked to
ski in the winter and hike in the summer and live a relatively
hassle-free, outdoor life most of the year. And it seemed to me
that it was even more starkly white in the '70s. The increase in
the Latino population hadn't begun; young workers from middle-class white families supplied the work force, and many of
them had college degrees. In my entire tenure in Aspen I only
knew one African-American, an actor and singer of some talent named Tony. He stayed for one season, and moved on.

Tipi Cheryl remembers another African-American, Jim
Spann, who worked with Robb Van Pelt and was arrested one
night in the alley behind the pub for peeing on public property.
Spann's defense, in his own words, according to Cheryl, was
unique: "How could the cop see a black man peeing in a dark
alley?" Kathy Daily and Gaylord Guenin put the photograph
of an African-American named Hannibal Brown on the cover
of their book, *Aspen: The Quiet Years*. Born in Kansas, Hannibal was brought to Colorado by one of the rich mining families and worked around town as a janitor and bartender until
his death in 1952. There seems to have been a small African-
American community in the valley during the '30s and '40s, but
Hannibal is more of an anomaly than a representative of what
Aspen looked like back then.

But its homogeneity didn't mean Aspen was normal. That's
the only explanation for how Dr. Hunter S. Thompson nearly
succeeded in his electoral bid to become Sheriff of Pitkin County, on a platform to legalize drugs and replace the streets with
grass. That's the only way Katherine Thalberg could feed her
dogs nothing but vegetables and no one would take her away

strapped to a gurney. Besides, she was married to the mayor. And where else could the weird, distorted dreams of Dr. Sadistic thrive, finding a ready and loyal audience which saw itself reflected in his perverted lyrics? Reasonable people might have been drawn to the skiing, but living in Aspen was probably not an option for most of them. The town was just too unconventional, too non-American in its quirks to become a haven for the ordinary citizen. We loved to think of ourselves as aberrant, and reveled in our differentness in a smug, self-conscious way. Aspen was a little Republic. Yet even in weird Aspen, there were people who stood out.

* * *

Two such characters represented the extreme right-wing, and must have rued the influx of counter-cultural types and their unconventional ways. Bert Bidwell was a stocky Aspen merchant with a bull-dog's face. Pug-nosed and pugnacious, he resembled an ex-Marine. His crew cut, broad shoulders, and swagger added to this impression. He owned a building at the corner of Hyman and Galena, which included what was then Sonny's Rendezvous and would later become The Blue Moose. These establishments existed in what would usually be the basement, but a large open area had been dug out on the south side of the building facing Aspen Mountain, which served as a terrace offering open-air seating at tables with sun umbrellas. Above this, at street level, was a low brick wall to keep people from tumbling into the open area below. Stairs led down to the terrace and the front door of Sonny's with its windows facing the diners and admitting some light to the front of the club. As the corner of Cooper and Galena was a major intersection, we liked to sit on the wall of Bidwell's building and wile away

the hours waiting for friends to pass. Day after day, Bidwell
would rush out to flush the hippies off his property, grimac-
ing and hissing imprecations. The hippies hissed back, and it
became common practice to aggravate him by sitting until he
would rush out—then run away—only to return soon to tor-
ment him again once he'd scuttled back inside. This game lasted until Bidwell had iron spikes set into the top of the wall.
That wall reminded us of the spiked helmets of German soldiers during World War I. Today, it's topped by an innocuous
iron railing that keeps people from sitting there, but lacks the
menace of earlier days.

Bidwell's conservative counterpart was Guido Meyer, a
Swiss transplant who owned and operated the Swiss Inn directly across from Bidwell's. Guido kept a lower profile, but he
was every bit as radical as Bert when it came to the hippie in-
vasion of Aspen. Patrons of the Swiss Inn were encouraged to
take matchbooks with them as they were leaving, on which
GUIDO'S SWISS INN was emblazoned on the front. The back cover read: NO HIPPIES ALLOWED. You can imagine that to light a
joint with one of Guido's matches became a matter of countercul-
tural pride.

In 1968, a group of Aspen businessmen concerned about the
growing number of scruffy young people in town drew up a
petition demanding the police enforce local vagrancy laws. Besides being a restaurateur, Guido also happened to be the city
magistrate. He is famous for sentencing a fourteen-year-old
hitchhiker to three months in jail for having had the audacity
to stick out his thumb within the city limits. But the tide was
turning.

In 1969 a group of young progressives took over the city
council and Joe Edwards, Aspen's "hippie lawyer," ran for may-

or, only to lose. In 1970, Hunter S. Thompson ran for Sheriff of Pitkin County (and lost, but barely). In 1973, Edwards was duly elected as county commissioner. Steve Wishart ran a successful campaign to become a city councilman. Finally, in 1976, progressive Dick Kienast—backed by Hunter Thompson—ran for sheriff, and won. According to Bob Braudis, who later became sheriff himself, "Kienast, in his first active gesture in changing the [department's] culture, was to start hiring well-educated locals who had no previous law-enforcement experience. He felt that career policemen became cynical, if not disdainful, of the people whom they served." The idea was that Kienast would hire deputies for a few years, and then those same deputies would move on to other community jobs. The intention was that an enlightened, vigilant citizenry might be created and the incidence of crime—which was relatively low to begin with—could be regulated accordingly. During Kienast's tenure, the sheriff's department came to be referred to as "Dick Dove and the Deputies of Love."

The sheriff's department in 1970s' Aspen had an unconventional composition and governing philosophy. Town visitors always remarked on law enforcement's shiny, black Saabs. During summer months, people might be ticketed by a beautiful young woman in khaki shorts and aviator shades. It was almost a pleasure to be apprehended. There were no parking meters or traffic lights until the 1980s, and people were free to park anywhere, except near fire hydrants or on private property that had been clearly marked with signs. The attitude towards drugs and other offences during Kienast's reign, and later that of Bob Braudis's, was permissive. But you had to be smart. It was best to be discrete and keep out of sight. Egregious behavior would be dealt with promptly, and the sheriff's

department had no problem with tossing you in jail if you vi-
olated the statutes, or outraged courtesy and common sense.
Once, I saw a cop on Galena Street tell someone who was
lighting up a joint, "Don't smoke that on the street. Go into
that alley." Then she added, "Don't let me catch you smoking
on the street again!" Most people I know respected and obeyed
the law, or made an attempt to hide their felonies and misde-
meanors. As far as I can recall, no one I knew personally ever
spent a night in the city or county jail, except for "Stray Dog"
Dykann, who'd been picked up once for a DUI. And *his* sentence, as I've mentioned previously, was to write a dozen or
so new folksongs dealing with the history of Colorado and the
Roaring Fork Valley. Crime of any consequence hardly existed
in Aspen, until much later in the decade.

* * *

Aspen's public "clown prince" was an elderly skier named
Ralph Jackson. I don't know how old Ralph was, or where he
came from, but we loved the antics of a jester who seemed not
just old, but ageless. Ralph would carve wide, graceful turns
down the front of Aspen Mountain on his skis while wearing
a long fur coat, motley scarf, lime green or pink leggings with
leather shorts, and a black top hat that was easy to spot against
the blazing white of the snow. Sometimes he wore short skis
so he could execute wild spins and ski backwards. Like Hunter Thompson, he smoked cigarettes fitted into a slender plastic holder. Ralph was the ski industry's mascot, its living logo,
and appeared regularly in the newspapers and on the covers of
various travel journals and ski magazines. He was the ultimate
ski bum and lived on what appeared to be publicity alone. People would buy him drinks and take him to lunch. Ralph would

mug for the cameras, waving his cigarette holder theatrical-
ly. As with all clowns, there was something sad and desperate
about Ralph as he sought attention and tried make the tourists laugh. His skin was leathery, his hair white, and he rarely
looked directly at you.

When he died, something of the town's past died with him,
its original innocence. For a brief time, later in the '70s and early '80s, another clown named Hinton Harrison strolled Aspen's
malls wearing the harlequin outfit of his tribe. Hinton was a
tall, angular young man with pale skin, thin red hair and blue
eyes. He also emitted an aura of sadness despite his painted
face and jocular clothes. I never saw him do anything remote-
ly funny, but he brought me poems he had written, mostly for
children, and tried his best to lighten the hearts of Aspen locals
and tourists. He finally gave up and left. Aspen was a place of
laughter that was produced spontaneously by hedonistic pleasure, not pratfalls and outlandish costumes. Its residents were
anything but gullible. Or innocent.

* * *

Ivan Abrams struck many people as odd, but in a lovable,
avuncular way. I met him soon after arriving in Aspen, when
I visited his bookstore in the basement of the Hotel Jerome,
later to relocate to a Victorian on E. Hopkins. Ivan held court
and spoke easily with patrons who browsed shelves of books
he would sell only if he approved of them. Ivan was a member
of that vanishing breed—a lover of books. He wanted no literary chaff in his store, and appeared to have read every book
he owned. When I'd lift a volume off the shelf and crack the
cover, he'd wait a moment while he drew thoughtfully on his
pipe, and say: "That's a good one." He seemed to understand

that I had literary pretensions, and sought in his gentle way
to guide me. His manner was deliberate, but not gruff. Ivan's
opinions were offered on a take-it-or-leave-it basis. He moved
slowly, with a heavy grace, and punctuated his sentences with
spontaneous grunts. Writing on the Aspen Historical Society's
"Your Story" blog, Ivan's friend Andy Hanson wrote: "I did not
know that he had roomed with Brando and knew Jack Kerouac
from NYC days. I did not know that he was a Phi Beta Kappa
from Stanford." None of us knew much about Ivan, apart from
conversing with him in his bookstore, and he offered nothing more of himself than that. Hanson goes on to say: "Ivan
changed over the years from a classics scholar and deep reader of Dostoyevsky to a New Age believer in the star Sirius and
other extraterrestrial subjects. To visit him in later years was
to be subjected to his belief in the bead and beads he called
Crazy where the future was laid out."

As the years wore on, many of us noticed that his once-
charming oddness took a somewhat darker and disturbing
turn. Ivan's mind, serious and acute, drifted toward incoher-
ence, a kind of benign madness. Like Don Quixote before him,
reading seemed to have addled his brain. The last time I spoke
with him he blurted, "We're all spirits stuffed into sausages."
Perhaps Dostoyevsky himself was a bit mad, or at least de-
pressed in his later years and afflicted with a compulsion for
gambling. But Ivan had no literary accomplishments of his
own—none that I know of—and seemed to slide slowly but in-
exorably into a world of fantasies and delusions. He was harmless, though, and when he died in 2000, I don't doubt that he
retained many friends and admirers. In the 1970s, he was vibrant, engaging, and alert and added much to the town's literary character.

* * *

"Have you seen the blue lady?" For a few months one season in the early '70s, this question played about the lips of local inhabitants like rumor itself, but it was no rumor. A young Indian woman roamed Aspen's streets with dark blue skin that turned out to have been caused by a drug called "colloidal silver." It was prescribed by physicians to treat skin conditions, but can sometimes turn a person's skin blue. In our shock and ignorance, we thought it was a horrible birth defect and we passed her with downcast eyes, embarrassed by her appearance. She glared, swathed as she was in Indian silks from Bombay or Jaipur. The blue lady appeared and vanished in the space of a season, like a gaudy migrating bird.

* * *

Rich Texans were a dime a dozen in Aspen. Irene Morrah introduced me to one, Mako Stewart, a successful businessman who had a branch office in town. The Stewart Title Guaranty Company was a family business and had been in existence for nearly a century. Mako loved to display his wealth, and sometimes skied down Aspen Mountain in a mink coat and even mink shorts. Mako might have been taken for a gaudier version of Ralph Jackson. He owned a large condominium at the base of the mountain that became a haven for lovely young ladies who had no other place to live and who would stay with him for brief interludes. Mako's annual Valentine's Day party was notorious. The idea was that you had to show up at the door of his place in your winter garb. But once inside, you would shuck it off to reveal nothing underneath but a small red paper heart over your privates. Guests rubbed elbows and other body parts as the champagne flowed. I never attended one of his parties, so the high jinx there remain only a rumor to me, but I did visit his condominium one summer day during the writers' conference with the poet Bill Matthews, who was conducting a workshop on the premises. Mako revered Hemingway, and had decorated his place with animal skin rugs and a table whose base was a stuffed elephant's foot. Like Frank Butler, he was a wealthy eccentric and lived at a level of society where I found it hard to breathe. He had a ruddy face and, as I recall, a heart condition. An aquiline nose gave him the profile of a raptor. He was writing poetry, and a novel, with salty language and graphic sex scenes that left little to the imagination. His writing was so turgid that I found almost nothing to praise, and we never really became friends.

* * *

A masseur named Conan plied his trade around town to those who wished to be rubbed and manipulated by his talented hands. He had olive skin and long, dark eyelashes. He was ambitious, muscular and completely mesmerized by celebrities. It was quite a sight to see Conan decked out in cowboy boots, a tooled-leather belt, and a ten-gallon Stetson hat studded with rhinestones—something like Omar Sharif in Dodge City, though Conan wasn't "quite" as handsome. Arnold Schwarzenegger brought Conan along to the set of *Conan the Barbarian* as his personal masseur. At least, that's what our Conan said. Perhaps Schwarzenegger simply enjoyed the fact that his masseur shared his character's name.

* * *

In Snowmass, entrepreneur Ron Young owned and operated The Tower Fondue Restaurant for a few years, and later Ron's

Bar & Grill (where the old Leather Jug used to be), as well as the Mesa Store Bakery on Main Street in Aspen. His spats with Jack Cole, head chef at the Meadows Restaurant, were legendary.

Half farce, half in earnest, the two would sneak into each other's establishments to wreck, steal, derange, or otherwise cause whatever mischief they could. One night, Cole snuck into one of Young's restaurants in Snowmass and began trashing the place. Chairs flew, equipment was savaged, glasses broke. And all of this, according to rumor, took place in complete darkness, as Young had cut the lights in order to make Cole's job more difficult. For hours, it was said, the two men hunted each other in the rubble like commandoes on a night raid into enemy territory.

How much of this actually happened, and how much was pure fiction? Who knows. But it made a good story and reflected the real cultivation of a friendly competition, if not a downright feud. Much later, in the mid-'90s, the game—at least for Ron Young—turned far more serious. According to authorities, Young was still living in Aspen in 1993 when he got involved with a divorcée, Pamela Phillips, who had been married to a businessman in Tucson, Arizona. Young was already in trouble with the police for theft, forgery, and embezzlement of funds; he'd become a petty crook who had long since lost his restaurant holdings in town. He fled Aspen in August, 1996 but was later sought in connection with the murder of Phillip's ex-husband in Tucson when his car blew up in a country club parking lot. Ten years after that, a tip phoned in to the television show *America's Most Wanted* pinpointed Young in Fort Lauderdale, where he was captured and jailed on first degree murder and conspiracy to commit murder. Police records describe how Pamela Phillips hired Young to murder her husband for the life insurance. But back in the '70s, Ron Young was a rich, dashingly handsome business speculator whom many admired.

Another character in Snowmass Village at the very beginning of the decade made a sharp impression on many of us. If I remember correctly, Billy Super was an ex-state-trooper from New Jersey, and might have been the younger brother of Bert Bidwell, as far as his attitude and politics were concerned. Back in Jersey, Billy had been known as "Super Trooper" for his uncompromising, gung-ho ways. Billy had been hired by the owner of the Leather Jug to manage the bar which meant, among other things, riding roughshod over the waiters. He sported short black hair with bangs, and a cop-stash—strictly regulation. No one could have been more out of place in Aspen then. Billy walked around with an English bulldog on a leash. "Don't mess with me!" said the bulldog, in so many words, its face flattened like a fist. "Super," apparently, was Billy's real last name. Perhaps he took himself too seriously. And Billy had a wife, a tall long-legged beauty with silky auburn hair and large brown eyes who could have been a *Playboy* bunny. She would come in and sit at the bar to laugh at us when Billy fulminated at our petty mistakes or dressed one of us out for arriving late or leaving early. There wasn't a man among us who didn't want to fuck Rebecca on the spot, and Billy knew it. Her presence conveyed a message: "This is what you get if you are a full-blooded American male and you play by the rules." In those days of counter-cultural liberation and freedom, Billy was a super-patriot, a man of rigid conservative principles. He seemed oblivious that he commanded a bunch of misfits, runaways who were deaf to all orders and blind to rules. We marched around the restaurant in the American flag ties he'd handed out on his first day, pretending to be normal, while Billy glowered from behind the bar. Half of us were stoned, the other half confused, laughing at each other and at Billy, our would-be leader, like Colonel Klink in *Hogan's Heroes*.

* * *

A different band of misfits populated the old town of Lenado in the mountains above Woody Creek, though to call it a *town* is a bit misleading. According to local history, a few hundred people built cabins at the end of the nineteenth century so they could mine deposits of lead and zinc. The town was largely abandoned after World War I, but in the 1950s, the Forest Service built a logging road to Lenado to take advantage of the area's fine timber. In the 1970s hippies, who were more than happy to re-inhabit the deserted cabins, had repopulated the town and began to make use of its small timber mill. A burly man with blond hair whom everyone called "Lumberjack" cut and delivered wood to Aspen homes and restaurants.

Poet and naturalist Robert Markham also lived in Lenado, along with Frank Peters and Daniel Delano, later owner of the Hotel Lenado in downtown Aspen, next to Whitaker Park. Markham wrote a book of poems about the Lenado area, *The Song of Larkspur Mountain*, which the Aspen Literary Foundation published in 1980, shortly after Markham's premature death from cancer. With a long disheveled beard and grizzled ponytail, Markham looked like the old man of the mountains himself, which earned him the nickname "Mayor of Lenado." For a brief period, he worked as a breakfast chef in the kitchen at Al Aban. His specialty was eggs rancheros, which he cooked in a particular way that he never divulged to anyone. I visited him one day in the hospital in Denver while he was being treated for his illness to tell him of our intention to publish his book. He was a gentle soul who had once been a Speedball bike messenger in the streets of Chicago. The whole town of Aspen showed up for a benefit in the side yard of the Hotel Jerome to raise money to cover his hospital bills. I recall Steve Wishart holding the phone out of a window on the third floor of the Jerome so that Markham—lying in his hospital bed in Denver—could hear the music and the roar of the crowd as it danced hopefully below.

* * *

Tipi Bob sold drugs, but as far as I knew he wasn't a major dealer. Bob dabbled in the trade, and as likely as not was selling part of his own stash to make just enough to buy more product for himself. Lots of small-time dealers operated this way, to keep themselves in stock. Bob was a short man with blue eyes, brown hair, and a warm smile, and radiated nothing sinister. In another time or place, Bob might have been selling you a car or a blender, and would likely have been the president of the local mercantile association. He used to hang around The Pub with a few ounces of grass in his pockets to sell to his favorite customers. He'd use a booth as an office. Like Cheryl, Bob lived in a tipi, but he'd erected his up the Castle Creek Road; I stopped in there once to say hello and see how he lived. He had a dog, a cat, and a roommate whose name I've forgotten. The four of them lived the simplest life possible, cooking beans and meat on a small central fire and venturing into town only when necessary.

* * *

No one knew where Honest Al or his nickname had come

from. He was one of Aspen's first drug dealers, and it's possible the sobriquet "Honest" came from the practice of his brisk, if shady trade. When first I heard of him, a further epithet had been added, giving his name a decided lilt: "The kiddies' pal." The suggestion was that he was something like the neighborhood ice-cream man, dispensing his delicious wares to make eager children come running. This meant marijuana and hashish, and all the kiddies came running, eagerly. With his dark skin, a mustache that curled up on the ends, and piercing green eyes, Al looked like Captain Hook or Salvador Dali, and when he smiled there was little warmth in it. Still, he was soft-spoken and, other than his looks and unkempt clothing, inspired nothing like suspicion or dread. Al was a New-Age entrepreneur, a psychedelic hobo, and had found the perfect way—as far as he was concerned—to make a living. I don't think Al could have survived holding down a regular job. He liked to sit on the stone steps of the Wheeler Opera House where he could bask in the sun and sell to whomever came stumbling up or down the stairs to The Pub below. He carried his inventory in a plain brown paper sack, which he must have copped from City Market to use as a pharmaceutical saddlebag, and to look as harmless as possible if spotted by the police. Anyone who saw him stretched out in the high mountain sun would have assumed he was simply a drowsy hippie headed home with a bag of groceries. When business was slow, he'd hop on his rickety bike and pedal through the neighborhoods, ringing his bell. It was small business at its best, and we were his clients, though no one knew who his supplier was, or what he did with his money.

There was another ragged, stoned-out hippie in town named Phil who never seemed to work or eat or sleep any-

where in particular. You'd see him turning a corner, or crossing the park, a bit skeletal and undernourished. He had the
look of someone who was truly in trouble. Something about
him made you draw back. I was passing the Paragon on Hyman Street when I saw Al about to enter the double doors that
led upstairs to the old, mostly empty, apartments on the second and third floors. Al had his bag cradled in one arm, and
he invited me to go upstairs with him to meet a couple of his
friends.

"Come on," he said. "You'll see."

We climbed the stairs to the second floor, and walked halfway down the hall to a door on the left with a broken number
on it. Al knocked, softly, and pricked up his ears. A muffled answer came from within.

"Yeah?"

"It's Al," he said.

The door opened and a burly man with ripped jeans and
worn-out sneakers asked us to come in. I had never seen him
before, and never saw him again after that day. There was a
look of pure desperation in his eyes. The only other person
in the room was Phil. There wasn't much furniture, a ratty
armchair and busted couch, not even a single rug on the floor.
There was a small bedroom with a mattress on the floor and
some soiled covers. The kitchen on the other side of the apartment was empty except for a refrigerator. There were two east-
facing windows that admitted a couple of squares of pale light.
Phil was slumped in the armchair when we entered.

"Who's this?" he wanted to know, nodding in my direction.

"No problem," said Al setting his bag down and introducing
me to Phil and his friend. "This here's Pighead," said Al. "He's
big, but he's a sweetheart."

Pighead glanced at me, then back to Al. "You brought the stuff?"

"Sure," said Al. "Whataya think?"

Al reached into his bag and brought out a small container with some white powder. I was nervous, but fascinated too. I had never seen heroin nor watched anyone shoot it. I was fighting the urge to leave, and trying to act casual and disinterested. Phil went to the refrigerator, where he retrieved some hypodermic needles and a carton of milk. He took a swig, and handed the needles to Al.

"Not me," he said. "Here, Pighead, you do the honors."

Pighead produced a spoon and Al poured a little powder into it. While this was going on, Phil sat up in his armchair and slipped his belt out of his pants, then strapped it around his upper arm and pulled tight. Within seconds, his veins bulged, bruised and bluish in that pasty skin. Pighead knelt beside him and lit a match under the spoon. When the heroin was bubbling, he let it cool, then drew it out into one of the syringes. Phil took the syringe and poked the needle into a vein. He emptied the heroin into it, loosened the belt on his arm, and closed his eyes. Suddenly, he stood up, wavering before us like a drunk, then fell on the floor, completely inert.

"He's okay," murmured Pighead. I was appalled. What if he were dead? Would I go to jail with the rest of them? In about thirty seconds, Phil opened his eyes and sat back up.

"Good stuff," he slurred, smiling faintly. His whole body seemed to relax and he spit up a white froth of mucous that glistened for a moment on the bare wood. Then he slumped back into his chair. I had never seen heroin in Aspen, and no one I knew ever used it or any of the other hard, dangerous drugs associated with big cities. I wondered if Aspen would

now become a haven for derelicts and hopheads like Pighead
and Phil. I wanted no part of it. Muttering an excuse about
meeting someone, I left as Pighead was preparing to shoot
himself up, making my way back downstairs into the street.

But I would never see heroin in Aspen again, or anyone
like Phil or his disheveled sidekick, Pighead. They must have
moved on once they realized that Aspen was no place for that
kind of deadly addiction. In fact, Aspen was full of healthy,
pleasure-loving, vigorous people and apart from marijuana
and various hallucinogens, hard drugs would never really gain
a strong foothold in the Roaring Fork Valley. I stayed away
from Al after that. Before long, Honest Al "The Kiddies' Pal"
disappeared from the Aspen scene, and I heard later that he
had died in a car wreck. No one was shocked. Guys like Al are
not long for this world. They're just passing through.

King of Hearts

A wiry hyperactive New Yorker of Italian descent, Tom DiMaggio had inherited from his forebears the habit of yelling when he talked. I thought this was a trait peculiar to him, until years later when I saw four Italian men playing cards in a little café on Campo de Fiori in Rome. What a ruckus of voices! What fake anger and mock indignation! There was no threat in their complaints, no substance in their boasts. Like them, Tom DiMaggio made a virtue out of being loudly assertive. He never answered the phone with a polite *Hello*, but rather would yank the handle out of its cradle and demand *What!* as though the caller had interrupted him in the middle of a sentence or confronted him indecently on the street. He was a lightning rod, a lick of flame, a sphere of energy bowling down the street.

Consider our first meeting, in the dining room of the old Leather Jug in Snowmass. Here he comes from the kitchen, wearing a blood-stained apron and a T-shirt with a photograph of a woman's breasts printed across the front, lending the impression he's some kind of hermaphrodite, or a character out

of myth—Tiresias, perhaps—who knew what it meant to be
both man and woman. He looks like a cross between Groucho
Marx and Frank Zappa, a mustachioed imp, an organ-grind-
er's grown monkey, with a crowning mass of black curls into
which he plunges a hand above his right ear, and out of which
he plucks a joint that had been hidden in its depths.

"Got a light?" he smiles.

You strike a match and offer it to him as he regards you
from under that tangle of hair. Then he troops back into the
kitchen, a joint dangling from his lips, to shuffle pots and wield
knives, a bundle of barely controlled mayhem in greasy sneakers and a chef's toque.

DiMaggio had been hired to assist the Leather Jug's head
chef, David Bernheimer, a German Jew who had worked at
a country club in Santa Barbara, where he staged elaborate
brunches. You'd see Bernheimer emerge from the kitchen with
a harried expression, barking, "Where's Tommy?" But no one
would ever tell him, even if they knew. And you could hear
Bernheimer bellowing at DiMaggio from the second floor of
the building, as though he, Bernheimer, were being tormented
by a pack of infernal demons. DiMaggio loved to play practical
jokes and could pop up when you least expected it or wanted
it. He'd done his stint in the army, and learned to cook early
when his father took him to greasy spoons in Hell's Kitchen
during the 1950s. Everyone called him "Tommy Freak," and he
didn't seem to mind. When he first came to Aspen, he lived in
the Independence Lodge, across the street from Guido's Swiss
Inn and, of course, learned of Guido's bitter aversion to hippies.
DiMaggio would sneak down at night to plant marijuana seeds
in the flower boxes outside the Swiss Inn, then watch from his
window on the third floor of the Lodge a few weeks later as

Guido would race out, cursing, to rip the plants up by their roots. DiMaggio's pranks were aggravating, not malicious. "I may be kinda crazy," he would say, but "I'm insanely responsible."

His sense of responsibility, ebullient personality, and natural cooking talent assured that he would always be in demand in Aspen. Once, he worked for Ron Young at the Mesa Store Bakery on West Main Street. I'd drop by in the morning on my way into town, and he'd toss me a free muffin or a croissant. When Young learned to fly and purchased his own private plane, he flew DiMaggio to Freeport in the Bahamas to work at a restaurant called The Boss Bird. According to DiMaggio, it was a knock-off of Kentucky Fried Chicken, and Young needed someone to run the store. "I wish I'd saved that chicken recipe," DiMaggio says. "It was excellent."

When he returned from the Bahamas, he worked for Young again in Snowmass at Ron's Bar & Grill, which had only just opened. I like to imagine Tommy and Ron up in that small plane exchanging small talk as the engine droned and clouds billowed immensely around them like oceanic foam. No hint, then, of the petty crook and murder suspect Young would become; no sense of DiMaggio's future home in Tucson, Arizona where he would operate two restaurants of his own before ditching it all to run a goat-packing outfit that would take tourists up into the Dragoon Mountains, where he'd cook over an open fire while telling stories of Geronimo and Cochise and the Chiricahua Apaches who once inhabited the area.

DiMaggio worked with me at the Golden Horn, one of the early gourmet hotspots, this one specializing in varieties of Swiss-German cuisine—mostly milk-fed veal—fried with butter in copper pans. Its owner, Klaus Christ, had emigrat-

ed to the United States from Davos where he served his ap-
prenticeship as a young chef among rich, stylish Europeans.
What Christ hadn't anticipated, however, was the American
lack of reverence for service. Christ had grown up in a culture of professional waiters and cooks whose jobs depended
on strong work ethic and deference to a social hierarchy within the food world. If DiMaggio brought David Bernheimer to
a rolling boil, he sometimes drove Christ to the edge of madness with his pranks and mercurial personality. Here's DiMaggio in the kitchen among clouds of steam, a cowboy's kerchief
tied around his head as a sweatband, flirting with the waitresses and singing along with a radio that blares rock while he or-
chestrates fiery operations on the stove. All of this on one drug
or another, while sipping beer and sneaking out into the alley
behind the restaurant to meet one of his girlfriends to make
plans for later that night. And all of it, too, without missing a
single order, or cooking it wrong, or failing to serve his dishes
up on time and in the proper sequence. Here's DiMaggio out at
the bar, sipping a beer and surveying the crowd, being chased
by Christ back into the kitchen with a raised fist and a string of
Swiss imprecations whose meaning none of us could decipher.
When Christ hired Jimmy Cambridge, another certifiable zany
who complemented DiMaggio's wit and energy with his own,
the kitchen at the Golden Horn became a stage for nightly installments of *Abbot and Costello* reruns.

As an avid collector of Indian jewelry, Christ traveled in
the off-season to Arizona, Texas, and New Mexico seeking the
most artfully wrought turquoise and silver trinkets he could
find. His collection was precious and expensive. To hide it
from all eyes but those whom he wished to impress—wealth-
ier friends and patrons—he locked the items in the safe in

his office, which was just off the kitchen. One night, he forgot to secure his treasure properly and when DiMaggio entered to retrieve something from the storeroom—which could only be accessed by passing through Christ's office—he noticed the door of the safe was slightly ajar. This was an invitation to madness, and in no time, DiMaggio and Cambridge had stripped to their underwear and festooned themselves with glittering belts, bracelets, and armbands—the entire cache of southwestern art—then took up their positions again behind the stoves. When Christ returned to the kitchen, he was thunderstruck trying to comprehend the meaning of the scene. There were his wacky American chefs serving schnitzel and Beef Wellington and shouting orders, weighted down with buckles, necklaces, and rings while the rest of the kitchen staff howled with laughter. Christ imported a professional chef straight from Switzerland to oversee kitchen operations, but to no avail. DiMaggio and Cambridge continued to make Christ's life miserable, though they worked like slaves and rarely made a mistake. They had become professional chefs in their own right, and were faster and more knowledgeable about local tastes than a foreign manager could ever be.

* * *

Sometime in the early '70s, William Peter Blatty bought a house in Aspen up the Castle Creek Road, probably from proceeds of *The Exorcist*, which had appeared in 1971. On the strength of its sales, Blatty wrote the screenplay for the movie that would follow in 1973, and premiered it—for free—at the Wheeler Opera House. DiMaggio was there, along with Crissy Daley and Tipi Cheryl, who admitted to having been scared out of her wits. All three were so terrified, in fact, that they spent the night together innocently—like three chaste babies in the same bed. Tipi Cheryl had met Blatty when he hired her to create a special quilt to be hung on a bedroom wall in his new house. Cheryl worked on the massive quilt for weeks before installing it and, in the process, she and Blatty became friends. Apparently, Blatty had been collecting unemployment checks while writing *The Exorcist*, which would soon lead to the movie and a wildly successful career. Through Tipi Cheryl, Blatty met DiMaggio and his girlfriend, Joyce McMullen, a fetching young hippie runaway from Colorado Springs who lived in a cabin on the back slope of Aspen Mountain. The cabin had dirt floors, which Joyce sensibly covered with area rugs, and stained glass windows. The road up to the cabin began close to Blatty's lot, and Joyce became friends with Blatty. "He really took to me," said Joyce. "It [Blatty's house] was practically my second home." Joyce recalls being in the house on the day Blatty returned from Hollywood, where he had received an Oscar for his *Exorcist* screenplay. He handed her a heavy velvet bag. Inside was the sleek, golden homunculus that weighed over eight pounds, gleaming expensively like success itself.

But it was DiMaggio whom Blatty would appoint as caretaker of his new house whenever he had to be out of town on business, which was often enough for a newly famous writer and filmmaker who must have been in high demand. On one of Blatty's trips abroad, DiMaggio and his friend, Bob Macbre, decided it was time to throw a big party. Word spread like a stiff breeze through an Aspen grove. By the day of the party, there were twenty kegs of beer and five roasting pigs that had arrived in a refrigerated truck from California, courtesy of Macbre's uncle who was in the meat business there. For some reason, DiMaggio and Macbre thought it might be a good idea to dig up part of the driveway with a backhoe so the pigs could be pit-roasted over a bed of burning coals. Unfortunately, the ground was still frozen and the coals never reached premium roasting temperature, so that on the morning of the party, the pit smelled of half-cooked meat. By the time the crowd flooded the premises, a new fire was built and people were cutting hunks of meat off the smoldering carcasses to roast over the open flame. The house was under siege. There were people on every floor, in every room, stuffed into bathrooms and closets, wedged into the hot tub, shoulder to shoulder and hip to hip. Michael Iceberg arrived and transferred his entire "Iceberg Machine" into Blatty's living room, which soon resounded with the strains of trumpets, clarinets, guitars, electric drums, animal sounds, an entire string orchestra, and the recorded voices of a celestial choir. Wally sauntered through the house in his floor-length raccoon-skin coat, distributing cocaine and marijuana liberally, like a priest at a raucous and profane black mass. Crowds of people came and went in shifts as the day wore on. The hours melted into one another, the light outside waxed and waned. At one point I saw a young couple— I think it was in the laundry room—the two of them groping each other in a frenzied embrace. Other couples danced, or dipped their bodies in the hot tub, or simply lay on the furniture. There were so many people on a deck overlooking the garage that it collapsed onto the garage's roof. No one was hurt and the party raged on without further incident. By mid-afternoon a line of cars and trucks backed up the driveway all the way out to the main road, so the police arrived to make sure the highway was kept clear. I can't remember why they neglected to come down to the party itself, but by a small miracle—or the intervention of the Lord of Misrule himself—they

didn't. The following day, while a few stragglers were still getting themselves together to make the short trip back to Aspen, DiMaggio received a call. Someone, a neighbor perhaps,
had reached Blatty—wherever he was—and alerted him to the
fact that his house was being used as the site of one of Aspen's
more notorious parties.

"This is Bill Blatty," he barked over the phone, "and I'm
pissed!"

DiMaggio, still high on acid twenty four hours later,
snapped back, "Oh yeah, well this is the Great Gatsby. Too bad
you couldn't come to your own party." Later, DiMaggio and
a few now-sober party goers cleaned up as well as they could.
They filled the hole in the driveway, and stacked the lumber
from the now-collapsed deck. Of course, Blatty fired DiMaggio when he returned and banished him from the house. Blatty
never forgave us, but we sure threw one hell of a party.

* * *

WHAM! WHAM! WHAM!

The sound is muffled, like someone firing a gun underwa-
ter.

BROWN! WHAM! WHAM!

I'm awake now, in my little underground crypt beneath
Hans Grammiger's complex of apartments on Monarch Street.
It's April, so there is no snow blocking the windows under the
wooden walkway above and a sickly light trickles through into
my room. A ghostly shimmer on the wall tells me it is early,
very early.

"BROWN!"

I get out of bed and limp to the door, only a few paces away,
and open it wide. There's DiMaggio in rubber hip boots and a

thick, red plaid Pendleton shirt regarding me with a look of exasperation.

"Get dressed," he says. "We're going fishing."

In no time, I've wedged myself into the passenger seat of his green Volkswagen and we labor up the valley towards Independence Pass, shivering in the cold and gazing through the windshield as the earliest rays of the sun flush the ridges to the east gold and turn the swath of sky above us a pale, fragile blue. The slopes of the valley, the higher we go, are clad in evergreens under which mounds of snow still survive from the past winter, glinting here and there among the boughs. My head is throbbing, and the pain I feel is only compounded by the radio's loud rock. DiMaggio laughs, shifts gears, obviously delighted by my distress. I don't know where we are going, and I don't want to ask. Probably some secret bend or stretch of water only he knows about, hidden among bracken and alders that line the Roaring Fork River at this altitude and keep most sensible people at a distance.

Suddenly, he pulls off the main highway onto a dirt road that leads, eventually, all the way to Grizzly Reservoir, a glittering emerald lake. But we are not going that far. Within a minute, he swerves into a picnic area to the left of the road, just before a bridge that crosses the river, and parks under a spruce near a weathered picnic table and an old fire pit.

"You gather some wood," he says, leaping out of the car and yanking the hood open in front to extract a fishing rod, tackle box, and other gear we will use later to cook our breakfast. He wades out into the stream as I scour the surrounding woods for stray branches, which I haul back by the armful. When I'm ready, I strike a match and touch it to the nest of newspaper I've added. It smolders for a second, then catches, quickly engulfing the branches. I do this in order to get warm, but by the time I've finished, DiMaggio has already caught two trout that are laying on pine needles by the bank. I clean them while he puts his fishing gear aside and heats a cast iron frying pan over the flames, then tosses in some butter and five or six strips of bacon. It pops and sizzles, and its salty tang permeates the air. He fries the trout in the bacon grease and, when they've turned from silver to a rich, golden brown, he cracks open four eggs and scrambles them quickly in the same pan. When he's done, we sit at the picnic table and eat the trout and the eggs and bacon on tin plates, with a few slices of bread and some hot coffee from a mug. The sun looms over the pass, spreading warm yellow light through the trees. The ground is just beginning to steam as it thaws. When we're finished, I scour the plates clean in the river while DiMaggio repacks the car and in a few minutes we're barreling back down the pass towards Aspen.

"I've gotta go to work," he tells me. "I can't mess around anymore."

He means the bakery on Main Street, where they've already begun to heat the ovens and roll out the dough. He drops me at the corner of Hyman and Galena. I'm still shivering a bit, but my stomach is full and my head has cleared, and I'm happy, standing there as DiMaggio roars off in his little VW. Sunlight floods the streets, painting the sides of buildings with a pinkish glow. It's eight o'clock in the morning. People are just waking up in the apartments around me, and in the large remote houses on Red Mountain whose windows, too, tremble with elusive flame. I light a cigarette and start walking.

The day has only just begun.

Doctor Gonzo and All That

I was not a friend of Hunter Thompson's, nor was I a hanger-on, or even a real fan. I was just someone who lived in Aspen all the years he lived there, and now and then our paths would cross. He was a famous American writer, and I respected that. Hunter had a way of making his presence known, though I suspect at times he would have liked to remain anonymous. His great race for sheriff of Pitkin County has been widely documented. In the fall of 1970 Hunter decided he would run for Sheriff against the incumbent, Carrol Whitmire, and the idea caught fire, calling out freaks and bohemians from miles around. We had all heard of Hunter Thompson and some of us had read his books; we identified with his idea that a counter-cultural figure, one of us, might actually be able to capture public office and revamp the local government in his own twisted image.

The Germans have a wonderful word which applies to people like Hunter: *bürgerschrecke*, which refers to those who "delight in tormenting the bourgeoisie." Hunter's campaign for sheriff was an exercise in *bürgerschrecke* if there ever were one.

The very idea that hippies from all over the country might head for Aspen in order to vote for Hunter sent waves of hysterical premonitions throughout the community. The good citizens of Pitkin County mobilized as never before, and in the end, nearly lost. My friend, Joyce McMullen, told me about the great debate between Thompson and Whitmire that would take place in the old Isis Theater, in which we'd all watched the hilarious and subversive film *King of Hearts*, where asylum inmates take over a town, and where we'd also recoiled in horror at Ridley Scott's masterpiece, *Alien*. It seemed an appropriate place for the absurd drama that was about to unfold in front of a packed house that snowy October evening. In the end, while there were no big surprises, no monsters emerging from Whitmire's chest, the evening was not without its moments of humor and political slapstick.

Joyce and I met in town and walked to the Isis together, excited about the evening's prospects for drama. "There are freaks coming from everywhere," Joyce said, her eyes wide. "I hope we get there in time to find a seat."

There was a line extraordinarily long stretching down East Hopkins Avenue. Once we managed to get inside, the atmosphere of merriment and *bürgerschrecke* was palpable. Bohemian Aspen had turned out in force; the crowd was unruly but willing to remain seated in order to view the spectacle. We knew Whitmire and we knew Thompson, and the idea of a clash between the two promised to be surreal—Whitmire was an old-time county sheriff with a quiet voice and a respectful manner, a perfect representative of the good burghers of Aspen and Pitkin County. He was middle-aged, courteous, well-groomed, and dressed in a coat and tie as he took his seat behind a long table at one side of the stage. Thompson stepped out into the lights from behind a red velvet curtain to take his seat at his own table. He had his famous cigarette holder clamped between his teeth and his head was shaved into a perfect egg of smooth, white skin that made him look more menacing than usual. Oddly, only the BBC showed up to film the event. Perhaps American news organizations deemed the debate unworthy of coverage. There was more than a hint of theatricality about the event that made it fascinating and fun. We believed Hunter had a chance of winning, and that hope galvanized us.

During the debate, Sheriff Whitmire listened quietly to Hunter, and spoke softly into his microphone when it was his turn. I can't recall what points he made, but compared to Hunter's journalistic flair and pizzazz, we hated Whitmire and thought he was a dunce. This was inaccurate and unfair, but he represented the establishment—rules, conventions, punishment, propriety—while Hunter represented freedom and all-out good times. When Whitmire admitted he didn't have information about the sheriff's office that someone had requested, Hunter piped up: "I do!" and shuffled some papers until he found the page he was looking for. This made us laugh at Whitmire's incompetence and applaud Hunter's preparedness. He seemed so much more well-informed than Whitmire, whose only charm was his placidity, and his wan smile.

At one point, Hunter introduced a new governmental term, something of which none of us—Whitmire and the other city officials included—had ever heard: Ombudsman. The office of Ombudsman existed in various places across the United States, but we didn't know that. A thrill went through the crowd when Hunter told us it was a political office with a particular kind of power and charged with a particular kind of authority,

an idea he'd adopted from Sweden. Sweden! Hunter presented
a large placard on which he had written OMBUDSMAN in huge
letters, and under which he'd listed the office's duties. We were
excited by the idea that an ombudsman represents the public
by investigating individual citizen's complaints against bad
or dishonest administrations, especially—and here we hung
on every word—that of *public* authorities. As the new sheriff,
Hunter said he would appoint an ombudsman to his department. We cheered, wildly.

Then he moved on to his next agenda item. Hunter said
he had no problem with drugs, only with people who sold *bad*
drugs. *They* were the real criminals, he avowed, and he would
order a set of medieval stocks to be built and placed on the
lawn in front of the Pitkin County Courthouse with a basket of
old tomatoes replenished each day so that the good citizens of
Aspen could come by and pelt drug offenders until they were
bloody with the juice of the rotting fruit.

Thompson then said he would tear up the pavement on
downtown streets and replace it with grass sod in an effort to
preserve the pastoral character of the town, a place which had
become a target for developers and real estate agents. He was
half joking, of course. Thompson was a political showman, so
he knew how such a bizarre proposition would strike his exuberant constituency.

Hunter's most eloquent moment was a short speech he gave
claiming that the laws against marijuana were backward and
ridiculous. He said the laws had created "a generation of fel-
ons" which, to his mind, was evil and counter-productive. Any
law that ran counter to the public's wishes—and which was de-
monstrably unpopular—ought to be repealed.

It was a brilliant performance, all the way around. I can't

recall a single thing Sheriff Whitmire said. Hunter turned him into a stooge, and though we should have felt sorry for the man, we didn't. However, many people *did* support Whitmire, and were unafraid to make their sentiments known. The more conservative and law-abiding citizens of Aspen did not mean to take any of this sitting down.

As we filed out of the Isis, we felt sure that Hunter would be elected. Perhaps this tiny social experiment would transform the entire country, town by town, as local authority fell into the hands of young malcontents and visionaries everywhere. It was a heady idea, but we also felt a sense of foreboding. If Hunter won and the things he promised were initiated, how long would it be before authorities from Denver or Washington, D.C. stormed the town to squelch us *savagely* (one of Hunter's favorite words) with an iron fist? For the powerful were sure to challenge what could be accomplished under the law in a free and open election. We had not forgotten the riots and demonstrations of the 1960s. We had not forgotten the massacre at Kent State. Our excitement and high spirits were tempered by our knowledge of the past and how the highest powers had a way of destroying anything that threatened their authority. Local politics is one thing, state and federal politics another. Aberrations must be stamped out quickly and effectively before they caught on elsewhere. The fire in Aspen was a bright, but feeble flame.

* * *

As it turned out, none of our aspirations or anxieties mattered. On election night, Hunter's campaign manager, Michael Solheim—who also owned and operated the Hotel Jerome Bar—set up headquarters in one of the spacious rooms upstairs in order to monitor returns and begin celebrating should Hunter win. The room was packed with hippies, campaign personnel, reporters for the *Aspen Times*, and a crew of television cameramen from the BBC, along with various stragglers. Tommy DiMaggio had asked me to go with him. He was a photographer as well as chef, and he ended up taking hundreds of photographs that evening. Had DiMaggio not lost all the photos from that night, he'd have a collection that would have shown a festive crowd, packed shoulder to shoulder under a fog of cigarette smoke, sipping drinks, and whose faces glowed with excitement.

Earlier that day, at Hunter's request, Joyce had served as a "poll watcher," charged with overseeing the balloting and making sure the process unfolded without a hitch. Though she was too young to vote, Joyce could at least contribute something to Hunter's campaign by helping to verify election results. There were poll watchers stationed at various polling stations around town, and at Buttermilk Ski Area for anyone down valley who wanted to vote without having to find a parking spot in town. Joyce told me later that Hunter had showed up to warn her of what he believed was an imminent threat to the process.

"We're expecting trouble," he said. "The Hell's Angels might show up any minute," and with that, he thrust a loaded .45 into her hand. When she protested that she didn't know how to use a gun, he took her out into the parking lot and gave her an impromptu shooting lesson by firing several rounds into the base of the mountain as a demonstration of what to do in case the paranoid, distorted image of violence in his head came to pass. Who knows what Hunter had been on at the time, but Joyce wanted nothing to do with the .45 and so handed it to one of the other poll watchers for safekeeping.

By the time Hunter showed up at his campaign headquarters in the Jerome Hotel wearing a gray Thomas Jefferson wig made of fiberglass, and the American flag draped across his shoulders, we were primed and ready for anything. I stood in the back of the room and took it all in. Hunter looked tired, semi-coherent, flushed. His admirers eddied around him as the lights washed him in a garish glow. His cigarette holder stuck out of his mouth at an odd angle when he wasn't waving it around wildly. A constant susurrus of chatter enveloped the room, broken by gleeful shouts. Then a call came in and the whole place collectively held its breath: Hunter was leading by a small margin. The crowd broke into raucous applause. It was in the bag, no doubt about it. But there were still votes to be counted down valley, where most of the conservative ranchers and rich Republican transplants lived. The returns we had received were from the city of Aspen itself, largely populated by young voters and liberal merchants. No surprise that *they* would vote for Hunter. How many down-valley residents would cross over and vote for him as well?

The answer was not long in coming. As the throng at the Hotel Jerome grew rowdier, votes were being tabulated that would sober us up. When the phone rang again, a hush settled over the room. The young woman who answered listened attentively, her face showing little emotion as the final results were poured secretly into her ear. She turned to us and announced a number that revealed Hunter had lost the election by fewer than three hundred votes. We sank into ourselves, and you could almost hear the escaping hiss of our collective disappointment. We shuffled around, avoiding each other's eyes. Some people left. Then the cameras were trained on

Kurt Brown

Hunter once again. Still wearing his wig and American flag, Hunter sounded philosophical and undaunted. After the interview, more people left, including Hunter himself. Soon, there were only a few of us skulking about the room. The downstairs bar had begun to fill and the noise level rose to a jabbering crescendo. If we couldn't win, we could still get drunk and laugh and toss it all off as though it hadn't really mattered. By two a.m., we had dissipated entirely—both as a crowd and a voting bloc—and when the following morning dawned we rose, not with high hopes for the establishment of a new, utopian society, but with pounding heads and red, weary eyes.

* * *

One Fourth of July evening, some friends and I had spread a blanket out on a bank above the intersection of Gibson Avenue and S. Mill Street to watch the fireworks shimmer and explode over Aspen Mountain. Most of the city's population gathered in Wagner Park, practically beneath the scintillating shower of fireworks themselves, but we found our vantage point less crowded and the fireworks more easily viewable. From where we sat on the other side of the narrow valley at the foot of Red Mountain, we could view the pyrotechnics at a comfortable forty-five degree angle. A few people who lived at the Silver King apartments behind us came out to watch, too, carrying lawn chairs and coolers stashed with beer and other party-enhancing items. The air, laced with pine and lilac, soon filled with marijuana smoke.

As dusk advanced, Hunter's long, low, white Cadillac flashed down the hill below us on Gibson Avenue. *That's Hunter!* someone yelled, pointing to the car that passed beneath us. We could see right down into the vehicle, a convertible—in which two figures sat. Hunter was driving, one hand slung over the steering wheel, the other gripping a drink, and his signature cigarette holder standing in the wind like a small mast. Hunter practically fishtailed down Gibson Avenue, careened around the corner of N. Mill Street, and headed back towards the center of town.

* * *

From time to time, it was possible to spot Hunter at the Hotel Jerome bar. But mostly, he stayed relatively hidden down valley on his Woody Creek ranch. There, he might be seen drinking at the Woody Creek Tavern, cursing or cheering the television screen as the fortunes of his favorite football team ebbed and flowed. But I had nothing more to do with him until we decided to bring out the special "locals" edition of *Aspen Anthology*. I don't recall how I went about contacting Hunter for a contribution of material. I probably broached my request through Michael Solheim, one of Hunter's best friends in Aspen and someone who saw him often. I liked Solheim. He was personable and accessible, though as the owner of the Hotel Jerome bar, he was also watchful and aloof in order to preserve his equanimity in a scene that was often on the edge of being out of control. As the owner, he couldn't make too many friends, because everyone wanted to be his friend and wanted something from him: free drinks, ready cash, favors of one kind or another.

However it happened, I received a message from Hunter that he would be happy to allow us to publish the introduction to his new book, *The Great Shark Hunt*, due out from a big New York publishing house within the year. We couldn't believe our good fortune. Our podunk magazine was going to have a piece of writing from the grand wizard of Gonzo himself, and we would be the first to publish it. This was a coup we couldn't have predicted and we celebrated it, fittingly, by drinking at the Hotel Jerome for the rest of the afternoon while, ostensibly, conducting an editorial meeting. But a week later, I was back at the Jerome bar for lunch and felt the need to visit the men's room while waiting for my order. In the hallway that led to the restrooms, there was a community bulletin board, and I happened to see my own name scribbled on a torn piece of brown paper. I stopped dead in my tracks, then turned back to the board. Yes, there was my name and a note.

> "Kurt Brown—Do not publish the introduction to my book under any circumstances. My publisher will rape my wife, kill my dog, destroy my house and cut off three of my fingers if it appears anywhere."—Hunter Thompson

It was something to that effect. I wish I'd saved it, published it as an example of Hunter's over-the-top, unabashed style. Instead, I removed it from the board and carefully re-read it. How could Hunter have possibly known I would pass by and see that message? I never received any other message from him: neither a phone call nor a letter, or even a word from Solheim asking for confirmation that I had seen it. I was crestfallen. To have such a prize snatched away from us, to return to the office and have to tell the rest of the staff that there would be no article by Hunter Thompson in the pages of our magazine, was bitter indeed. But somehow we received a consolation—the right to publish perhaps the only poem Hunter has ever written, and which appeared nowhere else, we were told, a free-verse ditty, "Collect Telegram from a Mad Dog." Deeply "twisted," suitably obscene, and filled with colorful—or off-colorful—phrases which only Hunter could have written, the poem began:

> Not being a poet and drunk as well,
> leaning into the diner and dawn
> and hearing the jukebox mockery of some better
> human sound
> I wanted rhetoric
> but could only howl the rotten truth
> Norman Luboff
> should have his nuts ripped off with a plastic fork

It appeared on a page opposite a graphic by Tom Benton, the now famous two-thumbed fist clutching a peyote button and the handle of a knife, all of it printed in the severest black ink we could find. On the issue's cover, we used a photograph of Hunter wearing his wig and the American flag that had been taken by Tommy DiMaggio on the night of the failed election. We were happy to have Hunter's poem, no matter how unconventional or odd. Like everything Hunter wrote, it was exaggerated, cartoonish, and distorted beyond all reality. But it was fun, too, the primal nightmare of a trashy world where people acted out their aggressive fantasies and the Id raged without restraint. We were open to almost anything, as long as it was well-crafted, original, and energetic. And Hunter was *energetic*! No doubt about that. A year or two would pass before I saw Hunter again, years in which our little magazine grew modestly and we continued to add to our literary programming. Hunter and his antics seemed a far cry from what we were doing and he receded, for us, into the background.

* * *

One spring afternoon in May around four o'clock, I was sitting in the Jerome Bar up near the front window where the bar
bends around to form a private nook, from which I could command a full view of the room. The bar was almost empty—
a woman sat across from me at a large table under the other
front window; two ragged hippies conferred at mid-bar, dirty
enough to have slept in the mountains the previous evening;
another patron sat near the back munching on a hamburger
while he studied the *Aspen Times*; and the bartender, setting
up for his coming shift. As I sipped my beer, Hunter and Michael Solheim entered from the rear door and took seats at the
bar a stool or two away from the tattered pair of hippies, who
were mumbling to themselves, obviously drunk and probably
stoned. Solheim asked the bartender for a couple of beers, and
he and Hunter, wearing sunglasses even inside the dim confines of the hotel, sipped thoughtfully and spoke little, seemingly content.

Suddenly, Hunter jumped from his seat, grabbed one of
the hippies closest to him by the collar, and flung him backwards off his stool onto the hard white tile floor. In a moment,
Hunter was on top of him, savagely beating him in the face,
while Solheim dragged the other hippie to the floor, punching him wildly, if not quite as violently. Hunter's man began to
bleed from the nose and mouth. It was sickening to see what a
beating he took, practically docile and unable to defend himself. Chairs flew, beer mugs broke, the air rang with curses.
Then Hunter floundered to his feet and grabbed a nearby bar
stool. In an instant, he had brought it down roundly on the
man, who was lying on the floor beneath him. Again, he lifted
the barstool and brought it down, until Solheim—sobered no

doubt by the thought of lawsuits and endless hospital bills and death—began struggling with Hunter to make him let go of the stool. The bartender helped subdue Hunter, and after a few minutes, they managed to get Hunter to drop the stool and retreat to the back of the room, then out the door, all the while snarling curses and glowering malevolently at his adversary, inert on the blood-spattered floor. Solhiem reappeared, yelling at the hippies to get out as they wobbled uncertainly to their feet, protesting feebly that they had done nothing wrong. *Out! And don't come back!* For a moment it looked like they might not comply, displaying what dignity they had left after being so thoroughly brutalized. But soon they were gone.

I hadn't moved, appalled as I was at the intensity of the violence, looking away only briefly when Hunter began the barstool portion of the beating. It had all happened in less than a minute. The image of Hunter, straddling his man and repeatedly bludgeoning him in the face, left me shocked and queasy. I can see it now: Hunter's left hand gripping the man's shirt and lifting his head off the floor, then Hunter's right fist pounding the man's face so that his head snapped back again and slammed the floor. I can smell the blood and spilled beer, hear the hiss and groan of the combatants. The man at the table in the back of the bar had stopped eating his hamburger, stunned. When I looked for the woman who had been sitting by the front window, she was gone.

* * *

Not long afterward, I ran into Sandy, Hunter's wife. I didn't know her well, but liked her for her warmth and directness. I was just leaving the bank and saw her coming toward me, so I nodded and stopped to say hello. Our conversation shifted from the weather to local events to more personal topics. I must have asked her how she was, because she confided that Hunter was often angry and violent, though she never said he had hurt her, or their son, Juan. It was just that she was afraid, that she might have to return to Florida, where she and Hunter had spent time, a place that held fond memories and where she felt safe. I don't know why she chose me as a confidante; I imagine she was confiding in other people at the time, too. Maybe it was because she knew I was a writer and thought—mistakenly—that Hunter and I were friends. Her eyes became red and teary, and she tipped her head in a gesture of helplessness, downcast and scared. She was small, with short blonde hair and blue eyes, pixie-like, and there was nothing in her that I could see that might inspire hatred or violence. I felt sorry for her, but felt I had nothing to offer, that I was just another rootless, immature bachelor floating around the carnival that was Aspen. Sad and somewhat ashamed, I left her on the street,

When Sandy eventually left Hunter, their marriage dissolved. I always wondered how I would have felt if some real violence against Sandy had occurred. But she found a way out, and Hunter went on to remarry. I met his new wife at a reading once, and liked her right away. She had the same warmth and dedication to Hunter that Sandy had shown, and was with him when he committed suicide at Owl Creek Ranch. I have no idea what Hunter's life was like after Sandy left, but I heard stories of people who surrounded him, an endless parade of visitors—Jack Nicholson, Johnny Depp, Jim Harrison, Ed Bradley, and Keith Richards, among others.

Hunter appeared infrequently during those final years. I saw him speak at Aspen High School to an auditorium packed with the faithful, but even with a microphone, it was impos-

sible to decipher most of what he said because he chewed
his words and swallowed them up with his famous mumble.
Hunter seemed distracted and bored. He sat alone at a folding cafeteria table by himself, with a paper cup and a bottle,
fielding questions from the audience. We listened politely to
his answers, which were neither enlightening nor coherent.
The point of the evening, it seemed, was to catch a glimpse
of our hero. It was clear that Hunter was no longer at the top
of his game. Not nearly as witty or articulate as he had been
that night in the Isis Theater when he'd debated Sheriff Carrol
Whitmire and sent the crowd, tittering and delighted, off into
the cold October night.

* * *

With his emphasis on the bizarre, the Gothic, the grotesque,
and the obscene, as well as his obsession with self-destruc-
tiveness, big cards, Dobermans, guns, and violence, Hunter
Thompson represented one kind of American adolescent who
found it impossible to grow up. This is an American type we
love to celebrate. As long as they are talented, anything goes.
Paradoxically, however, Thompson's best writing originated
from his adolescent fantasy-life, while his real life was somewhat despoiled by it at the same time. This is the tragedy with
respect to all boy-men (or women) who choose to self-immo-
late in public, whose careers are *built* on self-abuse and the desire to become legendary at all costs. Thompson lasted longer—far longer—than most. It is no coincidence that Ralph
Steadman quickly became Thompson's friend and official
portraitist—Steadman's work, while startling, resembles the
skulls, skeletons, monsters, freaks, and chimeras of the skate
board artists who would follow and who produce their imag-

es for the delectation of pre-pubescent teens. Such art is meant to shock, titillate, and disgust, which is exactly what defines the psyche of many teenage boys in their wish to break free of their parents.

Bürgerschrecke begins at home.

But not all teenage rebellion is marked by originality and talent. Most is marked by mere imitation of idols—the ones with real talent, whose brilliance propels them to the head of their generation. Thompson was undoubtedly one of these. His outrage at political corruption, at tepid conformity and complaisance, at the jaded values of a self-satisfied bourgeois culture that, in his estimate, had become nearly comatose in the materialistic flush of post-war prosperity, galvanized a huge readership and set him apart as a witness and reporter. His single-handed creation of a new kind of journalism marked him as a new voice in American letters, even if that creation itself has now been corrupted in its turn, leading to the strident, self-important, opinionated blowhards who dominate the media. Like all the greatest satirists, Thompson was able to raise hyperbole to the level of art, and make a comedy of human folly in which, however distorted, we could see ourselves unmistakably reflected.

Sex, Drugs, and Sushi Rolls

Everyone wanted to fuck everyone else all of the time. Liberated by the pill, we navigated blissfully between the inhibitions of our parents' generation and the approach of AIDS. For a brief twenty-year period, we could indulge ourselves in sex that was free of guilt, conception, and disease whenever, wherever, and with whomever we pleased. No condoms, patches, diaphragms, cervical caps, coils, spermicides, pessaries, sponges, films, foams, or jellies. All of that pre-revolutionary paraphernalia seemed like so many intra-uterine buckboards to us. And who would even *think* of tying their tubes or undergoing the perils of a vasectomy when the pill, the lovely egg-annihilating, consequence-conquering pill, would take care of everything? All that was required were the old arts of desire and seduction, as long as both parties agreed and there was no coercion of any kind. We weren't Victorians any longer, but neither were we brainless knuckle-dragging Neanderthals out to satisfy our lusts. Respect and mutual-consent were still things we valued. And where there was no love, mutual consent would do. We believed in pleasure for its own sake, anoth-

er way of breaking free of former constraints and exploring the
ecstasies of the flesh, as drugs allowed us to explore the phan-
tasmagoria of our minds.

The problem in Aspen was opportunity. Not the lack of
it, but the utter accessibility of it everywhere and at all times.
Walking in town one day with the poet Karen Swenson—as
face after beautiful face floated past us—the topic of Aspen's
youth culture came up. "Aspen is like a garden," she said, "you
can just reach out and pick the flowers anywhere." We were
simply *surrounded* by it, and the invitation to gather flowers became irresistible. The "problem," then, wasn't availability.

I knew of a few married couples, but only a handful. And a
few weddings took place, many of which were later annulled.

A few babies were born. Most people I knew were single,
though partnerships formed and dissolved regularly. Aspen's
population grew, but not because of an increase in births. It
grew because of the arrival of new recruits, those who were
seduced by the beauty of the place and its acceptance of hedo-
nism and casual freedom.

* * *

In the mid-'70s, we heard a rumor that someone was making a porn film in town using amateurs from the community.
This galvanized our more prurient instincts. The film was to
be shot on a particular night downstairs at Galena Street East,
under the Elk's Building. Several of the waitresses I worked
with at the Gold Horn intended to take part, and they named
people from other restaurants and bars who planned to appear
as well. The rest of us were dying to know who else was involved, and to get into the shoot so we could watch the film-
ing, but Galena Street East was locked on the night in question

and as far as I know, the film was never produced. The local porn film became one of those Aspen stories or myths that no one was able to verify or disclaim, but the fact that the story became such a source of speculation is indicative of the prevailing sexual atmosphere in Aspen during the time. Quite a bit of steam rose from hot tubs all over town, but the idea of actually splashing our escapades across the silver screen didn't appeal to our middle-class sensibilities. Sex was a great thing, a natural thing in which we indulged frequently and without qualms, but exhibitionism was largely viewed as petty and perverse. We were less liberated than we claimed to be.

In 1983, *Playboy* came to town with the idea of producing a spread called "The Women of Aspen." Several women I knew took part in that project, clothed, if scantily. A pair of girls, barely out of their teens, caused a minor sensation when they roller skated around town clad in bikinis. The appearance of *Playboy* in town was, I suppose, inevitable. Hugh Hefner's brother, Keith, lived down the street from Bruce Berger's cabin, and Hugh's first girlfriend, Barbi Benton, moved to Aspen sometime in the 1970s, and apparently still lives there today.

And then there were the nature lovers. It wasn't unusual to come upon a person, or sometimes, a couple in the mountains hiking *au naturel*, or sunbathing on a rock under a chaste Colorado sky. Once, when one of my friend's mother was in town, we drove up Independence Pass and took the road south to Grizzly Reservoir to show her the beauty of the lake, and the towering cliff wall that loomed beyond the water. As we came around a bend in the road, we urged my friend's mother to turn to her right so she could see where the underground waterfall spilled the Roaring Fork River's headwaters down into a stony pool through a narrow opening in the rocks. At that mo-

ment, two naked bodies lay entwined by the falls, gleaming-
ly exposed to our view and unperturbed by the sound of our
van passing not fifty feet away beyond the willows. Our heads
swiveled forward again and we went on our way to the reservoir as if we'd seen nothing out of the ordinary.

I once had a lover who preferred trekking through the Utah
desert near Moab in nothing but her hiking boots and socks.
She'd strip about twenty minutes into the hike, then lead me
into the wilderness for what would often prove to be a prickly
encounter. I heard of a couple caught skiing out of bounds on
the back of Ajax Mountain sans anything but skis, socks, and
poles.

But the greatest extravagance was probably the Penny Hot
Springs down valley, which lay on the banks of the Crystal River between Carbondale and Redstone, off highway 133. Nights
in January or February, we'd drive down after work to shuck
our clothes and plunge into the hot spring, which was housed
in a small shed, then jump into the frigid river not twenty feet
away. We'd race back and forth, exposing ourselves to a series
of temperature extremes some holistic nut among us swore
was good for our circulation. To be honest, we cared nothing
about circulation. We loved gallivanting naked under the stars,
rubbing against each other, six men and six women in the indifferent goose-pimpled night.

Hot springs and hot tubs were a great excuse to frolic naked
together and assess each other's bodies. One of the more popular hot springs required some effort to reach, and to plunge
into its sultry waters was considered a reward for hiking so
far. In fact, Conundrum Hot Springs is really a series of small
pools, the largest about three feet deep, perfect for wallowing.
A nine-mile hike brings you to the springs, at an altitude of

twelve thousand feet. If you have come during a cool part of the year, you will luxuriate in water that reaches 102° and will quickly thaw your chilled bones. You can float naked at Conundrum. But in Glenwood Springs' huge public spring, you have to wear a bathing suit as you bob in a rectangular concrete pool that spans two city blocks, accommodating hundreds of bathers.

For more private encounters, we sought the hot tubs and Jacuzzis that adorned almost every hotel and large dwelling in Aspen. Joe Popper—a.k.a "Joe-the-Door"—remembers coming home to an apartment he rented with others on his very first night in Aspen to find an orgy right outside his living room door. Though hot tubs were invented in Scandinavia to invigorate health, we Aspenites rarely used them with good health in mind. Hot tubs were essentially water beds without the bother of rubber mattresses, or the trouble of filling them up with a hose and then having to treat the water inside to stave off a proliferation of bacteria. The luxurious water in a hot tub provided us with the sensual pleasure of being warmed on every surface, caressed by the little waves and currents even the slightest agitation creates. But the truth is that hot tubs can become boring. Their novelty and superficial excitement wears off in a hurry.

There were famous lotharios and wild women, sexual athletes and ski gods, playboys and amazons, rakes and roués enough to suit any taste and keep anyone of either sex busy. Prostitution, in such a permissive atmosphere, was essentially nonexistent. A prostitute working the bars in Aspen would have earned a meager living. Then too, a small but largely invisible caste of homosexual men led lonely lives until the gay community finally began to organize itself in the 1980s. But in general, Aspen's residents and tourists indulged themselves, guilt-free, in pleasure domes and fleshpots, a brief interlude before the reality of AIDS set in and the sexual revolution came to an end.

* * *

When I began the Aspen Writers' Conference in 1976, I learned that people away from home in a festive and beautiful environment are liable to take advantage of their unaccustomed liberty. Those who were single often met other singles in their workshops and began affairs that might last the length of the conference, or beyond. Several of our couples continued their affairs after they returned home, some even marrying (and some, of course, divorcing). We took our writing seriously, but since the average age of the conferees was about thirty, it was inevitable that attractions would spring up, followed by assignations and consummations. As the director, I committed myself to a strict discipline when it came to conferees and faculty: no sex with anyone at the conference, a vow I was actually able to keep for a few years. It's true that summer conferences are often vacations as well as opportunities to work on the craft of writing. I wanted the conference to be taken seriously as a place where people grew as artists and would return home to pursue careers that would lead to publication. But adults are adults, free to do what they want.

* * *

Often, in Aspen, I would hear someone bragging about having multiple partners during the course of a single day. The period of a single day seemed to be the measure of virility most respected and, as I recall, someone boasted of having had seven different partners over a mere twenty-four hours. How this feat was accomplished—in addition to eight hours of work, plus meals and sleep—is anyone's guess. Experience was what mattered most. Life, as the old cliché would have it, was a banquet and we wanted to stuff ourselves with as much experience as possible. Thoreau's famous warning still resonated. We wanted to make sure that as we came to the end of our lives, we wouldn't find we had never truly lived. This is a generalization, of course. Not everyone felt the same, and there are people who held back, or responsibly paced themselves, or didn't share our omnivorous philosophy. And for good reason. Many of us had not learned how destructive and painful pure, unrestrained lust could be. For the most part, it was all good clean fun, a halcyon era of uninhibited play and experimentation.

* * *

If free sex was a result of the pill and its ensuing revolution, then alcohol and drugs were its catalysts—the lubricant and elixir, respectively—that could bring us to the heights of physical sensation. Marijuana, that staple of the '60s with its largely innocuous effects, was still the drug of choice in the following decade. Like anyplace else in America, in Aspen marijuana was plentiful and easy to obtain, and a local mom-'n'-pop cartel ensured that it was available most of the time. Dealers like Tipi Bob and Honest Al genially distributed their wares to a community that used marijuana to heighten any experience— eating one's favorite foodstuffs, watching a movie, attending a concert, wallowing in a hot tub, plunging downhill through blankets of fresh powder, glorying in the spectacular effects of a Colorado sunset, and having sex. Any occasion involving the senses might be reason to break out a bag of weed.

Wally was the head of a group of hippie entrepreneurs who imported marijuana from Mexico and other venues to meet

the demands of Aspen, and just beyond. In order to understand
Wally and his friends, it is necessary to dismiss the image of
the sleazy, sinister figure of popular myth who lurks around
schoolyards trying to get young innocent kids hooked on
drugs. Wally was a respected member of the community who
abhorred violence and corruption as much as the rest of us, and
loved life too much to take any pleasure in destroying it. Wally
and his merry band saw themselves as benefactors of society,
not its enemies. To bring the flame of expanded consciousness
to their fellow creatures was an ideal they not only preached,
but earnestly practiced. Marijuana was an unquestionable
good, a positive development on the order of polio vaccine or
penicillin, not something to be suppressed or reviled.

But in the eyes of the law, they were criminals, and they
lived outside the bounds of polite society, like the members
of any demimonde dispensing a desired but legally forbidden
product. At the highest levels of their "industry," there were
real outlaws, violence and murder, and Wally himself was often in danger, not only as a client of the South American car-
tels, but as a man wanted by the DEA. Dealing drugs was no
laughing matter, and the dangers were everywhere and real.
Joyce confessed to me that for a brief period, she had served as
a runner by taping thousands of dollars to her torso, then flying out of the country to deliver it safely, and on time, somewhere in the depths of South America. I heard stories, too, of
people being thrown out of private planes over the Arizona
desert because some of the crop had been lost, or a payment
hadn't been made, or had been short for one reason or another. There are no excuses in the drug trade, no refinancing
plans. Betrayals were dealt with summarily, and law enforcement agencies were tireless in their efforts to identify, trace,

and catch drug dealers wherever they operated. I can remember several sweeps through Aspen by federal agents who were
intent on cracking down on the drug trade. Wally *was* eventually caught, though not in Aspen, and served several years in a
state penitentiary.

But in the 1970s and on his own turf, Wally's activities
seemed benign enough and you hardly ever bought drugs directly from him. Once it filtered down to local salesmen like
Tipi Bob and Honest Al, law enforcement agents hardly paid
any attention. They were small fry as far as the DEA was concerned, and certain local sheriffs over the years didn't consider
smoking marijuana a crime at all. Not in Aspen. *Live and let live*
was the ethos of the time, but this ebbed when cocaine sup-
planted marijuana as the drug of choice. Cocaine was expensive. Moreover, it was a "hard" drug, one whose effects and
physical consequences were far greater than marijuana's. By
1975 or 1976, it seemed like everyone was snorting cocaine off
every hard surface they could find; for fashion-conscious users,
tiny glass vials and silver spoons were plentiful and chic. Most
people laid out their lines from small paper bindles, which
held an ounce of cocaine and sold for about a hundred dollars. No one I knew could really afford a hundred dollars for an
ounce of something that might, at best, last for an evening. We
wouldn't spend that much for a bottle of great French wine, or
invest that much in something we really needed, like health
insurance or the security of a savings account, but we did buy
cocaine at least a couple of times a week. Cocaine's primary appeal was the rush of energy it supplied, however short-lived. It
also satisfied our desire for the illicit and dangerous, the aura
of romance that surrounded anything illegal and the thrill of
secrecy it required.

Aspen had become a capital of glamour. But while we may have wanted to take a walk on the wild side, we didn't have a death wish. None of my friends, nor anyone else I knew of, ever died of cocaine. There were a couple of close calls. I once found Joyce at home with her curtains drawn against the sunlight, manically clipping articles from magazines and tossing them into a pile in the middle of her floor while at the same time vomiting pools of a milky substance that reminded me of the frothy mucous Phil had spit on the floor that day in his apartment at the Paragon. Joyce got the message, and promptly recovered. She'd lost a lot of weight, and she was a fairly thin woman to begin with. We were amateurs, recreational users, and we knew where the edge was. We wanted life, only life, heightened by any means that would not actually kill us.

* * *

One summer I was sitting in the Hotel Jerome Bar with a friend of mine—let's call him Bill—a visiting writer whose work I admired. Bill worked at a respectable school back east and had been a professor for some years. He smoked a pipe and sported a beard, like many poets. Cocaine was so acceptable in Aspen that to offer it to someone amounted to a social courtesy, not something scandalous or uncouth. So I suggested to Bill that we leave our drinks at the bar and go into the elevator to do some coke.

Before its restoration, the hotel had a rickety antique elevator that allowed you to open its sliding door between floors, promptly bringing the car to a halt. Looking out, you could see nothing but a brick wall, so it was perfectly safe to snort a little cocaine, let the door slide shut again, and get off at the second floor. Then you'd walk back down the wide set of stairs to the bar and resume drinking, as if nothing had happened. My friends and I had done this many times without incident, so Bill and I had no reason to be wary. Stopped between floors, I had just scooped up a bit of cocaine in a tiny spoon and was offering it to Bill when a loud pounding came from above, and the car was shaking.

"What's that?" Bill looked alarmed.

"I don't know," I said. "They must be working on the building upstairs."

I snorted more coke and another flurry of blows shook the car. This time, we heard a muffled voice, someone shouting from somewhere above us words I couldn't decipher. I stuffed the vial into my pocket and let the door slide shut. Something wasn't quite right, and Bill looked anxious. When we reached the second floor and the elevator door slid open, a short, stocky man in a vest and porkpie hat glared at us. I had never seen the bulldog-faced man before and it flashed across my mind that perhaps he was merely a patron of the hotel, not the source of the pounding. But then he yelled, "You can't do that! You can't do that here!" He looked indignant and menacing, and for a moment I froze. Bill was absolutely terrified.

"Do what?" I said. "What do you mean?"

I was cautious. For all I knew, he could be a DEA agent. My reputation, and the Conference's, as well as Bill's career, were all at risk. I cursed myself for putting us in this position. I had no way to defend myself if he threw me up against the wall to frisk me, or if more agents emerged from doors or hidden recesses down the hall." You can't do that in this grand old lady!" he shouted.

This strange phrasing threw me off; maybe he was a crazy street person, living a delusion. But then it hit me: he was referring to the hotel. Would an authority speak that way?

"Who are you?" I asked, growing bolder by the minute."

"You can't do that!" he bellowed again, unable, it seemed, to adjust his intensity to the level the situation required. Whoever he was, he seemed harmless, maybe an antique-lover or someone obsessed with old hotels I glanced at Bill.

"Come on," I said, "Let's go down and finish our drinks."

"You can't . . ."

"Get the hell out of my way," I barked. And then I laughed. He was still blustering at us as we made our way downstairs to take our seats again in the bar. But then I thought better of it, so we exited out the front door on Main Street and circled around to the back of the hotel, where I shoved my little vial of coke under a tuft a grass, beneath a tree.

We went back inside to have our drinks. But Bill was still shaken, and it didn't help when the odd little man showed up in the bar and talked excitedly to Michael Solheim, who was nodding and glancing in our direction. When the man left, Soldheim came over to explain.

"He's the house dick," Solheim said. "They just hired him this week, so maybe you'd better cool it for a while, okay?"

The hotel had never had anything like a detective, but I felt I had better cooperate with Solheim. Bill was riled up again.

"Don't you think we ought to leave?" he asked.

"Look," I said, "Solheim is a friend of mine, and I've been coming here for years. I'm the director of the conference, and everybody in town knows me, even the sheriff and the cops," I bragged. "Even the mayor! We've got nothing to worry about. I'd love to see that little weasel try something."

Then, as we were sitting there with our drinks, an Aspen police officer walked up to our table. He was someone I knew only vaguely, and I was slightly nervous. Solheim came over and explained that everything was under control, there was no need to worry, and the officer nodded his head in agreement. Then he turned to us and asked us politely to leave. He said we could come back in a few hours, after things had died down. I was indignant at first, but my rage subsided and we reluctantly paid our bill and left.

Later that night I retrieved my vial from the clump of grass behind the hotel and entered the bar again. I lifted my glass and toasted to the local gods, the gods of tolerance, unwarranted good luck, and high times.

* * *

After cocaine, more classes of drugs filtered in and out of the community. Methamphetamine, which we called crystal meth, or crank, made a brief appearance. The drug is a psychostimulant, and can boost sexual performance and enhance pleasure. But it can also ravage the body and kill you, horribly and quickly. Before I knew much about it, a friend offered me some meth while I was still living at Joyce's house when she was off exploring the jungle. Methedrine rockets you up to a tremendous high, but doesn't let go. There is no falling off twenty minutes later. Your body and mind simply lock into a high level of energy and alertness and you feel you can do anything—hike for a hundred miles, read a thousand books, run up and down a mountain without even breathing hard—and the feeling may last for up to twenty-four hours, well into the day after you've taken it.

We greeted dawn, my friend and I, after a night of hyperintensity and focus, jabbering like baboons, and didn't return to earth until late the following day. It had been a spectacu-

lar ride, but I knew that there would be a price to pay for such
a voyage. Anything that powerful would have to affect your
body negatively. It only stood to reason. I set my feet back on
the ground, and never thought about taking methedrine again.

On the opposite end of the pharmacological spectrum,
"downers," or depressants, made a brief appearance in town.
Barbiturates were popular among the laid back crowd, a way
of being on the precipice of sleep, letting the world pass dreamily by. There were many brand names—Valium, Seconal, Lu-
minal, and more—but nothing was quite as popular as Quaaludes, a substitute for barbiturates that had been developed in
the 1950s and already in widespread recreational use. Billed in
medical circles as a sedative, hypnotic, and muscle-relaxant,
these pills were advertised on the Aspen streets as "horse tran-
quilizers." The drug was so strong it could turn a grown man
into a blob of drowsy flesh. Someone offered me two Quaaludes one night in Jake's Abbey and because I was off-duty and
had nothing better to do, I took them. For the next few hours I
bounced around the room, trying to steady the unaccustomed
elastic of my legs as my muscles gave way and my head lolled
on my shoulders like a bubble in a carpenter's level. The effect
was not so much unpleasant as downright embarrassing as I
lumbered stupidly around, hardly able to lift my glass or talk.
For all I know I was a drooling, inarticulate moron and, like
methedrine, I never took Quaaludes again. By the early 1980s,
Quaaludes had been banned in both the United States and Europe due to its widespread abuse and the dreadful effects of
overdose.

* * *

LSD had enjoyed its heyday in the 1960s, but was still in use, though not as frequently. As a hallucinogen, peyote was a more "natural" substitute and had the caché of being used by some Native American tribes in religious ceremonies. For a person with a New Age sensibility, this gave the drug an aura of purity and magic that no chemically synthesized drug could beat. Peyote was a cactus, after all, and therefore a naturally occurring part of God's own creation, not something that had been engineered in a scientist's lab. Native Americans and everything they did were lionized by the hippie generation as a throwback to the "noble savage" of the Romantic period. I can recall seeing dried peyote buttons in Aspen on only a few occasions. The buttons were chewed, or boiled to make hallucinogenic tea. Sometimes, because the buttons were bitter, Peyote's active ingredient, mescaline, was extracted by grinding the dried buds into a white powder that the user could then measure into gelatin capsules for easy consumption. Mescalin was available in Aspen, if you wanted it. Not many people did, though it's true that Tom Benton's famous Gonzo poster for Hunter Thompson pictured a two-thumbed fist clutching a peyote bud. Like LSD, however, mescalin was saved for special occasions, not used on a daily basis.

* * *

One dazzling Colorado morning after a fresh snowfall, a group of us decided to take magic mushrooms and shuffle up on cross-country skis to visit Cheryl in her tipi. Radiant sunlight, streaming through minute particles of floating ice, creates the impression of a fairyland, a dazzling, magical display not unlike a child's snow globe. The purity of untracked snow against the evergreens, beneath the high-flung dome of an azure sky, added to the effect, making it possible to expe-

Kurt Brown

rience intense, sensory euphoria without benefit of any drug. When you add in psychedelics, however, the experience can be almost unbearably lovely. Psilocybin, the active ingredient in magic mushrooms, can make whatever you see, hear, or touch extraordinarily vivid. Even non-living objects seem to pulse with life, so that everything in sight shimmers and breathes. In such a world, laughter—often uncontrollable—seems the only plausible response.

We began our trip by ingesting the mushrooms while sitting in a friend's van in downtown Aspen. My friend opened a jar in which the mushrooms gleamed, stewing in their own occult oils.

"Here," he said, offering me a spoonful.

They tasted fleshy, and slightly objectionable.

"Ugh!" I said, drawing back. "I can't stomach this."

"Try it with a spoonful of honey," he suggested, producing a small jar and mixing it with the mushrooms. This made them far more palatable, and we each ate our share—about a spoonful apiece—then drove out to the end of Ute Avenue to begin our journey. At that time, the road simply petered out at the edge of the forest on the far side of the Roaring Fork River, east of Aspen Mountain. A makeshift trail led up the valley from there, paralleling the ridge above. It was not an official trail, and some of it wandered through private property, so it was not well marked. We kept the river to our left and broke through the snow, sending clouds of sparkling flakes up into the light. It is hard to describe the giddiness we felt as we sloughed through pristine mounds of powder, luxuriating in the sun's rising warmth, breathing the immaculate air. The trees cast blue shadows on the snow.

After a while, we stopped to eat cheese, and squirt wine into our mouths out of a skin I'd been carrying. By the time we reached Cheryl's tipi on the other side of the river, we were ready to rest and eat lunch. We unhooked our skis, hurled them like spears into a drift on the opposite bank, then tiptoed across a fallen log in our cross-country boots, careful not to fall into the icy water. Cheryl served us homemade soup while we warmed our bones sitting around her Franklin stove.

Later, back in town, we continued to feel inordinately happy. The effects of psilocybin can last up to eight hours, and all afternoon we wandered the streets elated, smiling at everyone, laughing inappropriately, and often. Those who met us thought we were crazy, and we were.

* * *

Pleasure takes many forms, and the true hedonist will explore them all. This includes fine food and wine, and Aspen in the 1970s was on its way to becoming a capital of gustatory delights. When I first arrived in town in 1970, eating establishments and bars then were almost all of the common American variety: meat and potatoes at reasonable prices; fried eggs, coffee and ham; bland, indigenous beer, jug wine, peanuts, and cheap scotch. The Shaft, on the corner of Hunter Street and Cooper Avenue (under what is now Boogie's Diner) featured steak and baked potatoes in a faux mineshaft. The dining room was decorated with dim lighting, a set of tracks with an old ore car, exposed wooden beams, Styrofoam rocks painted gray, and flickering lanterns on tables that were dressed in red-and-white oilcloths. There was a salad bar, which offered shredded iceberg lettuce, tomato chunks, and if we were lucky, onion or cucumber.

The Steak Pit (still open in a different location), was located beneath City Market, next to a pancake house called FlapJax.

An A-frame on Durant and Hunter served hot dogs, while the most exotic item on The White Kitchen's menu was corned beef hash. The Hotel Jerome served breakfast, lunch, and dinner, and the original Chart House, another steak emporium, added lobster and seared tuna. The Mesa Store Bakery, The Epicure, Jake's, The Red Onion, Pinocchio's, La Cocina, Toro's, Andre's, Little Annie's, The Hickory House, The Mother Lode, Abatone's, The Anchorage, Johnson's Temptation, Bruce LaFavour's Paragon, The Weinerstube, The Magic Pan: all good, all serving basic fare at affordable prices for ski bums and tourists on a budget.

This is what the culinary landscape looked like before the slick, restaurants that served nouvelle cuisine popped up in town in the 1980s and '90s. Syzygy, Ajax Tavern, Il Mullino's, Cache Cache, Piñons, Montagne at Little Nell—and its twenty thousand bottles of wine—Caribou Club (where I saw Diana Ross dancing on New Year's Eve), and Mezzaluna (Lou Diamond Phillips once gave me a neck rub there; George Hamilton was a regular customer): The list of pricey eating establishments is impressive and lengthy and has made Aspen, along with its food and wine festival, a mecca for gastronomes and connoisseurs.

Our sense of a gourmet restaurant in the 1970s reached no higher than The Golden Horn and The Copper Kettle, fine establishments serving delicious food, but beef-heavy and sauce-reliant compared to the revolution in nouvelle cuisine that was to follow. Sirloin tips over buttered noodles was out, hot oysters in a sauternes sabayon or roasted strips of duck magret with Mirabelle plums was in, and establishments like the Horn and Kettle began to feel the pinch. People were eating healthier food, and less of it.

A sure indication of this culinary shift in Aspen was the opening, in the early 1980s, of Takah Sushi, downstairs on the Hyman Street Mall. I recall the enthusiasm with which the advent of sushi in Aspen was greeted by the old hippie generation, once so enamored of Andre's and The Shaft. It wasn't such a long step, it seems, from the brown rice and kale soup that passed for "health food" during the hippie era to the flying fish roe, yellowtail collar, and California rolls of our more mature years. On any given night, I might find a host of my friends lined up along the bar at Taka Sushi munching crisp, pearly slices of giant clam, followed by fatty glistening strips of tuna belly. Takah Sushi was challenged, in pretty rapid succession, by Kenichi's and Nobu's, both opened by rogue chefs first working at Takah Sushi who thought they could do a better job and rake in more of the profit on their own. But the advent of sushi heralded more than a fundamental change in diet. It was part of a general drift, a growing consciousness that the carefree idealism and raggedy freedom of our youth was drawing to a close, and a taste for better things had arrived. We were becoming domesticated, socially conscious, provident, and aware of our responsibilities and the choices we had to make in order to maintain ourselves in the future. The 1980s would be a time of life-changing choices as we slipped easily into our thirties and saw our forties looming on the not-too-distant horizon. Many people left town to pursue postponed careers in other places. Some remained to become local entrepreneurs. A few of us returned to school in order to further our educations and attempt to better our chances in the expanding labor market of the Reagan years. The sudden shock and terror of AIDS put an end to the sexual revolution, and the new culture of greed ended any idealism the 1960s may have spawned. If the 1920s was one long party predicated on seemingly endless prosperity and the cult of youth—the "Jazz Age"—then the 1960s has to be thought of as the "Rock Age," a time that returned the cult of youth to its former glory, when the party raged on again for a decade.

Murder in the Mountains

"Hey, wasn't that Ted Bundy running down the street?"
It was a gorgeous June day, and only a few patches of snow still glimmered on the upper reaches of Ajax Mountain. The artists had taken up their posts at the big round table near the front window at the Jerome bar, and I think it was someone sitting there who had called out in disbelief. We'd all seen an ordinary looking man, limping slightly as he ran. He could have been anyone running to catch a friend, or to cross the street before the light changed.

"Nahh. Just some guy. Bundy's at the courthouse."

"You're crazy!" someone else said, and we laughed and went back to drinking beer and discussing art.

But a few minutes later, news came over the television that Bundy had escaped from the Pitkin County Courthouse where he'd been standing trial by jumping from a second-story window above the front door of the building and racing away. He'd injured his ankle when he hit the pavement, so he couldn't run as fast as usual, gingerly favoring that foot and then—we heard later—slowing down and walking normally

so as not to attract attention to himself until he could make his
way out of town, somewhere near Shadow Mountain. During
a break in court proceedings, Bundy had asked the two officers accompanying him if he could go inside the law library to
check on something. Because Bundy had been a law student at
the University of Utah, the officers agreed, and allowed him to
enter the library alone. Bundy opened one of the windows on
the front of the building that flanked a statue of Lady Justice,
slid a few feet down the peaked stone façade roof, and leaped
to the ground. Several minutes elapsed before anyone noticed
he was missing. He had been extradited from Utah, where he
was convicted of kidnapping and assaulting a young woman
in late 1974. Shortly after that, on January 12, 1975, authorities
believed he was at the Wildwood Inn at Snowmass, where
Caryn Campbell had been vacationing with her fiancé and his
two children. Campbell had left her companions in the dining
room and taken the elevator upstairs to get something when
she vanished from the hallway, somewhere in the fifty feet between the elevator and the door to her room. Campbell's body,
we heard, was found frozen, beaten, and somewhat ravaged
by animals about a month later in a field not far from the Owl
Creek road.

* * *

Of the many attractive features Aspen offered in the 1970s, the
relative lack of crime was foremost, a crime rate so low most
of us took no notice of it at all. Aspen was a land of plenty, so
why would anyone want to steal anything? Residents seemed
so happy and well-adjusted that violent crime—other than the
occasional scuffle at The Pub—rarely occurred. When crimes
did occur, they were often petty and farcical, bungled burglar-

ies and misunderstandings fueled by alcohol. But a few crimes, some deadly and some just a grim reminder that Aspen was not immune to the maladies of society, changed the perception of Aspen as a crime-free haven.

The first violent incident I can recall involved two European chefs who worked in the kitchen at The Red Onion briefly in the early '70s. They apparently had a falling-out one afternoon, and one stabbed the other with a paring knife in the alley behind the restaurant. The altercation began in the kitchen, spilling out into the alley later that evening. No one was killed, and I can't remember if the wound was serious or not. But the incident was so unusual, so out of character for Aspen, that it shocked many of us with a somber reminder that violence *could* occur even in our beloved Rocky Mountain paradise.

Not long after that, a bag lady was seen prowling Aspen's alleys, which were anything but shadowy and menacing. My friends and I traversed alleyways all the time; they were shortcuts between streets and business establishments. We noticed the bag lady as she rummaged leisurely in the town's dumpsters, picking out items and stuffing them into a sack she had slung over her shoulder. I saw her one afternoon sorting through the large metal bins behind the Wheeler Opera House. The sight was so astonishing that she became the talk of the town for almost a week before she vanished again as mysteriously as she had appeared.

The most celebrated murder in Aspen during the 1970s occurred when French actress and singer, Claudine Longet, "accidentally" shot her lover, championship skier Spider Sabich at their expensive chalet in Starwood where the couple had been living with Longet's three children. Certainly the mood among local residents turned decidedly against Longet. It's important to note that Aspen was a ski capital and loved, above all, its ski champions, especially if they were as young and dashing as Spider Sabich. Sabich had many more admirers in Aspen than Longet, who seemed, to many, to be an outsider, someone who had ridden to fame on the coattails of her first husband, crooner Andy Williams. None of my friends were professional skiers; their interest in the sport was recreational at best. I had no way of gauging the mood inside the professional ski community, but it must have been fairly intense to color the mood of the rest of us and turn it, so vehemently, against Longet. I recall feeling she must have been guilty, and so I despised her without sufficient evidence or reason. I hadn't known either one of them before the shooting, nor did I know many people who *did* know them. I hadn't attended the trial to learn of any evidence, one way or the other. I was carried along on the tide of contempt that engulfed the town both before and after the verdict was handed down.

The event had repercussions far beyond the walls of the Roaring Fork Valley. Longet was an international celebrity, a kittenish young beauty whose mellifluous voice and delicate features made it all the more bizarre that she would ever be involved in anything as sordid as a murder, or be a murderer herself. Sabich's flame burned brighter on the ski slopes around the United States, but especially in Aspen, where he had been adopted as the town's premier athlete. Mick Jagger's song, "Claudine," openly critical of Longet and all but accusing her of premeditated murder, had to be cut from the Rolling Stones' album, *Emotional Rescue*, because it was deemed too controversial and a possible legal liability. *Saturday Night Live* performed a skit about the murder called "'The Claudine

Longet Invitational Ski Shoot." The skit featured footage of skiers falling down after wiping out during a slalom competition, accompanied by the sound of gunshots while Jane Curtin remarked to Chevy Chase: "Uh oh, he seems to have been accidentally shot by Claudine Longet!" We thought this was hilarious, and it added to our disgust for Longet, as well as our firm belief that she had murdered Sabich.

The steady whittling down of her punishment served to exacerbate our vehemence. To start, she was charged not with murder, but with reckless manslaughter, a crime which carried a maximum sentence of ten years and a thirty thousand dollar fine. This charge was then mitigated by the jury to negligent homicide, taking it from a felony to a misdemeanor, and which carried a sentence of just two years in prison and a five thousand dollar fine. In the end, the presiding judge reduced Longet's sentence to thirty days, to be served at a "time of her own choosing," and a $250 fine. Looking back, it's hard to say whether our anger was justified or if we were simply influenced by a lynch-mob mentality that had seized the town. For me, the trial quickly faded and I moved on to other considerations.

* * *

In the 1980s, two newsworthy events took place that would add to Aspen's string of sensational murder cases. The first of these, in April 1983, involved a rich businessman and politician who had moved to Aspen to live on money he'd inherited from his family (a documentary film, *Inheritance*, was later made about his life and released at the Fort Lauderdale Film Festival). I didn't know Michael Hernstadt personally, and by the time he was murdered I no longer lived in town, but I do recall that he had a reputation for high living and spreading money around. His brother, Bill, was a state senator in Nevada, and according to the *Aspen Times*, Michael Hernstadt, along with a group calling themselves "The Aspen Street Railway Company," donated six antique trolley cars to the city in hopes that a light rail system would soon be installed in order to charm locals and attract tourists. That never happened, but Hernstadt continued to live the high life until he managed to infuriate his on-again off-again friend, Keith Porter, owner of Dr. Feelgood's, a sex and head shop that was somewhat of an anomaly in a town dedicated to sport, fine food, easy living, and high culture.

Unluckily for Hernstadt, Porter had also been a sniper in Vietnam, so when the two argued at a party on Silver King Drive one coke-and-alcohol fueled night until almost six in the morning, Porter went home, retrieved his AR-15 assault rifle, and returned to take up a position on Red Butte, which overlooked the house where the party was just breaking up. When Hernstadt left the party with another friend who had offered to drive him home, Porter fired a single shot through the windshield from almost two hundred yards away, wounding Hernstadt in the chest. As the driver fled, Porter descended the Butte, firing all the way, until he reached the car, where he emptied his last clip into Hernstadt.

There were no mysterious circumstances surrounding this event, and it was certainly no accident. Porter was sentenced to eleven years in prison for committing a crime of passion, and he returned to Aspen after his release. In 1999, he was arrested for threatening to kill another man, this time brandishing a knife, at the bus station in Rubey Park. Murder had come to Aspen, finally and openly, in a big way.

* * *

It wouldn't be long before another lurid incident usurped the headlines and monopolized the town's attention. Steven Grabow cut a dashing figure in a town that was known for its style, at least among the moneyed ski set where expensive equipment and skin-tight blazing lyrca ski suits advertised a person's economic stature. Among the hippie set, he was positively freakish, with his overly-groomed appearance and gaudy attire. Flamboyant and hard to miss, Grabow had graduated with honors in finance from the University of Miami, then moved to Aspen sometime in the early '70s and began to live like a pasha by sporting almost two hundred ski suits and thirty pairs of custom-made shoes, some reportedly worth $1,200 a pair. He had a plush house in Aspen Grove on McSkimming Road, a swanky black Porche and, according to local gossip, two jeeps: one with snow tires, and one without so he'd never have to go to the trouble of changing them when the seasons turned. All of this, with "no visible means of support," according to Bob Braudis, who would later become the sheriff of Pitkin County.

The first time I saw Grabow, he was gliding through the old Paragon Bar on his way to the restaurant on the other side of the building. He was startling with slicked-back, jet black hair, puffy fur coat, fashionable calf-length boots, and a one-piece cream-colored disco suit, open to the navel and sporting gold chains against his hairy chest. He wore wrap-around sunglasses, and exhibited a tan as deep and uniform as a cordovan shoe. I almost laughed out loud, at the sight of someone so out of place. Apart from casual sightings, I had no reason to think much of Grabow one way or the other.

When he wound up the victim of a car bombing in the

parking lot of the Aspen Club, the town took notice. Accidents and crimes of passion aside, this was a premeditated murder. A pipe bomb had been placed underneath the seat of one of his jeeps, detonated by remote control. Unfortunately for him, the bomb shifted slightly when he abruptly backed up, and he was not killed instantly. The jeep did not burst into flames, nor fly apart. Instead, a small sliver of metal rocketed through the floor and into Grabow's body, causing excruciating pain and a flow of blood that would kill him within the hour. By the time police and paramedics showed up, he was staggering around the parking lot in shock. The paramedics rushed him to Aspen Valley Hospital, where he died "a particularly ugly death," according to a 2009 *Aspen Sojourner* magazine article.

At the time, Grabow had been under federal indictment for importing somewhere between twenty-five and thirty-five million dollars of cocaine a year into the Roaring Fork Valley. According to the government, Grabow had been the lynchpin in a drug ring that included several other Aspenites, who eventually pleaded guilty in order to receive lighter sentences. But not Grabow, who had continued to insist on his innocence up to the time of his death. When agents raided his home on January 9, 1984, almost a year before his indictment and a month before the bombing, they impounded $1.4 million in hard cash, the Porsche, two jeeps, and 243 Krugerrands, but found little in the way of drugs, either in Grabow's house or in the houses of other suspects in his ring. The Grabow case has never been solved, neither his alleged activities as a local drug lord nor his murder in the parking lot of the Aspen Club. When police arrested Ron Young in Florida almost twenty years later for the car bombing in 1996 of a man in Tucson, Arizona, they thought they might be able to connect him with Grabow's murder. The circumstances were similar, and according to an Aspen police officer investigating the case, Young and Grabow "ran in the same circles, and they knew a lot of the same people." But circumstantial evidence is never an effective way to build a case for murder, and police were unable to tie the two cases together. Grabow left no children behind, and his widow eventually married the actor James Caan.

* * *

All the notorious cases aside, nothing would affect Aspen so immediately, and so personally, as the Ted Bundy escape from the Pitkin County Courthouse on June 7, 1977. After he made his way through town and up Aspen Mountain, Bundy took shelter in an abandoned miner's cabin as scores of Aspen police and volunteers combed the area in hopes of recapturing him and bringing him back to stand trial for the murder of Caryn Campbell. (While investigating murders in Utah the previous year, a detective searched Bundy's apartment in Salt Lake City and found a guide to Colorado ski resorts, with a check mark by the Wildwood Inn in Snowmass, from which Campbell had been abducted.) Ultimately, it was revealed that Bundy had been attempting to make his way over the mountains to Crested Butte and from there, planned to flee the state altogether. We heard, too, that Bundy had come upon hikers and asked them for directions, and that he had encountered one of the armed searchers and somehow talked his way out of being arrested.

While he was missing after the Aspen escape, a pall of terror settled over the town and no one was quite sure what would happen next. While Bundy traipsed through the mountains trying to make his way over to Crested Butte, sprained ankle and all, we huddled together in the town below, preparing ourselves for the worst. I remember locking the doors and windows in Joyce's house before going to bed, listening for noises outside the window, though I don't know what I would have done if I had heard any. Many Aspenites owned guns and kept them loaded should Bundy try to enter their homes. We talked of nothing else in the bars at night but his escape and whether or not he had been caught, or speculating about how or when the police would catch him. The men in town were less apprehensive than the women, because Bundy had never assaulted and killed a man. I kept a knife in my night stand, just in case.

For a week, the suspense was palpable, and picking up someone in a bar was never easier. Single women approached men at closing time and asked to be taken home. It may have been a macabre joke, but the fear was real. Had we known that Bundy was stumbling around the ridges of Aspen Mountain, half-starved and living on berries, leaves, grass, anything he could find, we might have breathed more easily. But as the event unfolded, we imagined him still in town, hiding in someone's garage or inside someone's home, crouched in a closet and just waiting to spring out to collect a few more victims.

In the end, the reality was far more prosaic.

Weak and disoriented after six days on the mountain, Bundy made his way back down into the valley somewhere east of town toward Independence Pass, possibly around Lupine Drive or North Star Drive. As I heard it, he managed to steal someone's Cadillac and was driving it back into town just after dawn when two Aspen cops pulled the Cadillac over as it wove erratically down the highway from lane to lane. According to local accounts, the officer, a woman, approached the car and recognized Bundy.

"Oh, hi Ted," she was reported to have said. "Get out of the car. You're under arrest."

As it turned out, this was not to be the end of Bundy's murderous rampage. Anxious that the Pitkin County jail was not secure enough to hold him—after all he had escaped from the courthouse already, embarrassing Aspen and the local authorities—Bundy was transferred down valley to the Garfield County Jail in Glenwood Springs. Yet Bundy outwitted Garfield County as well; he would escape *again*. He lost enough weight that he was able to slither out a heating vent in the ceiling of his cell before fleeing to Florida. There, he killed three more women before being apprehended for good. The Bundy episode would become part of local lore, but at least no murder had been committed on Pitkin County's watch. Everyone was thankful for that, and dismayed to learn of Bundy's further crimes in Florida. "It could have been one of us," was the unspoken response to these new, gruesome revelations when they appeared in the news. I remember feeling outraged and a bit ashamed that three more women had had to die. We had him, dead to rights. And we let him break free.

Local Color

Like any other small town, Aspen had its peculiar interests and odd local events. In order to celebrate their unique character and make use of whatever assets the local scene has to offer, small towns will often distinguish themselves by presenting annual contests or festivals that may not be found anywhere else. These events are broadcast from signs or billboards tourists spy immediately as they enter the precincts of the town. Strangers might be excited to know, for instance, that here, in this very spot, the 20*th* *Annual Knitting Festival* or *Pawpaw Eating Contest*, is about to commence, or glory in the fact that they are entering *The Ball Bearing Capital of the World*. Aspen displayed no such signs, which would have betrayed the city's basic anti-mercantile ethos: no buildings over three stories so as not to block the beauty of Red Mountain or the ski runs on Aspen Mountain, and the prohibition against neon to save downtown streets from looking like San Francisco or New York. But Aspen harbored its own homegrown, provincial pleasures and outlandish entertainments. It wouldn't be Aspen if it didn't.

The Soap Box Derby took place one spring on the steep hill

beyond Lift #1, sponsored by the Aspen Art Museum with the
hope of sparking creativity amongst Aspen's would-be artistic
residents. There wasn't anything particularly unique about Aspen's version of this annual American classic, except that the
contestants were all adults, who went to great lengths to construct soapboxes reflecting their own adult passions. The su-
per-sized Stoly bottle was just one of many colorful projectiles
that hurtled down the slope of South Aspen Street, miniature
juggernauts riding the implacable law of gravity. And the contestants and spectators alike clutched beer cans or sipped mi-
mosas out of champagne flutes, because it was not yet noon
and it would be unseemly to drink anything harder. The smell
of marijuana permeated the air, dissipating in the sunlight that
was just beginning to creep over the edge of Shadow Mountain. There was a classic entry in the form of an old European
racing car, which was made of solid rubber wheels and painted
lath. Someone else had cobbled together a soapbox that resembled a huge roller skate on which the driver lay supine wearing a helmet and goggles, steering precariously with his feet by
nudging the front axle this way and that as the whole contraption rocketed downhill to a rousing volley of applause. The
event portrayed was a determination to remain defiantly playful and child-like at all costs. The costs might have been high
had anyone shot off the course into a tree, or worse, into a giddy, semi-alert spectator. But no such tragedy occurred. Perhaps
the potential for such an accident may have persuaded the museum to drop it after a number of years.

* * *

The annual Fourth of July parade continues to celebrate the
advent of summer on the Western Slope. Here again, Aspen

is not unique in sponsoring a parade to commemorate the nation's birthday, but in the 1970s, everything about it—floats, activities, people—was unconventional. The parade would begin somewhere near Paepcke Park at noon, file up Main Street past the Hotel Jerome, and thread its way around a few downtown streets before returning to the Jerome, where it would take a turn down the hill toward Rio Grande Park to dissolve for another year. Announcers and judges would sit in chairs on the balcony of the Jerome, bellowing through microphones as they watched the spectacle unfold below, while others would throw water balloons from the windows at their favorite targets, enemies or friends.

Floats were sponsored by various businesses and were slap-dash affairs, jerry-rigged pickup trucks or small platforms pulled by trucks, largely devoid of decoration unless festooned with bunting and banners cheerily announcing their sponsors. People on the floats threw candy to the sparse crowd that was gathered for one block between Carl's Pharmacy and the intersection of Main and South Mill Streets. I always stood in front of the *Aspen Times* and watched the fire department tanker spraying the judges as it passed by.

It was mostly farce, reminiscent of a circus parade complete with clowns and horns, pretty girls, and the mayor in a gleaming open convertible waving to the crowd. The Aspen State Teacher's College Band would stagger past, beating on pots and pans with spoons while others tapped aluminum beer cans together to mark time and someone else crashed garbage can lids together as cymbals. Onlookers would stand at the curb, clutching beer cans they'd plucked from icy coolers. A few parents hoisted children on their shoulders for a better view, while dogs threaded their way among the many-legged crowd. An occasional firecracker would fizzle and pop. It was burlesque, parody, an Aspenized version of a real Fourth of July parade. Later, as dusk settled over the Roaring Fork Valley, a larger crowd would assemble in Wagner Park to watch the fireworks as they burst above Aspen Mountain. But the parade was always a truer gauge of the town's idiosyncrasies for me, a reflection of its harlequin soul.

* * *

In the very heart of winter, another event occasioned parades and celebrations, quickly becoming an Aspen tradition. Brain-child of a couple of civic-minded residents who were sitting around the empty barroom of the Hotel Jerome one dreary January in 1951, Wintersköl (originally called "Aspen Winter Carnival") was created to fill a gap in the town's business cycle, the precarious drop in profits that occurred each year in January. Klaus Christ, owner of the Golden Horn Restaurant, told me that sixty percent of his business happened at the end of December, then all but vanished until spring skiing started up again in mid-February and March. Clearly, something had to be done to lure tourists back into town during what would otherwise have been a dead season, even though the snow was as good as ever and the city's establishments stood ready to serve visitors.

Wintersköl, then, featured two main events: a parade that wound its way through the downtown area from the base of Little Nell via Cooper and Hyman Streets heading, this time, toward the Jerome Hotel; and a torchlight descent that began soon after dark on the slope of Little Nell, when a line of skiers brandishing flares would spiral down the mountain in a long continuous loop of light. Bars and restaurants would pitch in, offering Wintersköl specials trumped up for the event, wild boar or suckling pig, caribou steak, anything to draw tourists back to the valley. Spectators would teeter on the curb, their bellies full of hot-spiced wine, as the parade rumbled past, its revelers stuffed into parkas and warm wool hats and beating loudly on pots with spoons and spatulas to raise a festive din. Scott Myers remembers riding in the back of a pickup truck with fellow musician Pat Flynn—they called themselves "Crossroads" then—playing up a storm, until someone who was positioned on a roof hurled an icy snowball, hitting Flynn squarely in the head and almost knocked him out cold.

Wintersköl was a far less sophisticated affair than it is today; then, it relied on the creativity of Aspen locals to make something loud and flashy and fun happen to fill an otherwise frigid Colorado night. Though Wintersköl began in 1951 as a "toast to winter" and to "celebrate Aspen's unique Nordic lifestyle," it remains a profitable event with its roots in the business community. In the 1970s, it was an uproarious affair with a small town flavor and a slapped-together air.

* * *

There were other events, too. "The Little Woody Creek Cross Country Ski Race and Dope Smoke" in 1972. The annual "Best Breast Bash," which is described by the blog Tru TV as a "racy but guileless celebration of the female anatomy." I didn't attend either of these events and so cannot attest to their veracity, but the descriptions I've heard have the hokey, thrown-together, down-home ring of early Aspen that inclines me to believe they did exist, but have long since vanished into the annals of history or memory or both.

Overall, Aspen locals detested the town's visiting Texans

and would often voice disdain for the loud, brash, demanding
tourists from Dallas, Fort Worth, and Houston who swarmed
up during ski season. To be fair, there was more than a bit
of hypocrisy involved in this display of disdain, since Aspen
thrived in part on the dollars that Texans spent liberally
in its restaurants, hotels, and saloons. So for the most part, locals would grit their teeth, roll their eyes, and extract as much
cash as possible from their boorish clients, mocking them in
private and longing for the day they would return to the Lone
Star State. Still, resentments simmered. There had to be a way
to vent those grievances in a socially acceptable way, some ca-
thartic ritual that could leave both sides satisfied.

The event that was contrived to satisfy this grudge took
place on the other side of Independence Pass, in the diminutive town of Twin Lakes. Twin Lakes had been a transporta-
tion hub for miners who traveled between Leadville and Ute
City. Following a model created in the little Spanish town of
Bunolin, where every year over one hundred thousand tons
of tomatoes are hurled by tens of thousands of people at each
other for two full hours, someone in Aspen came up with the
idea of the Great Tomato Wars, which pitted Colorado against
Texas and took place in the lakeside meadows and alder groves
just across Highway 82 from the general store in Twin Lakes
Village. I was sent to investigate the event and write about it as
western slope correspondent for *Rolling Stock*, a left-leaning literary tabloid published by writing professors at the University
of Colorado. The tomato war was an all-out melee. A couple
of dump trucks delivered the tomatoes, stacked high in wood-
en crates, and the fruits were distributed among the warring
parties and around the battlefield at strategic points. There
were officials in black T-shirts with the word "Spotter" embla-

zoned in red letters. The spotters paced like referees at the Super Bowl, ready for the battle to begin. Whistles dangled from cords around their necks. Part of the spotters' job was to stop the action in case of a foul or if someone got hurt. Their other function was to pronounce a player "dead" and out of the game once they had been spattered with enough red tomato juice. Once a contestant was "dead," he or she was relegated to the sidelines.

The two "armies," distinguished by different colored T-shirts, squared off in the meadow and waited for the signal. Once the first tomato had been hurled, all sense of order and civility broke down as contestants ran about wildly, hiding among the alders to ambush their enemies, or stood firm in pitched battles as each side pelted the other with juicy tomatoes. The fracas resembled nothing so much as a snowball fight except for all the "blood," and sweaty faces under the relentless July sun. I strolled across the battlefield calmly, surveying the carnage. I was safe, neutral in my white T-Shirt, the word PRESS in black letters across my chest.

I was impressed by the energy and passion with which the participants carried on the fight. If this was an affair contrived to vent the suppressed fury of two communities through a simulation of war, it also seemed remarkably "real." Participants took it seriously enough to equip themselves (some even had Walkie Talkies), plan and strategize, and curse vehemently when they were eliminated. Within an hour, everyone was completely splattered with tomato pulp, and the event was called as a draw. Those who remained washed themselves with the hose of a tanker truck, then repaired to the Inn of the Black Wolfe for a bite to eat, and to drink round after round of beer until evening settled over the lakes with a perceptible chill.

* * *

A more personal event took place when musician Michael Iceberg decided we ought to invite our parents to Aspen for a day or two, thereby transforming the town so that none of the sex, drugs, drinking or other behavior would be noticeable; Aspen would appear to be just another small American town going about its daily business, not the madcap community it actually was. This charade would include everyone, a city-wide effort to stage "Parent's Day." Residents would clean themselves up: new haircuts, laundered clothes, ties and dresses, shined shoes and starched shirts, the whole conventional milieu that would falsify reality while representing middle-America. Iceberg had noticed that no one among the working ex-hippie crowd ever mentioned parents, much less invited any of them to town. No one seemed, in fact, to *have* parents, or even a family, as though we were all orphans or aliens living crazily in our mountain hideaway, with no ties to the outside world. Most of my friends even chose to remain in Aspen to work during Thanksgiving and Christmas when the money was prevalent and the skiing was at its best. It wasn't that we didn't love our parents or remember where we'd come from or who we were. Our families just weren't part of our lives in Aspen

Iceberg and I went around trying to convert others to our grandiose plan, thinking it would be a fabulous joke, a vast municipal skit that might become an annual event. In the end, people laughed at our foolishness. Iceberg and I wound up inviting our own mothers, who proved to be better sports than we anticipated. The rest of the town went on with its revels, from which we shielded our mothers as well as we could. They smiled politely and looked the other way.

* * *

Another of Iceberg's bright ideas might have resulted in some
actual money—big money—had we been able to carry it off,
and had it not been crushed by one of America's large cor-
porations. The profit motive was inimical to our hippie aes-
thetic, but this scheme promised to be quick and easy, and if
we could pull it off we'd be millionaires overnight and never
have to work again! Or so we thought, in our naïve, hippie-ish
way. Iceberg, who had children by his first wife back home in
Illinois, noticed the toy trucks his kids loved to play with—
small replicas of real cars, graders, and dump trucks—made
by the Tonka Toy Company in Mound, Minnesota. There was
a capitalistic adage: *Whoever dies with the most toys, wins!* This
turned out to be prescient, heading, as we turned out to be, toward the Reagan era. Iceberg gathered a group of us to reveal
the idea, and to ask us to serve on the board of directors. We
met at the Jerome Hotel bar: Iceberg's wife, Nancy, me, and
Ron Sievert. We all called Ron "Seymour." He was an affable,
bearded follower of Guru Maharishi Mahesh Yogi, and was a
student of both accounting and the law.

"Everyone likes toys, right?" Iceberg began. "If we make
these decals, huge replicas of the Tonka Toy logo, people can
put them on real cars, trucks, even private planes. We could
sell millions of them without much effort."

"And manufacturing them?" I asked.

"Not a problem." Iceberg replied. "Decals are easy to make
and we could size them for cars, trucks, planes, railroad engines.
All we have to find is someone to make them. That shouldn't be
too hard. People sell all kinds of personalized stuff. T-shirts, coffee mugs, baseball caps. Decals are easy and cheap. They're just
thin sheets of plastic with some glue on the back."

That sounded reasonable, and we nodded our assent.

"Here's what we have to do," Iceberg continued. "Seymour, you and I will write up an ad to place in the *Aspen Times*, just a classified, to announce the decals—'*Life-sized decals for your adult toys!*' or something like that, with an Aspen postal address so we can see how many people respond. '*Put them on your Porsche, your Lear jet, your pickup truck!*' A kind of marketing survey. Then we'll sit back and see what happens. If we get enough orders, we'll find someone to manufacture them and we're in business."

I was skeptical, but if the joke caught on and people took to the idea, it might become a fad, even for a short time. Crazier things have happened, I told myself. So I went along with the idea, if only half-heartedly. Iceberg had some plausibility, having been a successful businessman back in Illinois before he let his hair grow long, left his wife and kids, and went on the road as the itinerant musician known as Michael Iceberg and his Fabulous Iceberg Machine. He had a mountain of keyboards, amplifiers, Chamberlains, Mellotrons, synthesizers, speakers, switches, levers and pedals, all of which allowed him to reproduce the sounds of an entire orchestra, live onstage, by himself.

Back in Joliet, he'd owned and operated a successful business that sold pianos and organs out of his Music World store. He'd once sponsored a piano-playing contest to see how long contestants could play the instrument without passing out. One mother kept her daughter in the competition even though she had a heart condition, but when Iceberg found out, he disqualified her. Another time, he sponsored a promotional stunt called "The Amazing Race" long before the reality show appeared on TV in 2001. Iceberg's race was the real thing, albeit

a zany affair, the only rule being that no form of onboard pro-
pulsion would be allowed on any of the racing machines. According to Iceberg, one contestant pedaled a contraption all the
way from Joliet to Lockport and back using only his leg muscles as propellant, while a truck with a fan strapped to its bumper pushed another vehicle with a sail down the road in front
of it, gliding placidly along like a schooner on the high seas.
In towns along the way, mayors gave speeches and children
flocked to see the carnival of jerry-built machines labor past
in quest of the thousand dollar prize. Local media covered the
event, following it by the hour along its predetermined route.
Anyone who could do that had some credibility as far as I was
concerned, and investing a few bucks in a classified ad didn't
seem too risky. So we wrote our ad, toasted our enterprise,
and took the napkin on which we'd composed the classified
next door to the *Aspen Times*.

A few days later, we reconvened at the Jerome to read the
ad together and celebrate our new endeavor. There was our ad,
our chance to see if anyone in town might be interested in the
decals. It was Seymour's task to check the mailbox, and after
a week, we'd begun to lose heart. Not a single inquiry had arrived, not a single order for what we thought was a humorous
and creative way to make money honestly and without harm-
ing either another person, or the environment. In the second
week, a letter arrived, but not the letter we'd wished for. It was
written on official letterhead from the Tonka Toy Company,
and though I don't recall the exact wording, the gist was clear.
We were to cease and desist in using the Tonka name and/or
logo, and if we didn't, legal action would be taken. We looked
across the table at one another, shaking our heads in disbelief.
How in the world had the Tonka Toy Company, in *Minnesota*,

discovered our plans, especially since that announcement had been limited to a small independent paper in a little town in the middle of a huge mountain range? Was it possible that Tonka employed spies, not only in large metropolitan areas, but in every hamlet across America, spies ready to pounce? This went beyond acute paranoia into nightmares of Big Brother and universal surveillance on the most minute level. We concluded that because Aspen was an international ski resort, someone from Tonka must have been visiting town over the Christmas holidays and had subsequently come across our ad over a cup of morning coffee. We scratched our heads and ordered another round of drinks. I imagined millions of dollars with white feathery wings lifting out of the Roaring Fork Valley to make their way south over the Elk Mountain Range, flocks of unreachable, migrating birds.

* * *

The ultimate hoax, however, had to have been the founding of Aspen State Teacher's College in 1974, the "No-Credit Fun College of the Rockies." This was a spoof that was so elaborate and plausible that it apparently drew at least a few real students to Colorado each fall, students who'd had the intention of matriculating among the peaks and crags of the Western Slope. Imagine the letters they must have sent to their parents back home after realizing they'd been tricked, and then announcing their intention to stay in Aspen anyhow, requesting money. Bruce Berger remembers that one of the gubernatorial candidates running for reelection at that time was asked for increased funding for the illusory school and promised to deliver it, which made for colorful headlines around the state once the ploy was discovered. A few enterprising locals used

Aspen State Teacher's College Student IDs around the country to obtain discounts from unwary businesses, thereby combining real spending power with extravagant comic delusion. The ASTC hoax was so deeply imagined, well-developed, and executed that it was able to draw in the dubious with the gullible, creating a farce that is still admired for its resourcefulness to this day.

Aspen had a real educational institution, a branch of Colorado Mountain College, directed by Janet Landry. It had offices in the Wheeler Opera House but no real campus, at least none that I recall. While today's campus is located in the Airport Business Center, across the highway from Sardy Field, in the 1970s, classes were held in various places in town. In my tenure in Aspen, I'd met very few people who'd actually attended classes at CMC, though that didn't mean much since I spent most of my time cloistered in my office, planning literary events, oblivious to the outside world.

It was entirely possible to mistake the grounds of the Aspen Institute for Humanistic Studies for a college, set as it was on the edge of town, and with a number of administrative buildings, seminar halls, tennis courts, a restaurant and an auditorium. Sometime in the early '80s, the University of Colorado actually considered purchasing the Aspen Institute and turning it into a satellite location. But in general, it was Aspen itself—the entire town—that inspired two entrepreneurial jesters, Marc Demmon and Al Pendorf, later joined by Jim Furniss, to establish the jape that would draw thousands of participants and result in the sale of sweatshirts, coffee mugs, pennants, bumper stickers, and other paraphernalia, all bearing the faux-emblem of the school: a pair of crossed skis bisected by a broom, flanked by an aspen leaf and a mug of beer. One of the founders, Al Pendorf, was a printer so it was easy for him to produce a magazine, *Clean Sweep*, that bore all the pertinent school news, as well as a *Handbook* with a "campus" map of Aspen's important locations in town, as well as a list of classes. The class descriptions were prime examples of the trio's imagination and high spirits:

SKI INSTRUCTOR ACCENTS 222
This series of seminars will give the student an insight on how to impress his or her ski school class by creatively using either an Austrian, French, or Scandinavian accent. Assoc. Prof. Hans Schtupp.

FLUID MECHANICS 101
This course teaches the student how to mechanically deal with the elementary fluids of his or her environment; i.e., draft beer, tequila, and peppermint schnapps. Lunch not offered during lab time. Prof. Kelly Hooker.

And finally, a practical course anyone in Aspen might have wanted to take:

SEASONAL PARKING 341
How to maintain a downtown parking space all day is the primary objective of this study. The erasure of tire chalk marks and techniques of shifting vehicle position within its space will be studied in detail. Prof. P. K. Meter.

* * *

Aspen's resemblance to a college campus had been noticed by many during the 1970s, including Michi Blake, who tried to interest Bland Nesbit, a reporter at the *Aspen Times*, in producing an annual "class yearbook" with the photographs of everyone

in town. But it was up to Demmon, Pendorf, and Furniss to ac-
tualize the idea of Aspen as an exclusive, high-spirited school
by adhering to a simple guiding principal: "The whole town
is a college. Classes are taught everywhere." Since Aspen was
populated mostly by young people barely out of college themselves, and who had brought with them not only degrees but
minds and bodies forged in the factories of America's higher
educational system, it didn't take a forbidding act of imagination to see the town's apartments, lodges, and condominium
complexes as dormitories for the "student body," or to visual-
ize the summer softball leagues and Rugby club as the school's
"teams," or Wagner Park as the "athletic field" where contests
of great passion and import took place on a regular basis. Nor
was it hard to envision Aspen's bookstores as places where appropriate "texts" might be purchased, or to see the ASTC offices
under what is now Pacifica restaurant as the "student union."
Aspen lent itself to interpretation and parody, a place of social
experiment and self-invention that had been at the core of its
character since its rebirth in the late '40s and early '50s, when
Walter Paepcke dreamed of it as a proving ground for his concept of the whole man.

   In keeping with its transformational spirit, then, Demmon
changed his name to "Slats Cabbage," while his co-conspira-
tors, Pendorf and Furniss, changed their names to "Fulton Be-
glely, III" (Dean of the College), and "Harold Center," respectively. They viewed everything that happened in town through
the lens of their magnificent ruse. Even now, after thirty years,
Aspen State Teacher's College retains some of its original wit
and allure, maintaining an online presence where people can
exchange memories and recall participating in this most complex of practical jokes.

* * *

The ASTC prank gave rise to others, like the Aspen Yacht Club
and its annual regatta race on Ruedi Reservoir, completed in
1968 when the headwaters of the Frying Pan and Roaring Fork
Rivers were successfully dammed in order to divert water for
the Arkansas basin on the eastern slope. Recently celebrating
its fortieth anniversary, the Aspen Yacht Club was conceived
of as a joke by Fritz Benedict in response to the founding of
Aspen State Teacher's College in the late 1960s. It was meant
as another hoax, but the yacht club soon became a strange reality as enthusiasts joined and began to glide above the serene
waters of Ruedi Reservoir eighteen miles up the valley from
the town of Basalt. It's quite a sight on a clear Colorado day—
a group of small boats, spinnakers bellying to the wind, under the evergreen-clad mountains that surround the lake high
above the Roaring Fork Valley. It would be about as surprising for a group of sailors on Cape Cod to establish a mountain climbing club with little but the surrounding sand dunes
to scale. Fritz Benedict owned fifteen acres of land on the
shores of the reservoir, and allowed his property to be used as
a launching point for the "yachts."

The water directly off this land has been dubbed "Benedict Bay" in honor of the group's beneficiary and founder. Now
sporting its own website, the club has sixty-five members and
an annual schedule of events from June until September, when
the lake is not ice-bound. I drove up to Ruedi one frigid winter day, and walked out on the ice to see what the lake was like
at the very dregs of the year. The ice was covered with a foot
of fresh snow, and the glare was blinding under a clear blue
sky. Almost total silence gripped the valley. I tried to imagine
boats cutting through the water where I stood, and the flash

of sails along the far shore. I cleared a patch of snow away and got down on my knees to peer through the ice into the depths below, where I fancied I saw a trout winnow past, its flanks splashed with color and sprinkled with stars. I briefly experienced the illusion of complete solitude such as the early settlers must have felt when they reached the valley in the nineteenth century, before a single house or roadway had been built. My spirit withered at the thought of such unrelenting isolation. But Reudi in winter is no place for dawdling and I returned to my car and drove back down the valley for hot spiced wine at the Frying Pan Inn and a few minutes of borrowed warmth in front of the fire.

In a singular example of a double comical payback, the Aspen State Teacher's College held an annual regatta of their own on the tiny artificial streams that flow through Hyman Street mall, wending their way among aspen trees and banks of planted sod. As these streams are no more than six inches wide, the "yachts" involved had to be smaller than a hand's width and set with diminutive sails the size of cocktail napkins. I watched one such regatta on a sunny afternoon in July, as groups of yacht owners raced alongside the streams cheering their boats on to victory at the far end of the mall while tourists gaped in amazement. Bruce Berger participated in a regatta on the pond in Glory Hole Park, where he and a friend launched a boat called Interpid (sic) to sail alongside the other craft. In any case, the double joke was a joke itself and might have metastasized into more examples of cross-referencing humor had there not been so many other things to occupy our time, like holding down full-time jobs. We had only so much time for this kind of foolishness. Our time might have been fractured, but our lives were full.

* * *

I suppose it was inevitable that someone would seek to record those lives, not as they were but in a farcical way reflecting the self-mocking spirit of the era. If the founders of Aspen State Teachers College noticed how much Aspen resembled a college campus, someone at Grass Roots TV noticed how much the town's public life, and the private lives of its citizens, resembled a soap opera. Accordingly, *The Edge of Ajax* appeared for a brief period of time, a series of hastily written, cheaply produced shows using local actors in an attempt to parody Aspen's legendary social scene. Many of us were struck by its crude, amateurish, low-tech quality, which is why I was secretly drawn to it while smiling outwardly at its distinct lack of sophistication. At least the producers of *The Edge of Ajax* had their tongues thrust firmly into their cheeks, and they knew what they were producing was parody—not only of "serious" soap operas on the major networks, but of Aspen's growing superficiality and glitz as restaurants, shops, and night clubs increasingly resembled Rodeo Drive as the decade advanced. This is in contradistinction to the more recent television series, *Secrets of Aspen*, and its glossy, overproduced weekly installments that make no attempt at parody, presenting its episodes as if they defined life in Aspen in some essential way. The staged aftershow interviews, which are really more of the same, are unintentional parodies of themselves. *The Edge of Ajax* aspired to nothing so lofty. It was all about fun, not money, which must invariably take itself seriously because of the risks involved.

* * *

The residents of Aspen during the 1970s had a sense of the absurd, a quixotic take on life that revealed a tragicomic view of

things. It seemed then, as it must seem to every new generation, that the world was winding down and that we might be
coming to the end of things. Or, at the very least, the country
might be coming apart. War, recession, racial violence, poverty, disease, assassination, rampant corruption: the 1960s had
been a time of extremes and it appeared to those of us who had
lived through those years that the only possible life-asserting
reaction might be laughter and self-mockery. Music was a consolation, like whistling past the graveyard. Drugs were medi-
cation, and might possibly lead us through psychic wormholes
to another universe.

Dressing up and pretending to be other than what we were
was yet another way to deal with the oppressive reality of
things as we saw them. We knew we were living an illusion
and that Aspen didn't represent the real world. "To educate
through observation of real life experience," was one of the
Aspen State Teacher's College's most telling mottoes. If Aspen
were a mirage, what better way to inhabit it than to take on
new roles for ourselves, and how best to honor it than with
curiosity and laughter? We knew it couldn't last, but while it
did, a sense of irony and a good imagination were crucial. For
a while, anything seemed possible. Oh, how we laughed as the
parade passed by.

Gimme Shelter

Illusion can be an uncomfortable condition in which to live as the years begin to add up to a big, empty dream. Perhaps for that reason, people in Aspen proved susceptible to many New Age philosophies that were finding adherents all over the country. Almost no one I knew followed any organized religion, but there must have been enough believers to justify the existence of the three or four churches that waited for parishioners on Sunday mornings when the sun rose over Independence Pass to illuminate the town.

Scott Myers was an ordained minister, having successfully finished Yale Divinity School and worked with the congregation at the Community Church on the corner of Bleeker and Aspen Streets. Built in 1890, the sandstone church features a turret on one corner of the building, which gives it the imposing look of a medieval castle. The Community Church began its long service as a Presbyterian church, switching to Methodism in the 1930s, and by the 1970s, was probably hosting as many secular events as religious services. I used the sanctuary upstairs as a venue for conference readings, and recall listening to Nobel Laureate Joseph Brodsky there, as well as Czech immunologist and poet Miroslav Holub, Allen Ginsberg, and the director of the Naropa Institute, Anne Waldman, who waved her arms and chanted her poem, "Skin Meat Bone" in a high, keening voice while the audience looked on, astonished. The sanctuary was used for all kinds of concerts, occasional lectures, and sometimes even plays, making it a truly communal venue.

"Not many people in Aspen were interested in traditional religion," according to Scott Myers, "but it was a town full of seekers, people who considered themselves spiritual in one way or another, which probably came out of their backgrounds as hippies. This kind of New Age spirituality also had its roots in the beauty of the place, the Roaring Fork Valley, and the mountain environment. I could never figure out why people would pay good money to investigate all these New Age philosophies without ever darkening the door of a church for free! When I'd talk with them, they preached to me more than I did to them. They were full of ideas about various practices and philosophies. The worst were people who thought cocaine was some sort of accessory to enlightenment, that it crystallized the truth. But in general, people in Aspen kept away from the church, because it was viewed as part of the establishment.

"There were never more than a hundred people at a service, and usually fewer. Half of the congregation were visitors on vacation for skiing, and the other half were old Aspenites who'd been coming for years. But the church in Aspen served some valuable functions not otherwise normally associated with the regular service. For instance, divorces. Someone even came up with a ritual ceremony for divorce (a kind of reverse image of the marriage ceremony) whereby you stood on the

banks of the Roaring Fork River and, after declaring your un-
vows, you'd tear them up and toss the pieces into the water to
be carried off downstream. Also, whenever someone died—in
ski accidents, or plane crashes—they'd look to the church in
terms of funeral services. So the church played some part in
the life of the town, but not much."

I passed St. Mary's Catholic Church on East Main Street
for years, but hardly ever saw the big front doors open. Attendance might surge during Christmas and Easter, which drew
a larger crowd, but St. Mary's was often used as a venue for
secular events, while catechism classes, baptisms, communion, and confession must have kept the church going the rest
of the year. St. Mary's provided crucial community services
by hosting weekly Alcoholic Anonymous meetings, and providing meals, shelter, and showers to itinerant hippies and ski
bums who might be down on their luck. There is a fine stone
rectory that stands on the corner of East Main and S. Hunter
Streets behind a quaint metal fence, surrounded by lilac bush-
es that bloom every spring and which draw congregations of
their own, clouds of insatiable honeybees. On Sunday mornings you could hear the bells in the square wooden steeple that
straddles the peak of the roof ring out over the town, though I
always heard in them a mournful, desperate note. The church
itself is an imposing building of brick, with vertical buttresses
set into the exterior walls, and arched windows with sandstone
ledges cut from quarries down valley in Basalt. Such a mountain of brick can appear rather lugubrious on gloomy days, forbidding, even, as old churches sometimes do. A white wooden
cross surmounts the steeple, a warning and a benediction to all
who will cast their eyes upward as they pass.

* * *

The Jehovah's Witnesses Kingdom Hall stands now beside highway 82 on the outskirts of town, but if I remember correctly, their first Hall was located somewhere in the tangle of streets that lie beyond Heron Park. Whoever you are, wherever you live, the Witnesses will appear one morning at your door, respectfully trying to convert you to their apocalyptic point of view by thrusting a copy of *The Watchtower* into your hands. If you aren't home, they will leave *The Watchtower* on your doorstep as a calling card. In an article he wrote about the early years of the Aspen Writers' Conference, Bruce Berger recounts how he and the poet Jane Shore were in his carport, about to leave in his Jeep, when a pair of Witnesses abruptly accosted them. Shooing them away, Bruce turned to Jane, who remarked: "What a missed opportunity! You should have pretended to rape me, or said, 'Oh, we don't live here, we're just robbing the house. Would you help us carry out the TV?'" Proselytizing from door-to-door may work for some, but for others it can be an outright nuisance and cause hard feelings. Bruce relates: "In the late '60s I lost my best friend in Aspen to them—one day he approached me in the mall with a German-accented teammate, both in dry-cleaned sweaters and trying to lay the Word on me, and I left running and reached the house in tears." Sometimes (most of the time) my own friends could not find out where I lived as I kept moving season after season from place to place, but that did not daunt the Witnesses. Wherever I lived—apartment, guest house, trailer, tent— smartly-dressed representatives of Jehovah would invariably find me and attempt to recruit me as a fellow booster for the End of Days.

* * *

The church that strikes me as the most spectacular sits on top
of a small hill just off Highway 82 as you enter Aspen from
the west. Built by Mennonites and dedicated in June, 1968, the
Prince of Peace Chapel is a model of Aspen's gregarious, ecu-
menical spirit. It is a temple to no faith, or all faiths, and prides
itself as a center for progressive theology and "creative forms
of worship." Its square, rugged steeple, made of local stone,
towers above the surrounding land and always looked like
something out of Germany or the Swiss Alps. The rock walls
of its sanctuary are set with vertical stained glass windows,
which avoid any clear depiction of traditional religious icons.
You have to look closely to see the abstracted figures of Jesus
or other saints. Crossed wooden beams overhead hint at vault-
ed cathedral ceilings, and a second story of glass is arranged in
varying-sized squares and rectangles to allow the sun in from
above. The effect is like a vitreous canvas of Vasarelli cubes,
or Mondrian's geometric shapes. Here almost any religious
faith might practice its rites in peace without getting in another's way. The Prince of Peace Chapel is often used for artistic
events. Its chapel has a permanent art gallery. I used the chapel for a couple of years in the mid-'70s as a venue for poetry
readings. I have a clear picture of poet Peter Sears standing at
the podium in June, 1976, reading his distinctly un-theological
poem, "The Lady Who Got Me to Say So Long Mom" as the
audience listened, rapt as any congregation.

* * *

Perhaps because it was an irreligious place in the '70s, and because the spirit yearns for some source of comfort and satisfac-
tion if it cannot find it in traditional theologies, Aspen became

fertile ground for the New Age movement. Erhard Sensory Training, or EST, conquered the town like some ethereal invading force. It had the dogged tenacity of a meme. At one point I hardly had a friend who wasn't involved in the training, and news of its activities spread through town, seemingly coloring all our thoughts, entering every conversation. The story goes that Werner Erhard (a.k.a. John Paul Rosenberg) experienced a revelation while driving across the Golden Gate Bridge one sunny afternoon in 1971 as he mulled over a hash of spiritual influences that included everyone from Sigmund Freud, Abraham Maslow, Carl Rogers, and Fritz Perls to the practices of hypnosis, autosuggestion, revivalism, psychodrama, Gestalt Therapy, yoga, and Zen. Out of such a rich mulch of information, then, sprang Erhard's revelation: the world is perfect just as it is. This tenet couldn't have been better suited to Aspen and its largely hippie-inflected population, and to think of it in retrospect amounts to a modest revelation of its own. A philosophy based on the idea that little effort, except for realization, has to be made in order to improve the tenor of our existence had to have struck a sympathetic chord with those whose disappointment was profound, as the war in Vietnam escalated, high level corruption spread, the economy wavered and tanked, and ecological degradation worsened every year. In the 1960s, we had tried to change the world. There was a string of bodies from Kent State to Saigon to Alabama, corpses which testified to a generation's wish to transform society and set out in a different direction. In EST, here was a new American avatar disseminating the notion that we had been going about it the wrong way. The world was perfect just the way it was, and all we had to do was to stop fighting it and change ourselves, our attitude towards reality, our perspective, and then our lives would improve. No need to shave our heads, undergo years of arduous spiritual training, lie naked in a field with heavy stones on our bellies, or grow thin in caves while living off locusts and wild honey. A shift in perspective might do the trick. Self-transformation would lead to world transformation, and we'd be back on track for Nirvana.

Maybe I'm being too hard on Werner Erhard and EST. Some valuable concepts and techniques for improving one's life *did* result from the training, judging by the testimony of friends whose opinion I trust. The EST buzz lasted for several years in the '70s. Echoes of the training reached me even in the fastness of my office on the second floor of the Wheeler Opera House. I never took the training myself, but the idea of accepting responsibility for life, rather than blaming others, interested me and drew my attention. When I heard statements like "It is in being transformed—in being authentically true to oneself— that one lives passionately free, unencumbered, fearless, and committed," I thought, *Who could argue with that?* Or this: "The truth is not found in a different set of circumstances. The truth is always and only found in the circumstances you've got." Patently reasonable, eminently practical. Being authentic to oneself seemed to be as old as the Oracle of Delphi's admonition etched in stone on her cavern wall: KNOW THYSELF. The problem I had with EST and the other self-realization courses that followed was their focus on the individual, on personal salvation rather than on others who might be suffering terribly and need help. Where was the idea of charity, compassion, social responsibility, and sacrifice? It was easy enough for someone living in Aspen at the time to assert that the world was perfect just the way it was, but what about the woman in Vietnam who ran terrified through her village with her baby in her

arms as fighter jets dropped Napalm? What about the man in
El Salvador who had to watch his wife being raped by soldiers
before he and his children were assassinated? Self-realization,
I thought, was fine, but social-consciousness was better. Those
with a conscience could hardly turn away.

It was because of the self-satisfying aspect of the training
and its inescapable sense that it redeemed the fortunate that
EST became the butt of many jokes and engendered more than
a few creative responses from those who saw it as an enlightenment scam for the privileged few. John Denver and Diana
Ross were passionate adherents. Noted educator and scholar
Warren Bennis, as well as actor Valerie Harper, followed suit.
Half the population of Aspen, including almost everyone in local politics, flocked to Erhard's seminars to improve the quality of their lives that, by world standards, were already excep-
tionally blessed. "I took EST training from Werner in 1972,"
Anne Burrows told me. "I had to do it in self-defense because
everyone in town was running around smiling and talking
about *getting it*. Turns out, *it* was that there really was no *it*."
Vic Garrett said, "I always thought it was hippies tired of being
stoned all the time, seeking enlightenment from something
other than psychedelics." Bruce Berger has an insider's point
of view: "I did attend EST, along with a couple of follow-up programs, though I didn't finish either of the latter. I found certain elements of it useful, numerous pits to spit out, and never
became an ESThole in the sense of recruiting others or going
on about it...I generally take a skeptical view of the New Age
comedies (having coined the phrase 'assholistic medicine',
which my chiropractor loves, though he was involved with
that stuff)." Once the term "ESThole" gained currency in Aspen, there was no stopping it and it's no wonder Dr. Sadistic

and his Silverking Crybabies would fasten on to it with a vengeance in their timeless marching song, "ESTholes on Parade," whose chorus begins:

We're ESTholes on parade,
We're the chosen one's who've made the grade
See our auras light up, watch our hang-ups fade
We're ESTholes on parade . . .

EST held sway for several years, but eventually outgrew Aspen and mutated into The Forum in the 1980s, having paved the way for other self-realization programs to come. The Inner Peace Movement passed through town in the wake of EST but caused barely a ripple. Then, in the early 1990s, a group calling itself The Alive Tribe required its adherents to change their given names to ones more suitable to their environmental message. Women might call themselves "Rainbow Spring or Serenity Flower, while men chose Waterfall Eagle or Sky Canyon. The group's leader fashioned himself Truth Paradise and radiated a warm, phlegmatic smile wherever he went, in keeping with the idea that communion with nature might transfer some of its tranquility directly into the souls of its human devotees. Apparently, he'd never seen a snake eat a mouse or a lion rip apart its prey. One evening, in Jake's Abbey, Truth Paradise arrived and during a break in the music approached Mark Moriva, saxophonist for the group Grown Men.

"Hi," he said, extending his hand. "I'm Truth Paradise."

Mark, who'd heard of the cult, clasped his hand, looked him directly in the eye and said, "That's a lie right there!"

Taken aback, Mr. Paradise could only smile and recount some of the advantages of pillow punching, primal screaming, parental de-conditioning, yoga fire breathing, and free form dancing that might lead to something called a "domain shift," whereby personal transformation brought about an "optimal care for one's own body and the body of the earth." But Mark's retort must have rung in Truth's ears for weeks afterwards.

* * *

Briefly in the 1970s, sensory deprivation tanks offered a way to relieve pain and stress, and even spark creativity. Floating in a sealed, soundless chamber in complete darkness on a pool of salt water the exact temperature of human skin, subjects might experience total relaxation, though seldom enlightenment. Flotation tanks *have* been found to be useful in reducing anxiety and stress, while showing improvement for those suffering from other conditions, such as depression and fibromyalgia. I recall having a conversation with someone in the Jerome bar who had just experienced a session in a flotation tank.

"What was it like?" I asked.

"Oh, much like this," she laughed, sweeping her hand around to take in the entire room where patrons sat drowsily sipping beer in the late afternoon sun. Sensory deprivation tanks—like Jacuzzis, hot tubs, steam rooms, and swimming pools—were a luxury most of us could not afford. A martini or two at the Jerome provided a much cheaper way to relax and reduce stress, though few of us drank enough to deprive ourselves of all sense. Perhaps because of the expense, flotation tanks never caught on, and we turned to other forms of self-improvement, if not indulgence.

These other forms included Rolfing and rebirthing, a two-pronged approach aimed first at realigning the body, then concentrating on getting the head straight. Rolfing, or "structural integration," was pioneered by Ida Rolf in the 1940s and '50s, but didn't take root in Aspen until the early 1970s. When it did, many of my friends, including Joyce, eagerly embraced its concepts and signed up for the course—a sequence of ten sixty-to-ninety minute sessions to "balance and optimize both the structure (shape) and function (movement) of the entire body," according to the Rolf Institute's own literature. Joyce explained it to me one day at a friend's ranch in Polecat Hollow just west of Buttermilk Ski Area, how gravity slowly pulls the body—spine, hips, legs, shoulders, the whole skeleto-muscular structure—out of balance as we age, so that the fascia, or connective tissue, sticks together and prevents the muscles from coordinating easily with one another. This, she told me, might be corrected by deep-tissue massage where the fascia become unstuck by a trained Rolfer, or super-masseuse, who is able to separate the fibers manually. I thought about this for a moment, and glanced at her.

"Sounds painful," I said.

"Oh," she purred, "but it hurts so *good*! We store certain emotions in our bodies at various points, in various muscles," she went on, "and when you get Rolfed those emotions are released as part of the process. So for me, when the therapist was working on my neck I suddenly started to cry—not because it hurt so much but because I remembered that my father had always grabbed me there, by the back of the neck, real hard when he wanted to punish me for something. I had completely forgotten about that until I got Rolfed and it all came out."

This was a radical departure from parents who carp about posture, telling their children to throw their shoulders back and hold their heads up, or to walk around a room while balancing a book on the top of their skulls. Rolfing might even result in unwanted effects, depending on your point of view. Vic

Garret remembers that his wife, Jan, had gotten Rolfed and the consequences, for him, were less than desirable: "It totally ruined the shape of her ass!" he told me with a rueful grin, "but we laughed about it later so it didn't affect our marriage."

* * *

As a kinder, gentler way of reducing stress and increasing energy according its practitioners, rebirthing enjoyed a brief vogue in Aspen though it never quite caught on like Rolfing or EST. It entailed a process akin to pranayama, or yogic breathing. Rebirthers claim that controlling and disciplining one's breath may effect change in everything from releasing bodily toxins to a list of more generalized benefits such as "healing the wound of your imagined separation" and "increasing one's experience of inner peace and surrender." It also "increases one's ability to feel and resolve the effects of one's past" because "through the use of the breath early rebirthers discovered the tremendous impact birth had on their lives." Rebirthers remind us, as do the yogis, that the word *breath* is related to the word *spirit*, as in *inspire* and *expire*. But these sorts of exercises are less dramatic than the experience of being Rolfed or the rigorous training of EST, where participants are prevented from going to the bathroom for long periods of time and called assholes if they don't "get it." I suspect that the patience and discipline required in practicing breathing techniques appealed less to the energetic, outdoorsy residents of Aspen in the 1970s than the speedier, quick-fix nature of other, more spectacular methods of self-improvement.

* * *

One of the most spectacular claims involved J. Z. Knight's assertion that she could channel the spirit of a thirty-five thousand year-old Lemurian warrior called Ramtha, and by so doing disseminate his ancient teachings around the world. The teachings assert that Christianity is "a backward religion," that murder isn't wrong or evil, and that you yourself are god. This would not endear Ramtha to the majority of middle-class Americans living in the Midwest, or the southern Bible belt. Even for so secular a place as Aspen, Ramtha's radical teachings proved to be too extreme. Not a single person I know ever talked to me at length about Ramtha, or became his disciple. But that doesn't mean his ideas didn't flourish elsewhere. According to an article in Wikipedia, Ramtha's channeler, J. Z. Knight, lives "in a 12,800 square foot French chateau-styled mansion on the outskirts of Yelm, Washington, which includes a spa, swimming pool, and stables, and recruits a staff of fourteen." This, on top of revenues brought in by Ramtha's School of Enlightenment and a line of products that would make even Walt Disney smile (kitchen utensils, women's apparel, cosmetics, pet supplies, and other products not related to Ramtha or his teachings sold both in her store in Yelma, and online).

Born in Roswell, New Mexico in 1946, J. Z. Knight is only one of several noteworthy natives of that infamous desert town. Americans will remember that a little over a year after Knight's birth, a supposed UFO—a spacecraft shaped like a disc—had crashed on a ranch outside of town. It turned out to be a high-altitude weather balloon, but that didn't matter. Something in the water of Roswell engenders such fantastical stories, as well as one-time residents who keep re-inventing themselves to become fabulously successful in later life. This includes J. Z. Knight herself (aka Judith Hampton), John Denver (aka Henry John Deutschendorf, Jr.), Demi Moore (aka

Demi Guynes) and Hall of Fame jockey Mike E. Smith (aka Michael Earl Smith), all born in Roswell but destined for greater things. Whether or not aliens ever landed in this dusty New Mexican hamlet, a number of noteworthy aliases have certainly hailed from there.

* * *

More lovable, and certainly more popular than Ramtha, a young boy from India who called himself Guru Maharaj Ji arrived in the United States in 1971 at the tender age of thirteen and quickly gathered followers from coast to coast. Born Prem Pal Singh Rawat, on December 10, 1957 in Haridwar, India, his father was leader of the Divine Light Mission, which put Prem Rawat on the fast-track as a spiritual figure. When he was three, he began lecturing to the initiates of the Divine Light Mission. At six, his father taught him the meditation techniques known simply as, "The Knowledge," and changed Prem Rawat's name to the much loftier Balyogeshwar Param Hans Satgurudev Shri Sant Ji Maharaj. When his father died, Balyogeshwar succeeded him as leader of the Divine Light Mission and was promptly dubbed Guru Maharaj Ji, the name by which he would become known widely in the West, especially in England and the United States. In September, 1971, he addressed a crowd in Colorado, where I suppose most of his new adherents from Aspen first heard him, and a chapter of the Divine Light Mission was set up in Denver. At sixteen, the charismatic young spiritual leader married a westerner and broke entirely with the rest of his family, which operated the original Divine Light Mission back home in India.

I suppose it was inevitable that a teenage guru would have appealed to the ex-hippie crowd more than the staid fathers

of most traditional religions with their lists of rules and pro-
hibitions, and their history of implacable power and violence.
We were the generation that had coined the preposterous admonition: "Never trust anyone over thirty," a dreaded mile-
stone we were quickly and nervously approaching. Here was
a young boy who loved the massive attention he was receiving, a playful creature who acted like any young boy at his age,
like *us* when we were thirteen or fourteen, only a decade or
so before Maharaj Ji's appearance in the United States. In his
book, *Sacred Journeys: The Conversion of Young Americans to Divine Light Mission*, sociologist James Downton records the testimony of one witness at a Mission event who said that Maharaj
Ji "played the whole time he was there...he played with squirt
guns, flashed pictures of himself for all to see, and took movies
of everybody...Love flowed back and forth between him and
his devotees." In fact, his followers—or premies—acted almost
exactly like they were in love, and newly in love, which is the
worst kind of behavior to behold objectively when you are not
in love yourself. Close friends of mine returned from a huge
weekend gathering in Montrose, Colorado with light hearts, a
kind word for everyone, and sappy looks on their faces. When
I interrogated them about their experience, they laughed fond-
ly, and smiled: "Oh, it was fabulous! I'm blissed-out, man! The
last night of the festival Maharaj Ji sprayed the crowed with
colored water as the sun was going down, and it was so far
out you can't believe it!" When pressed for further details, they
could only jabber about how beautiful it all was without utter-
ing a word of doctrine or explaining Maharaj Ji's teachings in
any coherent way.

Apparently jets of various colored water arcing over a
sweaty crowd did the trick for those willing to be baptized in

such a way by a thirteen-year-old boy. Stern criticism from older members of the religious community, plus a pie in the face hurled by a reporter from the *Detroit Free Press* when Maharaj Ji appeared there, failed to dissuade the young or cool their ardor as his message spread rapidly among disenfranchised members of the '60s counterculture. In the early '70s, the Divine Light Mission was the fastest growing religion in America and the ascendancy of Guru Maharaj Ji, or as Bruce Berger liked to call him—Nirvana Fats—seemed poised to take over the spiritual lives of young people everywhere.

* * *

For those of us who were less inclined to follow the leader, there was always nature to adore, books to read, music to hear, and movies to see in order to address our spiritual and intellectual needs. Nature was inescapable in Aspen. Even downtown, in the heart of the city, nature swept in with cooling rain or downy snow, trees and flowers grew, sunlight paved the streets and the walls of Red Mountain and Ajax loomed above us under skies so blue they seemed polished, turning purple and lavender in the dusk, set with stars even the municipal lights couldn't completely dim. Nature was a step away, up Shadow Mountain, or Independence Pass, off any secondary road leading out of town, in the manifold gold of aspen leaves every autumn, the willows and poplars of the west end, or Hallam Lake with its mallards and loons.

Once, in my very first year in Aspen, I saw hundreds of sheep herded down Main Street and up Aspen Mountain as ranchers brought their animals into town to graze on vacated ski slopes, in what used to be an annual event. The sound and smell of these herds turned Aspen into a Swiss village for a few

brief weeks, their bells tinkling softly as they wandered mo-
guls newly flush with grass. There were magpies everywhere,
pestiferous birds bold enough to invade any property and scav-
enge where they will. One day, I found a couple of magpies
tearing apart garbage bags in my garage in Snowmass. And
an early spring season spent house sitting for a friend of mine
in Old Snowmass Valley provided me with a front-row seat
on the natural world I can never forget. Deer splashed across
Snowmass Creek at dawn, hawks patrolled surrounding fields
and ridges, sunlight glanced off the frozen crust of snow, and
once, returning home from a night of carousing in town, I met
a porcupine at my front door and was forced to step aside until he waddled away, imperious and unperturbed. Even from
the confines of your car, traveling on any road in the area—including Highway 82—you might spot a coyote or fox or group
of elk making its way across a meadow and up into the trees.
We weren't living *near* nature, but squarely *in* it, as though Aspen had been settled only a few years before our own arrival
in town which, in geological terms, wasn't that far from the
truth.

* * *

When we weren't climbing up past Cathedral Lake to Electric Pass and back again before noon in order to avoid the daily afternoon lightning storms, or being tossed around in a
rubber raft on the turbulent rapids of the Colorado River in
Glenwood Canyon, we might be trekking across the desert in
southern Utah to meditate among weird sandforms in Goblin
Valley or under ruddy spans of rock in Arches National Park.
As Vic Garret recalls: "The desert was a big part of the culture
then...Most of us made several trips down there every year,

spring and fall, to hike, backpack, and seek mind expansion"
which among my friends involved rendering those weird land-
scapes even weirder under the influence of one drug or another to heighten the effect of nature's artistry. After the excesses
of Aspen, the sparseness of the desert seemed a perfect place
to be shriven by the wind, the sand, and the lunar emptiness
of the landscape surrounding Moab—a place to detoxify and
relax before heading back up into the mountains to rejoin Aspen's ever-lasting party. Always, it seemed, someone would be
heading out to the desert, or just returning—sunburnt, chas-
tened—ready for another go-around of debauchery, another
sensual spree. The desert was our hospital, our clinic, a much-
needed counter-balance to our hedonistic ways. But our physical activities, the constant stress on getting out and *doing* something, precluded obesity or any of the other health problems
plaguing the country today. We may have been self-indulgent,
but we were active and athletic at the same time, and young
enough to metabolize any excess, any surfeit to which our appetites might lead. More than that, a few days in the desert
lowered the static of our social lives, the chatter and noise of
contact with others. Every so often, it all got to be too much:
food, wine, sex, music, a continuous stream of events that
would eventually wear anyone down, so we'd head for the desert—nothing but the sound of wind against rock, and a few
glittering stars.

   And even in Aspen, a few hours of solitude might be
snatched from an otherwise hectic day in order to read, rest,
or just contemplate life's mysteries. One of the books that had
a great impact on the culture in general was *Be Here Now* by
Babba Ram Das (a.k.a. Richard Alpert). The book itself was everywhere, on everyone's shelf, and whether we talked about

its philosophy and teachings with anyone else, it formed a large portion of our thinking. For many of us, its predecessor might have been Jack Kerouac's *On the Road*, urging its readers to grasp the moment, to seize the day as it flowed inevitably through our fingers and vanished into the past. A famous passage from *On the Road* still echoed in our minds:

> ...the only people for me are the mad ones, the ones who are mad to live, mad to talk, mad to be saved, desirous of everything at the same time, the ones who never yawn or say a commonplace thing, but burn, burn, burn like fabulous yellow roman candles exploding like spiders across the stars and in the middle you see the blue centerlight pop and everybody goes "Awww!"

This kind of frantic experience, a call for devouring life, certainly figured into our lives in Aspen, but Ram Dass's message was more level-headed and sustainable. Unlike Kerouac, he didn't preach salvation through the body—an updating of Rimbaud's "willing derangement of the senses"—but through meditation techniques aimed at pacifying the mind in order to realize the moment, that sense of sheer being that was easy to miss if you were always rushing toward the next excitation, then the next. In the end, it would be as though you had not been here at all, and that is what Ram Dass wanted to avoid, like Thoreau before him. *Be Here Now* advised readers to tune back in, but with a Zen-like intensity on the moment, not a manic commitment to experience. We had seen our parents ground down under the burden of so many responsibilities, fretting always about the future, working to better themselves and their position in the socio-economic order until it seemed that their lives were empty and miserable, not fulfill-

ing at all. We couldn't see, then, that our own improvident philosophies would ultimately depend upon the hard work and
commitment of others, that Kerouac's mother housed him and
Thoreau's parents fed him, and Ram Dass held a degree from
Harvard and was able to support himself on the proceeds of
his writing, teaching, and personal appearances while we had
only our groovy ideas on which to rely.

Other books that spoke to us included Herman Hesse's *Sid-
dhartha*, which reflected the prevailing quest-ethic of the era in
a condensed, accessible way ("I don't know who I am, but life is
for learning . . .") and appealed to our sense of self-reliance and
freedom from the normal patterns of existence. As a writer, I
preferred Hesse's *Steppenwolf*, because it dealt with themes of
alienation and psychological crisis, ending in scenes from The
Magic Theater which, for me at least, stood as an analog for
the spirit of creativity and imagination itself.

For sheer fun and a story that recalled the fairy tales we had
loved in childhood, nothing could beat J. R. R. Tolkien's epic
cycle, *The Lord of the Rings*, and its introductory tale, *The Hobbit*.
We didn't know that Tolkien was a professor at Cambridge in
England and a noted Medieval scholar, and had we known, we
wouldn't have cared. For a while, it seemed like everyone was
reading *The Lord of the Rings* and somehow connecting with its
saga of personal redemption and world-saving glory. It helped,
too, that the protagonist was a humble character and that the
narrative itself took place in a land long ago and far away. In
some respects, it set the stage for *Star Wars*, that blockbuster
of cosmic proportions, whimsical characters, and improbable
self-discovery that would follow in 1977, galvanizing an aging
generation still seeking a morally uplifting fantasy in which to
believe.

For those of a more realistic bent, *One Flew Over the Cuckoo's Nest* confirmed Aspen's self-image as a wacky, unconventional place where the craziest people were actually the smartest, while the smuggest in society at large were actually the sickest, a deft reversal that made us feel better about ourselves if we had any doubts at all. Eco-warriors preferred Edward Abbey's books, manuals for environmental revolution defending the desert and, on a greater scale, the American West, which was suffering the depredations of politicians and developers, while intellectuals were drawn to Thomas Pynchon's *V* and *Gravity's Rainbow*, and visionaries like my friend Joyce to the work of Carlos Castaneda or Immanuel Velikovsky. For me, one of the chronically bemused, Richard Brautigan provided ample entertainment in the form of poems, stories, and novels that featured the zaniest characters doing the most preposterous things in a way that only Brautigan, with his original mind, could possibly have created.

Though it seemed like we wished to please only ourselves, to satisfy our own immediate desires, we were seeking a balance between self-indulgence and self-improvement, obliteration and enlightenment, irresponsibility and the demands of our own ambitions, as though we knew even then in the beautiful frenzy of it all that it couldn't last. By the close of the decade, many of us had already migrated out of town, though not necessarily back home which, in any case, would have been impossible (we were much too old for that) and would have amounted to a betrayal of our most fundamental beliefs. America, too, had changed once again—as it seems to change decade to decade—swinging back to a far more conservative mood with the election of Ronald Reagan and the announcement by Michael Douglas in *Wall Street* that "Greed is *good!*"

though it would take most of the 1980s to reach that stunning conclusion. Aspen was changing, becoming slicker and glitzier, with more multi-million dollar mansions being erected in all areas of town, and snazzier restaurants opening every season serving up the newest fashionable cuisine. Disco finally eclipsed live music, and many of the venues in town that used to support musicians—including Jake's Abbey which had become a beer-drinking sports bar—closed up shop as far as music was concerned and went back to other mercantile pursuits. Stores that used to sell records or blue jeans or fishing equipment transformed into emporiums for designer clothes, turquoise jewelry, and crystal candelabras for polished, twenty-foot cherry wood dining tables. A walk through Aspen evoked nothing so much as the environs of Rodeo Drive. Change is inevitable, and when it finally came to Aspen, it swept in like one of those reality shows to give an entire town a complete makeover. The secret was out. Rich people from all over the country had discovered Aspen and bought up land to build second and third homes at a record-breaking clip. The unique hideaway, the funky hole in the wall that had been Aspen in the 1970s, the safe haven we'd discovered for ourselves and inevitably lost, was no more.

Afterword

Part of what you were was here before
You came, and part of what you were is gone
—Thomas Hornsby Ferril,
"Waltz Against the Mountains"

I passed through Amarillo recently on a drive that took me across the country from New York to Los Angeles. My wife and I, with our two cats, were bouncing along in a rented RV enjoying the scenery when a storm kicked up from the south and began to buffet our vehicle, tossing it from side to side. It felt good to be on the road again, especially on such an extended trip, viewing America from ground level, every foot of the way from Middletown, New Jersey to a trailer camp in Ventura, California where we would meet our daughter and return the RV the following morning to an office in Agoura Hills. Transcontinental drives are fine with me. I have always loved sitting behind a wheel watching the landscape change, observing the weather—the play of light on mountains, the oceanic roll of plains, deserts with their withering, empty spaces—as lonely towns float past, water towers and used car lots, all to a

musical score of my own choosing. I love the sense that I am
going somewhere, that for a few unhindered hours I am free,
liberated from whatever schedule I had been following, and I
begin to lean forward as though that might help speed up the
miles and pass the time. And always, at the end of the journey,
there would be someone to meet me, and the chance to experience an unfamiliar place, one I had never seen before, or even
one I knew very well but hadn't visited for a long time.

But for the moment, I was concerned only with the sand-
storm approaching from the south turning the horizon gray,
then purple though not with rain clouds—but dust. Sand blew
across the highway in great sheets, crested above us in waves,
and whirled through each crack and gap in the RV into our
open mouths as we bit down on tiny pieces of grit. The windows and doors were closed, but it didn't matter. Dust has a
way of passing through solid walls to settle on everything as
though to lay claim again to what it rightfully owns. Dust to
dust. Now and then tumbleweed blasted across the desert in
front of us, dry tangles of twigs going nowhere. A few semi-
trucks had pulled to the side of the road to wait it out. No
sense gambling with the wind. A powerful blast—we heard on
the radio that gusts had reached sixty miles an hour—might
topple them, bring them crashing down on their sides like be-
hemoths. Even passing through Amarillo, stop signs shuddered, lights hung above the road swung crazily like hooked
fish. I should have stopped, too, but I wanted to push on to Santa Rosa, New Mexico before camping for the night. I thought
I could outrun the storm, as it was coming from the south and
I was headed due west. Maybe I could reach its far edge, and
calmer weather, before nightfall.

When I glanced into my rearview mirror, I saw Amaril-

lo about to be engulfed in a wall of sand. Then I thought of
Egan and Flo—him with his scraggly beard, her fussing with
the cat and smiling in her softly bemused way. In all the years
that had intervened, they had not changed. At least not in my
imagination. They were children, barely out of high school,
traveling haphazardly through a landscape completely indifferent to them and their fate. What *had* happened to them? Had
they reached the West Coast and married? Had they grown
old together, grown apart, wound up divorced and bitter, become cynical and obese? Had one of them died and left the
other alone? Which one? Had they become disillusioned and
broken, wandering the streets, worthless outcasts from a society that had no use for them? Or had they adapted themselves,
become successful? Had they relinquished their old ideals and
transformed into a conventional American couple by pursuing
careers while raising children and squirreling enough money
away for retirement? And *where* were they? San Francisco still?
New York? Dallas? Chicago? Or somewhere in between, one of
those bleak towns I had passed through on my way west?

I could still see them standing by the side of the road, just
outside Amarillo, with their rucksacks and cat, Egan's battered
guitar case, the vast American continent diminishing them,
annihilating them with its crushing distances; and then on the
shoulder of Highway 82, near Snowmass where I had left them
after I had decided to stay and they opted to move on. And I
got that feeling, a feeling of danger and dread that something
might happen, *had* happened, and nothing would ever be the
same. They weren't family, not even by marriage, and I had
only known them briefly, and even then, not well. Whatever
had happened to them was really none of my business, so why
should I concern myself at all? Yet, despite their ordinariness,

they represented something for me. A moment had arrived and passed, and they were part of it. They had remained in my memory for some reason, most of my life. Until I looked back and there was nothing but that wall of sand stretching across the southwest all the way from Amarillo to Bartsow, obscuring everything.

CPSIA information can be obtained at www.ICGtesting.com
Printed in the USA
LVOW091818170812

294811LV00009B/19/P